Praise for *Facing the Music*

"As I read Jennifer Knapp's beautifully written book, I felt like I was looking through multiple windows—a window into the Contemporary Christian Music industry and, beyond that, a window into the heart of a uniquely gifted musician, and, deeper still, a window into the heart of a gay woman of faith who dared to open the blinds to let others look in. It takes courage to write a book like this, and reading it will give others courage too—to face their music, to tell their story, to sing their song."

—Brian D. McLaren, author of *Why Did Jesus, Moses, the Buddha, and Mohammed Cross the Road?*

"Jennifer Knapp's lyrics come alive in the pages of *Facing the Music*, a vivid account of Knapp's journey to embrace herself, her faith, and her capacity for love. Neither a confession nor an apology, *Facing the Music* is a hard-won declaration that faith and love transcend our theologies of exclusion. In this deeply personal memoir, Jennifer Knapp offers hope to individuals struggling to overcome the rejection, shame, and insecurities so often experienced by LGBTQ Christians."

—Alison Amyx, senior editor of *Believe Out Loud*

"*Facing the Music* was a good kick in the pants to remind us that getting to know our Father in Heaven has far greater consequences than any trophy, any accolade, any perceived goodness we can lay at His feet. The book, not so gently, asks the question:

Why are we even debating this? These questions will arise in your mind as you read this book: Is Jen winning or losing? Is Jen good or is she bad? I hope somewhere in the deepest recesses of your heart you will recalibrate those questions and ask: What is God doing in Jen's life? And is there anything in Jen's story that can help me to know my Father in Heaven more intimately? I'm a better man for having read *Facing the Music*."

—Joey Elwood, cofounder of Gotee Records

"*Facing the Music* is a fascinating read on so many levels. Knapp is brutally honest about herself, about what she experienced, and about what was happening in her head and her heart as she grew in her relationship with music, Christianity, and her sexual orientation. It pulls back the curtain on the Christian music industry to look at the business behind the worship and the squeaky-clean image. It's a story that many of us will be able to relate to, in our own way, and readers of *Facing the Music* will find not only Knapp's story, but their own as well."

—Ross Murray, director of news for GLAAD

"With often dramatic language Jennifer Knapp describes the movements of her family life and loss, her discovery of faith and its challenges, the highs and lows of where her music has taken her, and the rugged terrain of being completely honest about all God has made her. And I applaud this force of nature for doing so."

—Mark Tidd, founding pastor of Highlands Church, Denver

Facing the *Music*

my story

JENNIFER KNAPP

HOWARD BOOKS
A Division of Simon & Schuster, Inc.
New York   Nashville   London   Toronto   Sydney   New Delhi

Howard Books
A Division of Simon & Schuster, Inc.
1230 Avenue of the Americas
New York, NY 10020

First Howard Books hardcover edition October 2014

HOWARD and colophon are trademarks of Simon & Schuster, Inc.

For information about special discounts for bulk purchases,
please contact Simon & Schuster Special Sales at 1-866-506-1949
or business@simonandschuster.com.

The Simon & Schuster Speakers Bureau can bring authors to your live event. For more
information or to book an event, contact the Simon & Schuster Speakers Bureau at
1-866-248-3049 or visit our website at www.simonspeakers.com.

Interior design by Davina Mock-Maniscalco
Jacket design by Bruce Gore
Front jacket photograph by Fairlight Hubbard for Eye Management

Manufactured in the United States of America

10   9   8   7   6   5   4   3   2   1

Library of Congress Cataloging-in-Publication Data

Knapp, Jennifer.
    Facing the music : my story / Jennifer Knapp.
        pages cm
    1. Knapp, Jennifer, 1974– 2. Rock musicians—United States—Biography. I. Title.
    ML420.K64A3 2014
    782.42164092—dc23
    [B]
                                                                            2014008731

ISBN 978-1-4767-5947-0
ISBN 978-1-4767-5949-4 (ebook)

For K.E.R.

Facing the
Music

one

Eight months after the Supreme Court ruling on *Roe v. Wade*, my parents found themselves unwed, pregnant, and expecting twins. Before they had even considered what their lives might look like, they were confronted with a challenging beginning as to how they were going to be a family, or if they even wanted to. My mother, a teenager, and my father, a post-Vietnam Navy veteran barely into his twenties, did as most honorable small-town Kansas folks expected at the time. They decided to keep their babies and get married.

My young parents' brief history together was colored by the social taboos they had challenged. Their seven-year age difference, their clandestine love affair, premarital pregnancy, and a shotgun wedding no doubt seemed like slim odds for a lasting relationship. Instead of finishing high school, my mother spent what would have been her senior year giving birth and nursing babies. After an adventurous summer with a pretty young girl, my father suddenly found himself responsible for the welfare of a wife and two children.

After two years, they would divorce. My mother, barely in her twenties, lost the custody battle to my father. The court reached an unusual decision, choosing my father as the parent most responsible to care for my sister and me. We were two toddlers still shaky on our feet, trying to understand what phrases like *child custody* and *visitation rights* had to do with why Mom wasn't there to tuck us into bed each night. Growing up, we would have to learn how to adapt to the pitch and roll of being shared between my parents' two worlds. Going forward, we were to live full-time with my father, while spending alternate weekends with Mom.

Mom only lived a few miles away in those early years, but everything seems bigger, longer, and farther away when you're little. Even though Mom might be living in the next county over, our journey there was always an adventure.

Fridays were the most important, highly anticipated day of the week for us. I would be in utter bliss when I knew Mom was on her way to pick us up for the weekend, and disappointed when I realized that I'd have to wait another week to see her.

The best Fridays were filled with the ritual of her coming. With anticipation, I'd get to pack a little bag of clothes and place it by the front door. I'd sit at the window, willing every passing car to be hers. What joy it was when through the darkness, a pair of headlights turned from the road into our driveway! Mom! At last!

Once I'd jumped into the car, I was in her world, a place in which we had developed our own traditions. I couldn't wait to show her every tomboy bump and bruise that I had acquired since we were last together, so that she could hasten the healing of each blemish with her tender kisses. Then, after every ache had been attended to, we would sing. I was torn between the excitement of joining in the chorus or just listening to her sing alone. Hers was the most glorious voice I had ever heard. Whether she led us in a rousing rendition of "Bill Grogan's Goat" or the Beatles' "Yellow Submarine," I was beside myself with awe and wonder over her talent. The longer the drive to our destination, the better. I welcomed the nights when the rain poured down and Mom had to drive more slowly. Rather than fighting the weather, we sang through it. Ours was the perfect cocoon of joy on four wheels.

During our short times together, Mom always made an effort to do something special for us. In the winter, she would join us in a wild snowball fight. In the summer, she'd start a water war by grabbing a garden hose and dousing us with cold spray. If we were stuck inside, she'd teach us to play a card game or how to make a batch of cookies. She found a way to be a part of our lives by making memories out of the most ordinary days.

If Fridays were the good days, Sundays were bittersweet, knowing that the minutes with Mom were ticking down, and that we soon would be parting ways. I was aware that she would be taking us back home. I was old enough to repeat the facts, that it would be two weeks until we could do it all over again, but two weeks, to a five-year-old, felt like a lifetime. It was difficult to imagine passing the time between then and the next visit, so I tried to make the most of the lazy Sunday afternoons before going home. I'd do my best to fight back the tears, aware that our weekend together was drawing to a close.

She'd drive us back home to the small farm where we lived with my father in rural southeastern Kansas, five miles east of a cozy little town called Chanute. Our house was a breezy fixer-upper nestled on a few acres between pastures and soybean fields. My sister and I spent most of our time outdoors exploring, looking for wild mulberries along the fence-line trees or working alongside my father in our old, red wooden barn as he tended to his horses. I found comfort in the simplicity of my father's world. There was always something constructive to be done around the farm, mending fences or feeding the animals. When the chores were done, he'd grab a rope and teach us how to lasso a sawhorse as if it were a calf, or maybe even fashion us a bow and arrow made from tree branches and baling twine. With Dad, there was always adventure with work and with play.

Among my favorite things to do was to help Dad shoe the horses. His skills as a farrier were fascinating. Whenever he brought out his tools and the anvil, I was right there to join him. Though I was still small enough that I could walk under a horse, I begged for him to let me in on the action. There were times where he might say something like, "This is too big a job for a little girl," but I wouldn't have it. I wanted to be just like him. So, he taught me, perhaps nervously, to pick up the hoof of our mare, hold it between my knees and file it down. It didn't matter that I only had the strength and coordination to last for a few seconds. He let me be a part of his world and I was overjoyed. While other little girls were playing with dolls and dressing up, I found my stride alongside my dad as a happy little tomboy.

My father faced his fair share of criticism for supposedly letting his pretty little girls run wild. I was as happy as I could imagine when I was knee deep in mud fetching the horses from the pasture. However, Grandma Knapp did not see it that way.

There were the odd Sundays when grandma insisted that we clean up, put on dresses, and head to church with her. Yielding to his mother's insistence that we should at least try to act like little ladies, she would squeeze us (against our will) into nylons and patent leather shoes, comb our hair, and send us off to Sunday school. I felt like a lump of meat shoved into an itchy sausage casing. I was the spitting image of Scout from *To Kill a Mocking Bird.* There was nothing more excruciating than to have to try to pay attention to the unwanted, boring lessons about Jesus and the loaves and fishes while trying to manage a pair of creeping nylons running up my backside. All I could think of was changing into a pair of jeans and getting back outside on the farm with my dad.

Much of the adult conversation in my father's world in those days was about how his little girls needed a woman's influence. The fear, I suppose, was that we would soon grow so wild and tomboyish, that we might eventually be unrecognizable as girls. My mother, with her allotment of four days per month, and my Grandma Knapp were doing the best to inspire femininity in us, but it wasn't enough. I think everyone felt a bit of relief when, after a few short years of being a single father, he would meet and introduce us to the woman who would change our lives.

I remember being excited about my father's new love. While I adored my father's laid-back style of living, there was some charm we were clearly missing without a woman on the scene. Up to that point, our country house was little more than a shelter, where we ate and slept. The only life we had known for the two years since my parents' divorce was that of subsistence. A life in which we all worked and played outside until we had nothing left, then retreated tiredly indoors, choked down one of my father's dreary hamburger hash concoctions, then prepared for bed, with the prospect of doing the same the next day. Though I loved my father and found comfort in his attention, I had no idea how much all of us still ached for a sense of family.

The early days of my dad's courtship were wonderful. Instead of the once dull, gray meals we ate alone with our father, we now had company to add excitement to our evenings. All of us together, joyfully preparing the dinner and sharing the happenings of the day. Dad seemed relaxed and his happiness spilled out for all of us to share. I found myself hoping that they would get married so that it would last. She was also a much better cook than my father, and I began to notice what a void those days were in between comforting weekends with my mother. I saw my grandmas and grandpas together, and I saw other children with their moms and dads under one roof and I realized that I had been missing out.

I remember thinking how beautiful my father's friend was. She had long, silky straight hair that fell down her back all the way to her waist. I was enamored of it, and often begged for her to let me run my fingers through it. I had never seen such long and splendid locks except on television, when the famed country music star Crystal Gayle sang on *Hee Haw*. After dinner, we would retire to the living room to watch whatever was on television, and she would let me play with her hair. She taught me how to weave the long tresses into braids. I felt so proud and loved when she would admire my work in the mirror afterward, turning her head this way and that, saying "What a beautiful job you have done!"

I liked her very much.

When they decided to get married my Grandma Knapp sewed two matching yellow flower girl dresses and, it seemed, we all got married together. I was five years old and starting to get into the swing of life with two sets of families—my mom's, whom I visited, and my lived-in home with my father and his new bride. I finally started to feel like I had an idea of what family was and could be. For a while, I couldn't have imagined it working out any better.

two

*B*y the time I started elementary school, my world, the place that I would forever call *home*, was with my father and stepmother. We had our routine firmly set. Every morning my father was the first to trundle off to work. He'd grab his lunch box and tool belt and head off to his job as a carpenter. My stepmother would fill the house with the smell of perfume as she dressed smartly for her work as a teacher. My sister and I would stand at the end of our long country driveway and wait for our dusty yellow school bus to take us to school.

We'd all come home to the same rituals each evening. My father would do the chores, feeding all our dogs, cats, and horses. My stepmother would make dinner and we girls would be busy with our homework. On the surface, it was a picture of the Rockwellian life.

Life was simple and routine during the week, but the weekends were the days I longed for. When we stayed home, Dad might take us fishing, or we might go with him on an adventure to the lumberyard. Like in the days before he remarried, the weekends were our special time to nurture our bond. A father and his two girls.

On alternate weekends, the same would happen in my mother's world. Off we would go for a glorious forty-eight hours of her undivided attention. We might go camping with our grandparents, or on a picnic. When my mother remarried, she would go on to have my two little sisters. There would always be something fun for us all to do together.

I loved both my families, but I struggled to make sense of the growing tension I felt being between them. I was becoming aware of how it felt to divide my affections. At school, I noticed that most of the other children lived with their mothers, even if their parents were divorced. When I talked about it with my mother, she tried her best to explain how our lives had come to this place.

"Why," I would ask, "can't I live with you like all the other kids live with their moms?"

My questions tore her heart out. She did her best to explain to a young girl how child custody works and how, if she had any choice, that things would be different. For the time being, I would have to try and understand that our lives were based on a court decision, not hers. The best she could offer was that when we were old enough, twelve years old to be exact, then the courts would let us choose.

When I brought my anxieties up to my father, the answer was different. He never discussed our situation much: "This is just the way things are."

All this began to weigh on me in the form of agonizing guilt. When I was about six years old, I became aware of how grateful I was to return back to the routine of my father's world at the end of our weekends away. I loved growing up on our farm. I enjoyed the excitement of going to school and all my friends there, but I also loved spending time with my mom. I had no clue as to how to manage the feelings of loss, watching her drive away each weekend. If I loved her, wouldn't I want to be with her? I loved my dad, too. I didn't want to *not* live with him.

With every visitation trade-off, I'd wade through the tears of my split affections. I loved them both. I wanted things to be different. I loved each life with equal measure, but I was a little girl, unable to put into words how difficult this was to manage.

The cost of this emotional struggle was starting to creep into our family psyche. As the halcyon days of my father's new marriage faded into everyday life and the visitation schedule taking its toll, my stepmother and I were clearly struggling with our new roles. The previous hopes that I had had about her acting as a kind of surrogate mother began to evaporate when we found ourselves in conflict.

It started in the little, predictable challenges of daily life. Maybe, one night we might be stubborn in getting to bed on time or complain about picking up our toys. When it came time for parental discipline to be enforced, we often lost our way. I wouldn't dream of challenging my father, but my stepmother was uncharted territory. I'd test her authority, childishly crying: "I don't have to do what you say!"

We would go round and round until our minor skirmishes eventually took on darker tones, and the language became littered with ugliness.

I'd get to the point at which I would scream: "You are *not* my mother!" and my stepmother's reply would be equally hurtful.

Like a glass capsule of cyanide, we put it between us and crushed it. Our awful words leaked out beyond the boundaries of our goodwill toward one another. We found ourselves at merciless odds, with each of us willing to go the distance into a spiraling darkness. Me, with all the rage of a confused little girl, and she with the constant reminder that I would never be her flesh and blood.

It became our cycle of hostility to go toe-to-toe in a war of words, in the hopes that one of us would come out on top as the victor. Neither one of us willing to relent. When the slightest grievance erupted to pit my stepmother against my sister and me, it seemed to leave my father torn between the loyalties of the women in his life, his wife and his children. Who was he to side with? The adult or the children?

It had to have been a difficult situation for him to navigate. Between my sister and me, I was often the confident ringleader, notorious for challenging boundaries. I'd fight until my last breath to stay the course of whatever path I had chosen, but I rarely came out the other side feeling as if I'd gained any ground.

My stepmother's account of contentious events usually won out, leaving me feeling crushed when my father appeared to choose her narrative over my own.

Growing up, I would struggle to keep hold of how he loved me when it seemed he was powerless to change the circumstances of our home life. Between the hours when he seemed swept away by the current of our family brokenness, there would be times we could find peaceful moments of rest. Little moments of respite, like mending a fence or grooming a horse. The everyday chores of the farm would predictably bend to our will and hard work. From him, I would learn a kind of patience in suffering, of living between that which we had the power to change and a determination to survive what we could not.

three

*T*ime spent alongside my father was precious.

I delighted in the Saturday mornings when he would invite my sister and me to join him on his trips to town. The simple pleasure of being by his side was joyful. Long before the days when seat belts were mandatory, we would stand up on the bench seat of the pickup truck so that we could see the world speeding by. He would give us the rundown of the day's schedule. A trip to the feed yard to buy oats for the horses. Out to Walmart for motor oil for our tractor. Then, off to the lumberyard to get supplies for repairs around the farm.

Oh, how I loved going to the lumberyard! It was a place where the necessary tools of my father's blue-collar world were laid out in full glory. I loved watching him in his element, potent and empowered among his like-minded peers. All the men would stand about in their worked-in clothes, paint spattered and dusty, talking about how they were going to tackle this project or that.

The smell of freshly cut timbers and chugging noises of forklifts only added to the excitement. I was in awe of the organized library of treated pine, two by fours of various lengths and wood types, stacked so high in the warehouse. There were stacks of brick, pallets of colorful tile, sheet rock, and plywood, and bins of nails, screws, brass hinges, and knobs. Each was mysterious to me, but all were the tools of my father's talent.

As he confidently called for the cuts of lumber he required, I stood back, taking it all in. I believed each man there to be deft and skillful in his craft, astounded by their knowledge of how to shape all that waiting wood with nails and power tools.

I saw my father as having the power to sculpt the world into shape. What would it be this weekend, I wondered? A nifty saddle rack? A ladder to the hay loft? Maybe a swinging barn door?

With a few planks of wood and a hammer, my father's skills inspired my creativity then as much as any Picasso does today. I'll always remember him pulling back from a newly completed construction, wiping the sweat from his brow to clear his eyes so that he could survey his accomplishments. Sometimes, I wonder if the artist that I grew up to be wasn't in some way inspired by his gift.

Among the most treasured gifts he gave me were the leftover wood scraps, near-empty paint cans, and rusted nails that I could make my own creations. Sometimes, he would lend me one of his precious tools to assist me in my project. Oh, the terror of sawing off a finger! He sat aside any worries that I might pound my thumb to a purple and nail-less pulp when he gave me a hammer. It was his way of instilling confidence in my own abilities, though I might have been but a little girl. He trusted me to learn by doing, even if it meant the odd bruise or splinter.

Those long hours that we spent, side by side, building our projects were our escape. We rarely spoke of the tension that came from the fallout of his and my mother's life together. Nor did we speak of how to manage the growing anger and resentment that was becoming an everyday reality between my stepmother and me. Instead, the reassuring noises came from the rhythms of our construction. The calm pulse of my father's breath in sync with the athletic *whaah-hee! whaah-hee! whaah-hee!* of the hand saw, or the *tap-tap-bang!* as he pounded in the nails.

THESE OUTSIDE NOISES were soothing compared to those that happened inside our home, where we were a family of conflict. By the time I was ten years old, my stepmother's mercurial personality was the force that we would all revolve around.

It is difficult to lay hold of what exactly put her in such a state of unrest, as both my sister and I were, by most general description, two ordinary children. Reasonably well behaved, we were neither extraordinarily precocious nor disobedient, yet we could never seem to win her affection. I felt that we were always being reminded that we were our mother's children. The implication was that we were born as evidence of my mother's youthful pregnancy—errors in judgment and, above all, unwanted.

If my sister and I did not adequately clean our room, or maybe forget to put away our crayons, she would snap, and, before I knew it, I was standing guard between her and my sister, who in tears, fell into self-preserving silence, while I held out for justice.

Though my father knew that we were at war, he seemed unable to secure any kind of lasting peace. The best he had to offer was in trying to keep us separated as much as he could. Encouraging us to keep a low profile. Pleading with us stay out of trouble.

I felt very isolated. My stepmother's awful words would echo in my head long after our arguments had ended. I had difficulty at such a young age to find the words to explain to my father, or anyone for that matter, how those fights were chipping away my spirit. I needed to be believed. Protected. Cared for. But our house had turned into a zone of either icy silence or earth-shaking rage.

I needed a peaceful place of my own to retreat, as my father found in his work. Going to school turned out to be my saving grace. There I would learn to read and write. Through the many books on offer at my school library, I found a way of floating away to other more pleasant worlds. From Bill Pete's "Scamp" in *The Whingdingdilly* to Lucy Maud Montgomery's *Anne of Green Gables*, I was fascinated by how each character prospered despite their trials. I wanted to be like those heroes, unfazed and victorious through adversity.

I related to the diaries of little Anne Frank. I recognized the feeling of being locked away, challenged by silence. I imagined that I, too, could grab a pencil and paper and write down everything that was going on inside my head.

Writing was one of the few acts in my life that I felt I could control. The pages helped keep me sane. I couldn't go to school and tell of my struggles at home. Who could I tell? What could I tell? I wasn't being beaten. I had a roof over my head, clean clothes, and well-balanced meals. There were no bruises to give evidence to my deepening wounds. Maybe I was just too sensitive? Maybe this was what life was like for other kids? Whatever the case, I couldn't seem to escape my sorrow and what felt like a rising tide of insanity. I didn't want to be another suicidal depressed kid sent to therapy so that I could be whispered about. I just wanted to get on with things. So, onto the pages it all went. My fears. My anger. My plots for escape. Even if I didn't have the courage to run away now, I could prepare myself for the possibility in the event of emergency. My imaginative contingency plans were invaluable in maintaining my sense of control. Maybe, one day, I could be just like Sam Gribley in *My Side of the Mountain*. Living on my own out in the forest, alone, challenged, but free.

I was surviving by seeing my thoughts become real, legible evidence of what otherwise seemed invisible. It never occurred to me how I would feel if anyone actually read my thoughts. All that was about to change.

It was subtle at first. I started to recognize that some of the comments coming from my stepmother sounded eerily like the worries I had squirreled away on my pages. It took me a while to realize that she was teasing me with my own secrets.

Recognizing how the taunts were in the vein of my hidden truths, it finally dawned on me. "Oh, my God," I thought, nauseated at the realization, "she's read my pages!"

I changed my tactics and began to write in code. I wasn't about to let her think that she had any power over me. I created my own unique scheme of symbols to replace each letter of the alphabet. They were simple substitutions that any fan of cryptic word games could solve, but it was my only defense. I wrote so much and so often that the second script became fluid and natural to my hand. At the very least, my stepmother would have to spend time deciphering it, and then she would know that I was onto her.

It must have gotten on her nerves, because one day she snapped. In an elaborate spring-cleaning ruse, she instructed me to go and clean up my room. As soon as I opened the door to my bedroom, I saw that my pages were littered all over the floor. Seeing my secrets out in the open, a chill came over my body and I could only stand there, frozen in fear.

She proceeded to rifle through my things, confiscating all my paper and pencils. Arcing toward an apoplectic fit, she shredded countless sheets into confetti, snowing my room with my private dreams.

I had never witnessed another human being so overcome with anger, and now, without the sanctuary of my pages, I had no way to protect myself from it.

My father heard about the incident when my stepmother told him that I had been falsely accusing her of malevolence in my diaries. I was grounded in my room for several weeks as a result, but in all, his response was muted compared to the tragedy it felt to me. He offered little acknowledgment that I was truly hurting inside. Several days would pass before I would realize that the significance of the episode had actually appeared on his radar.

Not long after, my father presented me with an old metal toolbox. It seemed a strange gift at first, but then he handed me a padlock and some paint to decorate it. Without a single word about what had happened with my stepmom, it was clear that he understood. He made a way for me to find safety as best he could. He couldn't rescind the punishment I was serving, lest he, too, encounter my stepmother's wrath, but he gave me the combination to the padlock. He directed me to a place in the barn, high in the rafters, where he had constructed a safe hiding place for my new treasure chest. In one of the most enduring and compassionate acts of his life, he gave me what mattered most, his best available love.

Now that I had a new place to keep my writing, along with the assumed protection of my father, the codes became unnecessary. Still, I had learned a valuable lesson. The secrets of the heart are vulnerable and more valuable than I had ever imagined.

For as much as the experience changed the spirit of our home, it began shaping my writing as well. I was maturing. My thoughts and dreams were becoming less childlike and more cerebral in tone. I was shifting from the daily news to the more philosophical and poetic. I was noticing the world around me. I was becoming increasingly more aware of my own ability to contemplate the world around me: *Who am I? What is life all about? What do I do with all these feelings I have inside of me?* I began writing with abandon, hopeful and refreshed that my voice mattered, that somehow, I was capable of being heard.

In many ways, what I wrote in those pages were like my prayers to God. My grandmother's forced marches through Sunday school must have made some kind subconscious connection. I began to find comfort in the idea that what I spoke of in my pages seemed to find a sympathetic ear. As if, somehow, though I could not see the Listener, I was being heard. Life suddenly began to open up, not to just the things I could see with my own eyes. There seemed to be a kind of spirit weaving it all together. A sensation. A knowing. A presence of some spiritual nature that acknowledged my existence in the universe.

I would find myself sneaking outside in the middle of the night to try to find it. I would lie on my back, beneath the big Kansas sky, and imagine myself as a single star. The distant waning howls of the coyotes seemed to echo my own prayers. I would imagine what peace looked like when I would come home tomorrow and will it to be so. I ached for grace, for ease. I would toy with my childhood understanding of God, search the black expanse of the heavens, and write.

Poetry became my new cipher. I could write a poem about how the tornadic spring storms would bring both terror and re-birth. I could use budding flowers as a metaphor in the constant and reliable cycles of anger and hoped-for peace in my real life. I could write about the strength of our horses as they galloped through the field as a symbol of freedom that I could only dream of.

My poems could be beautiful and wishful, or act as the dark vessels of all my sorrow. I could at last tell someone, anyone, at least a portion of what had long been mine to suffer alone. I could share these things with the outside world and maybe I would find a connection. With others? With God? I was learning that these experiences did not have to stay locked inside my head, eroding my spirit. I was learning new ways to survive. I was learning that I did not have to be captive to the grievous acts of others. I might never be able to change my stepmother. I might not be able to change all of my circumstances. But I was becoming aware that being alive is sometimes a conscious choice. No matter what happened, I wanted to be there, living.

four

If I wasn't ambling in the countryside, or nestled away somewhere scribbling in my diary, I was equally enthusiastic about being in school. Beyond the relief it provided in being away from home, there were so many adventures to be had. I could spend hours fossicking around the library for a new and exciting book to read. I loved it all, be it math, social studies, or history. The thrill of rising to the top of the class and getting praise for my excellent marks made me an unabashed contender for teacher's pet. It was a safe place, where I felt inspired to succeed. It was also the place where I fell in love with music.

One day a week, a music teacher would visit our country school. We had no proper music room, only the gymnasium. The same gym that served as basketball court during phys ed also served as concert hall and cafeteria, depending on the time of day. When it was time for music, our teacher, a spritely little woman, would throw her shoulder into the side of an old piano and roll it out into the center of the gymnasium floor to begin our lessons.

Heaven only knows how she managed to wrangle a class of energetic country kids into standing in place. I, for one, was more accustomed to running around outside, kicking balls, and climbing trees. The idea of standing in place for an hour at first seemed like a cruel substitute for entertainment, best reserved for rainy days. Still, she managed to keep my attention.

She always greeted us with her startlingly wide smile and vivid appearance. She was like Rapunzel meets Janis Joplin turned school librarian. Her long, wispy blonde hair cascaded down her back, where it seemed to join in conspiracy with her usual long, cotton print skirt.

There was always some part of her in motion. Her petite hands often guided us with light, feminine gestures, like a ballerina cum traffic cop. No matter that her directions made no earthly sense to us as she pointed and waved in rhythm with the music. When her hands were busy on the keys of the piano, her legs would tap and dance beneath her as she sat precariously on the edge of the piano bench, her hair joining in the perfect choreography of fully embodied sound.

So what if the songs we were singing had only one-part harmony? That she led us in rousing renditions of the latest Muppets movie soundtrack didn't limit her enthusiasm or purpose. For many of us, she was the first, and perhaps, the only, human being on the planet who could usher us into a world beyond that which was visible. That one day a week was a window into a world beyond our books, capable of launching us into a new realm of imagination.

Long before I would learn to express my insecurities by saying "I can't," she began to teach us how to read the language of music. With limited resources, she found a way. There weren't any blackboard or textbooks for her to use to help us decode the magical language of the music staff and black dots called notes, so she took to the hardwood floor. Ignoring all the markings of the basketball court, she found a clear spot where she could map out five perfectly straight parallel lines, with four uniform spaces in between. She called the creation a "staff." With the aid of a stuffed toy frog, she'd place it at various positions in the diagram and called out the representative letter that we would later call notes. The lines, we would learn by using the acronym "Every Good Boy Does Fine" and the spaces as "F.A.C.E.".

As we learned what to call the lines and spaces, she let us tap out these notes on the piano. I found it the greatest extravagance when I would have my turn to take the quiz. I would sit alone at the keyboard, where I could strike the corresponding key indicated by the stuffed frog. But one note just didn't seem enough; I felt the urge to link the notes together, in rhythm and order to make what seemed so fantastic . . . a song!

Eventually, part of our musical curriculum would come to include learning how to play an alto recorder. It's a plastic, flute-like whistle of sorts that looks somewhat like a small clarinet. Once I got my hands on my very own, I couldn't get enough.

Learning to read the code of music as fluently as the written word was like cracking open the door to a magic world. I was mesmerized that I could take those little black dots on the page and breathe them into life. What to some appeared as frantic nonsense scored on the page, was, to me, something that I had the power to sing into recognition. I just couldn't get enough of it.

Some way or another I got my hands on a book of old American folk tunes. I must have played the tune "Erie Canal" a thousand times in this state of amazement. I played that song so many times that I began to feel, in my soul, that I was there, on the canal, walking and pulling my burdens alongside the famed waterway with the aid of my trusty mule. My parents, on the other hand, found themselves quickly exhausted. And who could blame them?

I've got a mule her name is" (Wrong note, start again.)

—(Okay.)*I've got a mule her name is Sa—* (Oops, okay, start again.)

I've got a mule her name is Sal, fifteen miles on the Erie Canal. I would sing along in my head as I played the notes on my trusty recorder.

On and on it went until my poor parents, in hopes of maintaining their own sanity, demanded that I play no more than one hour inside the house and, if that weren't enough, I'd have to go outside. So, outside I went. I played under the shade trees and in the boughs of the trees. I'd go to the barn and serenade the horses. I'd crawl up into the hay loft, make a hay bale my music stand and play every last song I could manage.

Much to my father's amusement, my talents never reached the same magical effect as the Pied Piper of Hamelin. Though my playing failed to abate the never-ending raid of oat-pilfering field mice from the barn, as far as I was concerned, I was a virtuoso.

In those rare moments of youth, when we are oblivious to facts, logic, and our insecurities, everything is possible. Nothing is beyond our reach. I played my songs with abandon. I looked to the notes on the page, I sent my breath through my recorder, I moved my fingers, and the world came alive. There was not a dream I could conjure that wasn't possible. Every song was an invitation to an experience that would otherwise be too far away for a little girl from Kansas. It had never occurred to me that the music that I heard might be received as noise to another person. It never occurred to me to judge it as good or not good. It never occurred to me that I was performing for anyone's pleasure other than my own. Music was a part of my body, a part of my experience that allowed me a safe space to feel and express my heart. Before music, I was just another kid who cried when they didn't get what they wanted. With music, I was becoming a person who began to see emotion as the tangible, real stuff of being.

The feeling of freedom and escape was similar to when I found writing. Yet it seemed to assuage a burden that my writing could not. I could write until my fingers bled, but there were times when words didn't seem sufficient. There was still more inside of me. There were emotions that failed to be fully expressed without words.

Music seemed to give voice to what I knew in my heart but could not spell into being. I might write down words about sadness, but with the help of a minor key, I could make all the world vibrate with resonant empathy.

It's easy to wax poetically about it now, but, at the time, I was just a nerdy little girl who failed to have an age-expected obsession with Cabbage Patch Kids or My Little Ponies. Nope. I was enamored of a noisy hunk of plastic, that, along with my love of writing, would form the fabric of how I learned to communicate with the world.

As with my private writings, I had grown wary of letting my need for creative expression lead me to a place of vulnerability with my stepmother. While I found ways to keep my enjoyment in writing out of her reach, it was more difficult to keep my love of music a secret. By the time most kids' recorders were gathering dust and our music classes were no longer amusing, I was still blowing away. But, as I got older, my recorder appeared more like a child's toy rather than a proper instrument. If I wanted to expand my musical horizons, I needed to devise a plan to step up my skills with a more grown-up instrument. Doing so would mean taking a risk and appealing to my stepmother's own love of music.

My stepmother was a respectable piano player herself. In the summer, she played for the children's Vacation Bible School at the United Methodist Church in town. Some Christmasses she'd even take a break from our wars and play a few carols on the old piano she kept at her mother's house. Maybe, if I was convincing enough, she could see that I shared a similar passion? Maybe I could give her a reason to respect me?

I spent a season begging my parents for piano lessons. I wasn't particularly drawn to the piano, but there were other girls who spoke of their weekly lessons and periodic adventures in something they called "recitals." I didn't even know what a recital was, but I wanted it so badly. I wanted to play a grown-up instrument.

"Please," I bargained, "let me stay after school. I'll do whatever it takes. I promise I'll be good! I'll feed the dogs every night. I'll water the horses so you guys don't have to. I'll mow the lawn every weekend. I'll clean out the stalls." I named every loathed family chore I could think of, trying to convince my folks of my sincerity.

"The piano teacher is walking distance from my school. I'll do more chores. I'll dust. I'll do the dishes every night! *Please . . .!*"

Though I hoped my enthusiasm would spark my parents' sympathies, there was little discussion about it. My campaign was short-lived, the answer came down firmly: *No.*

It was risky business in my household to voice such an obvious desire for pleasure. To ask for anything that might have required an extra effort from my father and my stepmother seemed to always be met with restraint, if not outright denial. Through the years I had discovered that speaking up often came with the risk of upsetting whatever rare calm might have been. A simple request like asking to be allowed to spend a Friday night at the skating rink or to be taken to the movies had the potential to erupt into full-blown drama.

It's not that my sister and I were completely denied the pleasures of childhood. It was just that it usually came with a cost. There were times when my father would splurge. Joy would wash over us when he gave my sister and me a twenty-dollar bill and dropped us off at the skating rink. However, that joy would be short-lived. When we would return home, our parents would be in an all-out war. My father would be relegated to sleeping on the couch, my stepmother having locked herself away in their bedroom. My sister and I reckoned that it was our fault for having wanted to go play; it was because of us that our father was in trouble because he had given us money that would have been better spent on something more important.

Through the tension of it all, my sister and I learned to stifle our desires for adventures away from the farm, especially those which required a little spending money. I wasn't surprised at the denial, but I was disappointed all the same.

My sister and I began a ritual of bartering between us. We would draw straws to see who would have the unenviable task of asking our parents for permission for an activity. Only one of us could be crowned the loser. The winner was the one who pushed the other forward to be the lamb to the slaughter. I found the whole exercise to be an excruciating ritual of disappointment. I never wanted to be the one who returned with the report that I had failed.

The whole exercise was fraught with danger. Get a *yes* and there was potential for family turmoil. Get a *no,* and live out the reality of feeling isolated and unsupported. The only thing that seemed to help us handle the disappointment is that we shared the journey together. If we had success, we were equal beneficiaries. And, when we failed, at least we could entertain each other.

For so many years, my sister and I relied on our unified front. In a way, we were a single identity in our family unit. "The girls," we were often called. One body. One space. What was good for one often seemed to be good for us collectively. We were, after all, twins. But, as we grew, our individual personalities and interests each began to take their own shape.

I had already found a way to explore my own identity with writing and now, my interest in music was one that seemed to be my own as well. I found that I couldn't rely on my sister to speak for me in my desire for learning music. It seemed that it was unique to me.

By the time we were in the fourth grade, my sister and I were being allowed to spend entire summers living with Mom. Three whole months to release the cares and stresses of life back home. A place where we felt free to be our true selves. With Mom, we were encouraged to dream. We could ask for anything without worry of upsetting the applecart. We didn't always get what we hoped for, but there she was always inspiring us to see all of life's possibilities. I felt safe enough to tell her all about how I wanted piano lessons, knowing that even if it wasn't something she could afford, at the very least I would be heard. I could count on her to listen, to feel and appreciate what I was longing for.

One summer, she found a way. For the few short weeks that we were together, Mom managed to set enough money aside so that both my sister and I could take piano lessons. My sister seemed to like it enough, but I was beside myself.

After a few short lessons I began learning to read chords and play more complex music than I had ever imagined. To my delight, I ended the summer with an ability to pound my way through recognizable works from Chopin and Beethoven. I relished that I had my very own books filled with all manner of songs, each that I now had the skill to dance into life.

It was a life-changing gift. No matter what happened now, I knew that I would always have music. I couldn't unlearn it. As much as I knew how to read and to write to express myself, music had expanded how I experienced the world around me.

Back home, with my father, us girls had been moved from our country school to a school in town. For the first time ever, my sister and I would find ourselves separated during the day. Up until then, we had always been in the same classroom. Things were different in town. There were several classrooms for each grade, so we were assigned different teachers. As a result, we became more individual. She built a world with the friends in her class and I built one with mine. In doing so, we began to form a divide in our personal interests.

My identity with music was becoming decidedly my very own, and my new school had a lot of possibilities by which to explore it.

Unlike my country school, my new school had a dedicated

music room. Rather than the echoic, cold, and uncomfortable gymnasium, my new music room had carpet and permanent, tiered risers. The walls were decorated with posters of wildly gesticulating conductors and cartoons of composers like Bach, Mozart, and Beethoven. I didn't even know who any of these people were, but it didn't matter. They *were* music and the entire room was dedicated to them. No more duct-taped staves on the gym floor. Now, we had a blackboard painted with imperishable staff paper. And there were instruments, too! So many instruments, just lying around. There was a guitar and lots of percussion, like wood blocks, claves, and tambourines. I was in hog heaven! I was so ready to leave behind the childish lessons delivered by a stuffed toy frog. I wanted *more*, and everything about this room made my dreaming seem possible.

However, it was the music that happened after school hours that really stirred my lust. Every day of fourth grade, while I waited in line to board the bus back out to the country, I watched as what seemed every fifth grader from my school commandeered the auditorium. I watched, green with envy, as they unpacked extravagant instruments like saxophones, trumpets, snare drums, and flutes. All the noises of their bustling and tuning in preparation of a coming Sousa march had me aching with desire. Without question, I wanted in on the action. I couldn't imagine anything more wonderful than being able to have a saxophone all to myself. I still had my plastic recorder to go home to, but this . . . this was sexy!

It was all I could to do imagine how I was going to survive a whole year until I was old enough to be a part of the fun. If piano lessons were out, asking my parents to buy me an expensive instrument *and* make a way for me to stay after school was going to be a challenge of epic proportions. I couldn't be afraid of *no*. I had to find a way to press on.

FIFTH GRADE AND sixth grade blew by and, with them, what appeared to my dream of joining the band. My parents couldn't get out of work to drive me home after band, so I had to be on that school bus every day. Through every Christmas that approached, I would plead my case for the season, hoping, at last, that my joy would be found under the tree—to no avail. I did my best to behave. I paid more than the average attention to my grades. Everything I did, I did with the motivation of pleasing my parents so that they would have no choice but to reward me. Undaunted and still yearning, I continued to keep my hopes alive. Soon, I would be entering junior high, where band was a class that I could take during school hours. It no longer required staying after school. It meant that I didn't have to worry about whether my parents had to make any changes in their work routines; all I needed now was the horn.

I had always imagined myself playing saxophone. It seemed similar to my much beloved alto recorder, only much more curvaceous and seductive. I did all the research, constantly pricing just how much it would cost, and mapping a barter system for the household chores, so that I could show I was willing to earn it. My parents seemed to be softening a bit.

"I played clarinet in high school," my stepmother confessed. "Such a honky thing. There's no way you're bringing that screechy instrument into this house. You'll drive me crazy."

"Okay. Okay? Not saxophone then," I conceded. "Maybe something else then? Anything . . . I'll play anything. I just want to join the band."

"If you do this, it's got to be something we can afford. We can't afford all the broken reeds and what-nots."

Was this a light at the end of the tunnel?

Christmas that year came and went, but by spring the word came down. The words I had longed to hear for years.

"There's a program for private lessons through the city parks and recreation department this summer. Maybe it would be a good way for you to catch up with the other kids," my stepmother finally offered.

"*Yes! Yes!*" I thought to myself. I couldn't believe it. But the rush of satisfaction quickly came to a halt when I realized that I was facing an agonizing decision.

Summer was the time that I spent with my mother. As it stood, we scarcely had enough time together. One factor that had led to an extended visit was that she had moved farther away from my hometown, making it difficult to keep up what was once our bimonthly schedule. We compromised with fewer visits during the school year by spending entire summer breaks with her. It wasn't lost on me what a predicament I was in.

I tried to maneuver without loss. "Maybe I could practice while I'm at Mom's?" I hoped aloud.

As usual, my options came down with limited discussion. "You want to play; you have to stay here for the summer. It's an option for both you girls if you want it," she expanded. "We can go down to the music shop and pick out an instrument that we can afford, but it has to stay here."

There it was. I was twelve years old, facing what would ultimately be a life-changing decision. Which sacrifice would I choose? That of losing the summer spent with my mother, or never getting to play?

Before I committed, I consulted with my sister.

She didn't seem flummoxed by options. There would be no drawing of straws to see which way we went together. I tried to convince her to join me, but music didn't seem to have the hold on her that it did on me. Her choice was going to Mom's. Whatever decision I made, it was going to be a choice I made on my own.

It would be the crossroads that would ultimately alter both our lives. Never before had we experienced being apart for more than the hours when we were at school in separate classrooms. We were developing our own identities, each with individual and unique desires. My imagination was captured with the call of music in a way in which she did not share. Faced with the opportunity to realize my dream, the idea of deciding against it seemed a choice against myself.

I knew what I wanted, apart from anyone else's influence. I wanted music. I chose to stay and she chose to go. I didn't know it then, but those days before the summer came would be the last we would share under the same roof.

I WILL NEVER forget the day that my stepmother took me down to our town's only music store to buy my first horn. It was memorable in so many ways.

I was filled with excitement and unease in equal parts.

Strained as my stepmother's and my relationship was, we had little practice in how to share such a personal moment together. So fierce had words been between us at times, that I couldn't help but feel an overwhelming sense of caution. I wondered if I could trust her to know just how momentous this occasion was for me. I had dreamed about this day, but had never imagined that it would be she that walked me through it. I had always pictured my father taking me to the shop, having squirreled away his pennies, to help me in my endeavor. All that faded as soon as I walked into the store.

I had no idea what I was going to choose. It was already made clear that a saxophone was off the table, so what then? A flute? I picked one up and tried to play it, but it seemed awkward and too girly. Clarinet was on par with the sax, so no-go there. Drums? I didn't even bother. I wanted to make music; I didn't care about the beat. All that was left was the brass.

The trombone seemed pretty cool, alien with its slurry slide and it was as long as I was. The shopkeeper handed it over, gave me a few pointers in how to approach the imposing beast and I blew . . . *Phffflurrrrgh* . . . What came out was a noise akin to a dying calf. Hardly inspiring.

I began to sweat a little. There was a moment where I wondered if I wasn't made for this. How ridiculous would it be to have spent all those years pining and then have it turn out that I actually had no talent for it whatsoever?

"Maybe the trumpet?" the shopkeeper offered sheepishly.

He pulled the thing down from the display wall, cleaned off the mouthpiece, and handed it to me. Solid and heavy in my hands, it didn't exactly feel like the romance of music that lived in my head. Still, I had to try.

As directed, I put the cold, metal mouthpiece to my pursed lips and buzzed. To my amazement, what came out the other end was immediately recognizable. The noise I made actually sounded like the real thing. I pushed at the piston valves, making out differing notes.

I successfully voiced a low tone: *Whhuuaaaahh!*

Then, as I was instructed, pursed tighter and with more air: *Whheeeeee!*

Despite having no real clue as to what I was doing, the match seemed ordained. "It looks like we have a winner," declared the keeper. "So, whaddya think?" he said, turning to my stepmother, ready to make the sale.

Minutes later I was walking out the door with my very own Conn Director. It wasn't a brand new horn, she came preloved, but she was mine now. A striking beauty she was, too. Unlike other trumpets, which were usually uniformly plated with the familiar golden brass, she had a rose-colored copper bell to help her stand out from the crowd. With a little practice, we were going to make wonderful music together.

Once I got her home, I put my head down and got to work. I had twelve weeks before school started. I didn't want to embarrass myself when I got to band class, so I tore into my books. I challenged my poor, tender lips to keep pace with what I wanted to accomplish. I played every minute of the day that I could physically handle.

After only a couple of weeks of practicing alone, I tripped into my first lesson. My practice had apparently paid off.

My instructor assumed that I had been playing for a couple of years, similar to the course that was expected of my peers. When I told him that I had just started, he seemed confused. He tested my honesty. In his mind, there was no way I could be play-ing as well as I was in only a few weeks.

"You mean to tell me you *just* started playing? You didn't start in fifth grade with the other kids?"

"No," I maintained. I was equally surprised that he found it questionable.

After a momentary pause, he moved on. "Well then, let's find something to challenge you."

For the rest of the summer, he introduced and tested me with all manner of taxing exercises. Etudes, articulation drills, and slurring assignments. I ate it all up. I worked tirelessly at perfect-ing my skills and adored the work. It didn't hurt that my instruc-tor said that I had talent. I relished the fact that I had a kind of gift that made me feel worthwhile. His endorsement encouraged me to press on. I couldn't wait to put my newfound skills to the test when school started again. At long last, I was going to be a member of the school band!

The end of that summer felt triumphant. There was so much to be happy about.

Though life in our home had been difficult at times, this summer had developed a different tone. My stepmother seemed more relaxed and less prone to anger. We were getting along, al-most bonding even. The support that she had offered in helping me find my way to music seemed to open the door to a new un-derstanding between us. For the first time in a very long time, it seemed like we all might be able to live in harmony.

I looked forward to my sister's return to the fold. I couldn't wait for her to share in what seemed a positive shift in our home. It had seemed that, in recent years, she and I had been struggling to stay connected to one another. Our past family struggles came to affect us in different ways. I had found my hope through the lean times in reaching out through creative expression of writing and music. It wouldn't be until she came back home that I would learn about where she kept her own hope.

Our time apart had seemed to veer us in two distinctly different paths of survival. It turned out that my sister had kept her hopes stored in moving to Mom's once she was old enough to enforce her choice in the court system. During my last visit of the summer, together again at my mother's, I learned of it. Mom was clear that I, too, could make a similar choice, but she was also careful to make certain that I felt no pressure to arrive at the same conclusion.

"Your sister has decided that she wants to move here, with me. I want you to know that you can do the same, if you choose. But I want you to know, that I will love you no matter what. Whatever you decide, I will love you and support you."

I couldn't imagine what life apart from my sister would look like, nor could I imagine altering my current vision of following music. Through the years, I had often dreamed of running away, and had attempted to do so on more than one occasion. I had spent countless hours imagining that life would be better, more pleasant, more openly loving in my mother's world, but now that I was faced with the reality of actually making it happen, I couldn't get over the idea that I was in some way forced to choose between the music that had become my safety net and a life with her that I didn't seem to have the courage to test.

In the years to come, I would be haunted by the picture of my sister coming home and packing her things from the room where everything had always been ours. I would struggle with the strange conflicting feelings of being abandoned by her and the frivolous teenage joy of finally having a bedroom to myself. The idea that I had, for the first time in my life, made a clearly individual decision, independent of our collective personality, was empowering and, at the same time, a choice that made me feel a fool. I saw myself as lacking in courage in comparison to her. I couldn't help but feel that my choice was an act of betrayal to her love and to my mother's, but in the end I chose to stay in the place I had always called home, in my father's world.

five

Life, as it always seems to do, moved callously forward, oblivious to my need to regain my breath. There seemed to be a hole in my universe. My sister was gone now, and I was on my own. I was brokenhearted and trying to make sense of it all.

The idyllic summer of eased tensions with my stepmother came to an end, only to ramp back up to our usual cycle of emotional turmoil. We did not know how to comfort one another. We did not know how to love. Once again, every conflict of our home pressed on the bruise that was our family brokenness. We were either in all-out war or locked in icy silence. Whatever my family had been was crumbling.

I felt I could no longer rely on my father to bridge the gap of our family tensions. He began to express his sorrow about my sister's absence by hiding out in the barn, busying himself with this task and that. Like my sister, he seemed to disappear, leaving me feeling all the more isolated. I was stunned at feeling so alone, unable to find any way to connect with and communicate what I was going through. If it weren't for music, I don't know how I would have survived it all.

For the first time in my life, I hopped the bus to school alone. I was in junior high now, facing a new school and a whole new way of going to class. The sound and feel of it all was so foreign. It was all so noisy and alive compared to grade school. The hallways were teeming with teenagers, some of them seemingly twice my size. The school bell that alerted us of the changing hours rang through the building, along with the banging and bustle of all the students rummaging through the metal lockers that lined the hallways. Every new hour meant a new class, and with it a new teacher to lead the way. It was all so overwhelming, until, at last, I walked into the band room.

That was where I met Carol. The tall, lanky ginger of a woman that stood in front of the room hardly looked old enough to be a teacher, but here she was, our band director.

All the anticipation I had had for this day did not go unrewarded. She was a ball of enthusiasm, welcoming us to sit down, each to our sections, flutes in front, saxes and clarinets in the next row, and brass in the back. Most of the other kids seemed to know their place, making their way to seats in front of music stands already laid out with sheet music. I fought through my fear of the newness of it all and followed suit, taking a seat alongside all the other trumpeters.

Carol took her place atop her conductor's pedestal, raised her long, spindly arms wide and declared, "Okay, let's see what you've got!" With that, every student put their horns to their mouths and began to play under her direction.

I was shocked. I had never before played in a band, but I went with it. One note after the next. I couldn't believe it! I was in the *band!* I had always played my music alone, or maybe in a duet with my private instructor, but now I was playing, in harmony, alongside the other students.

Periodically, I would peek up from the page to see this widely gesticulating figure of a skinny, red-headed woman, flapping her arms to the beat. When she wanted us to play more softly, she would shrink to smaller gestures. When she demanded force, she would widen and wave with a gusto unlike anything I had ever seen. To my amazement, the whole room had no choice but to respond to her spell. I thought she was so brave and wild in how she seemed to move with such abandon. I couldn't imagine being so free, but I could tell, she *loved* music. I did, too, and I wanted her to teach it all to me.

I loved band class, but there were times when the music we played as a group seemed less than challenging. I would get bored, feeling like I was being held back by the rest of the class. So, I began asking Carol for more. I began showing up at her classroom outside our prescribed hours. Even when I wasn't looking for music, there were times when I was just looking for a friend. I must have been a pest of a kid, always bugging her apart from class, but I was serious about my instrument and she, above all people in the world, seemed to appreciate that. In an act of kindness, she took me under her wing.

She tested me a bit at first, giving me music that was usually reserved for older high school students, but I gobbled it up. I was young, and lacking in finesse, for sure, but I was plucky. There wasn't any music that she put in front of me that I didn't work on playing to the best of my ability. Though it wasn't part of the school curriculum, Carol began to make a way for me to prepare music for solo competitions similar to those of the high school students ahead of me. Somehow, Carol had managed get my parents' permission to sign me up and make a way for me to perform at music competitions throughout the state. At her own expense, she would drive me around Kansas on the weekends to universities in Wichita, Emporia, and Pittsburg so that I could play all the challenging pieces of music that she had put in front of me. Every competition that I entered, I walked away with a gold medal.

I had a lot of natural talent as a trumpet player, but I still needed instruction to grow. Carol was an excellent flutist and conductor, but she knew that I needed a proper trumpet teacher to help me move forward.

In my freshman year, Carol reached out to Dr. Gary Corcoran, who was then the acting band director at Pittsburg State University. Dr. Corcoran was the trumpet instructor for PSU students and, thanks to Carol's urging, agreed to give me lessons pro bono. The only problem with accepting such a gracious gift was that I had to figure out a way to get there. Pittsburg was sixty miles away, I wasn't old enough to drive, and my parents weren't prepared to make the commitment themselves. Once again, Carol found a way. She somehow managed to garner my parents' permission for the whole affair, agreeing that she would drive me the distance, two hours round trip.

I was stunned that Carol thought I was a decent enough player to warrant such an undertaking. But, even more, I was deeply blessed by her act of kindness in believing in me. It was the kind of outward encouragement that was empowering to me as a teenager struggling to maintain a sense of personal worth. Her generosity of time and inspiration was more than simply giving me an opportunity to do something *fun;* it was an investment in my dignity. It felt good to have a mentor who believed in my potential. The impact of that support gave me hope that I could be someone who was meaningful. I began to be aware of the necessary value of finding, within myself, a gift worthy of celebrating. At home I felt like a mistake, an afterthought, a burden, but when I closed my eyes, picked up my horn and played, I could breathe into life every dream and hope that was trapped, unspoken inside my heart. Music wasn't just something I found outside of myself, but rather, it was a song that was, and had always been, living inside me. To me, music was the voice of our inner spirit, that when we call out, answers our deepest longings.

What Carol did, both as mentor and friend, was give me permission to set that inner voice free. Through the countless hours of driving, we talked about falling into the gift that music had been for us. How it was the language in which we hear the call to be alive. She inspired in me the idea that in the things that we do, we do them not to just be excellent at skill for skill's sake, or even for talent's sake, but that we are in the process of reaching out into those places that give our lives meaning and hope. She often reminded me that I could play every note on the page with technical precision, but that all of life is more than just the execution.

"You can play with all the skill in the world, Jennifer," she would say, "but if you don't put your heart into it, it's just noise." Usually, a comment like this came after I performed a piece without flaw, but with no feeling. I'd want to perform without error so as to be praised for perfection, but I'd hold back the emotion, selfishly saving it for the times when I wasn't on stage.

As my friend, Carol knew that I had found an inner voice. What she was trying to teach me was that practicing wasn't just about making my fingers and lips do as I commanded. Music was also a journey into self-discovery that took courage.

"You can play every note right, but if you don't bring the joy out of the piece, you've missed the true purpose. You have to find that joy and let it live," she would say. The idea was terrifying, but alluring. I wanted joy, but what if I couldn't find it? To Carol, that was just as much a part of practicing music, facing the emotions, knowing them, *then* communicating them.

"I know you're a woman of depth. I can see it and it's a beautiful thing when you let it out," she said one day. "The gift isn't that you can make that trumpet sound good, it's that you know—you *know* how music feels. That isn't talent, honey, that's a gift. One that I hope you will always be willing to share."

Those words would stay with me for the rest of my life. Whatever I would experience in life, however deeply I felt my emotions, none of these were meant to be wholly absorbed and end with me. I wasn't meant to simply act as a sponge and keep it all to myself where it might fester. I didn't know it at the time, but she was giving me a lesson about life. None of us are at the end of what we experience. It may feel like we are at times the target of sorrow or of anger, but these things must pass through us if we want to survive them. We cannot keep joy to ourselves or love hidden away. Nor can we harbor pain so deep that it takes root. We can set the love we have inside our hearts free to be enjoyed by those we hold dear. We have in us the power to reshape the anger we experience into acts of forgiveness.

I was lucky that I found music and a compassionate teacher to help me see it as a form of lived grace. Music would be a gift that would help me understand that life is made up of all manner of serenity and despair, but that it is in how we choose to let those things pass through us that speak of our true character. I didn't yet know what kind of person I was going to become, but I hoped that in my journey toward adulthood, I could honor the person Carol had believed me capable of being.

BY THE TIME I got to high school, Carol had to move away, but she left with me the legacy of her kindness and a passion to dedicate my studies to music. Like her, I was going to be a music teacher, maybe even a conductor of an orchestra. Knowing that, school and academics took on a new significance. I had always been a good student, but now that I knew what I wanted to be when I grew up, I was determined to not just go to school. I wanted an education. I wanted to go to college for music.

I put my head down and got to work. Everything I did—every class, every elective, every afterschool activity that I gave my time to—was done with an eye toward gaining experience in fine arts. I was fearless.

Though I had never thought much about singing before, I enrolled in the choir. I talked our resident choir pianist to help me prepare and perform solo vocal pieces so that I could compete, as I did with my trumpet, at state competitions. In band, I took it upon myself to learn at least a little something about every instrument. With a little coercion, I got my new band director to give me at least a cursory lesson on each major instrument in the band. I understood that in college, I would have to learn how to play all of them at least to some kind of passing level, so I wanted to get a head start.

Though our school had limited resources, there were a few unused instruments kicking around. I found a dusty, brass baritone horn in the storage room, a heavily dented French horn, a trombone, and a soprano sax. I pestered my band director to instruct me about every one. Though he insisted that I keep my chair as a trumpeter during school hours, I eventually managed to convince him to let me play trombone during basketball games, baritone for state solo competition, and French horn when an odd score may have called for it. In exchange, I promised to never play saxophone in public. (Apparently, whatever musical gifts I have don't extend to reed instruments!)

Now, more than ever, I needed to find a way to afford the piano lessons, and the more complex music theory that came with them. I needed to find a way to stay after school and stay involved in all the fine art activities that were preparing me for college without the relentless, and usually disappointing, bartering with my parents.

To them, this music thing didn't seem all that important. They had invested in buying me a horn, but that was about the limit. I had hoped they would share in my enjoyment by coming to my various concerts and performances, but my parents didn't seem to recognize the significance that music was having in my life. There were times when I wondered if they even noticed just how much their absence left me feeling empty and disregarded.

I tried to explain to my father that all these things weren't just busywork for me. I had shared with him my vision of going to college.

"Dad, this isn't just something I want to do," I shared, "It's my future. It's what I want to be."

His response was more practical than emotional. "Well, if that's the case, then, you'll have to take responsibility for it. You want piano lessons? You need to find a way to pay for it. More than that, you'll need to get yourself there."

I don't think he understood my dream of wanting to become a skilled musician or how much his support as a father mattered to me.

Eventually, we struck a kind of deal. My parents would give me use of one of their old cars, keeping it insured and registered. In turn, I would do whatever it took to keep it running. That meant earning my own gas money, keeping up my good grades, and generally staying out of trouble.

"You can help around the house by chipping in with the bills. Pay for what you can. School books, music paper, gas money, movies—whatever," my dad said. "If you want it, you'll need to be able to afford it. Then . . ." he paused. "Well, that will help us save up for college."

"Done deal!" I took my oath and ran with it. I found part-time jobs that fit my busy school life and help to fund my passions. Whenever I felt the grind of not wanting to clock in for work or got bored with my school work, I reminded myself of the future.

I acted as if there were not a minute to be wasted. If I wasn't busy serving up egg rolls at the local Chinese restaurant, I was delivering pizza. When I wasn't at work, I was usually in a rehearsal, a lesson, or performing. It was even better when I was performing *and* working at the same time.

In the summer, I found work playing Haydn concertos at weddings. In the Advent season, the organist for the local Methodist church put me to work with all manner of challenging cantatas. I was even asked to be on call as a trumpeter for funerals at the local VFW. When the last report of the twenty-one-gun salute had fired, it fell to me to complete the honor by playing "Taps." Playing at the funerals was strange at first. I didn't know how to react while others mourned the passing of their loved one, but eventually found a kind of peace in offering the gift of music.

So much of my performance work in the community was happening in sacred spaces. All that time, being a part of and witnessing the spiritual impact of music during the weddings, funerals, and High Church ceremonies filled me with a growing sense of reverence for Divinity. I recognized the hope's longing that filled the hymns' refrains. I wasn't thrilled with the idea of religion, but I couldn't help but be moved by what seemed a distant, faint voice of comfort. Inside my chest, music and spirituality seemed to be made of the same stuff—as if sounding in the same voice. There were times when it felt like I was being called to. By who or what, I couldn't say, and didn't want to say. The idea of calling that sensation by a name—to call it "God" aloud to others—was too provocative for me, but it didn't keep my spirit from drifting into it. From time to time, I became aware that my imagination had wandered off into some kind of reassuring conversation with a distant being. I suppose some folks would have called it prayer. Part of me wanted to say that I believed in God because that's what good girls do, but my growing pride and sense of personal accomplishment was such that I wanted to push aside such notions. That business might have been necessary for some, but I felt I was managing just fine without it.

The truth was that I wasn't doing fine. I was slipping.

For four long years, I had kept my eyes on the prize of college. By my senior year, I was counting down the days until graduation. I had successfully auditioned for, and was granted, a scholarship at nearby Pittsburg State. PSU was a good back-up plan, but I wanted to follow in the footsteps of my mentor, Carol. The University of Kansas (KU), in Lawrence, was her alma mater and was the school that I had spent my days dreaming about. Every day, I would race to the end of our country drive-way to check the mailbox for the letter that would confirm their great desire to have me as an undergrad. KU's tuition was pricey compared to Pitt State, but I had the confidence that I had the grades and musical pedigree to warrant enough scholarship money to supplement what modest income my father had prom-ised to put toward my goal. For four years running, I was first-chair trumpet for the Kansas All-State Band. I had numerous State medals to my name in multiple disciplines and, clearly, enough ego to get me there.

I waited and waited, but the letter I had hoped for never came. Many of my peers had already decided and confirmed where they were going to school next, but I was still on the bub-ble. It had never occurred to me to actually go up to the KU cam-pus and audition as I had for PSU. The fact that I had auditioned for Pittsburg was actually an accident. I happened to find myself on campus for a State competition hosted by PSU. I was there anyway, so I figured it wouldn't hurt to go through the motions. Little did I know how fortuitous that audition would be.

In truth, though I had dreamed of college, now that it was time to start making it happen, I was finding it difficult to figure out how to proceed on my own. In the infrequent and brief con-versations I had had with my father about the matter, we spoke little more about it than we did our previous financial arrange-ment. I had honored my end of the bargain, but eventually it be-came clear that our agreement would not come to fruition as I had imagined it.

One day, not long into my senior year of high school, I came home and noticed a new horse in the paddock. The gelding was easily admired. Courtly, muscular, and immaculately groomed, he was the most beautiful horse that had ever set foot on our farm. This animal wasn't cheap and I knew it.

In that instant, I was crushed. I realized that there was no family plan for my future. It had all gone into the horse.

I held out hope that the steed belonged to someone else and that we were boarding it, maybe even training it for a season. But when I confronted my father about it, my worst fears were realized.

"What's with the new horse?" I tried to play down my internal panic while watching my dreams slip away.

Coolly, my father replied, "It's your stepmother's new horse." He paused, filling the gap with defeated silence. He took yet another beat and then: "She bought it."

"Seriously?" I asked with teenage sarcasm. I felt my body release all the chemicals of despair and rage into my bloodstream like a hot intravenous drip.

"How much? How much did you guys pay for that thing?"

It was unlike me to be so forward and prying into our family finances, but I wanted to know. He had promised me college support, but he and I both knew we weren't a family of great enough means to afford both. I wanted his confession.

"Fifteen thousand dollars, " he said flatly, then walked away.

I came unhinged. All the energy that fired its way through my body shuddered with a violence that felt sure to rip me apart. Overcome by panic, my body began to contort and twitch against my control. I rocked back and forth, grasping at my chest. My vision went black. I couldn't see, but I could hear my breath and a groan that seemed to come from a distant place, apart from me.

When the color began creeping back into the world, a thousand little voices came with it. A decade's worth of family quarrels replayed and echoed through my head. Every insult I had ever heard joined in chorus. Every insecurity that I had ever carried inside my little heart spoke at once. Every dark and evil voice that loved to come in moments like this confirmed I was what I had always feared . . . *nothing*. They all swirled about in a buzzing fury until I finally channeled them all into one meaning. One sentence to describe the absolute heartache I felt at that moment.

"He chose her," I said aloud. Calm now, and detached. It took a decade for me to see it, but it finally sunk in. My father had made his family, and though I was there to witness it, ultimately, I had not been grafted in. I just didn't see until that moment. I had been too focused on my own life, burying my head in music and dreaming, but, now, I couldn't ignore it any more.

My father and stepmother had two sons by now. I had two brothers, but I hardly knew them. I watched them grow in my stepmother's belly like an apparition that became manifest in our world, but I never dared to touch them. So distant had my stepmother and I become, the only serenity my family ever seemed to have was when I was separated, locked in my room, or busy with my own affairs. I felt that they did not need me. They did not want me. And, worst of all, it seemed that I would never be missed.

Over the last decade, my parents had built their family, but that day I understood that neither I nor my sister had truly been a part of it. It was as if we were appendages or acquaintances, rather than children. We were the remnants of my father's previous life, not the evidences of his current one. I began to see it all play back as if it were a movie, but the role I held in it began to evaporate. It was like when my sister moved away. Her person was literally forgotten. Her pictures removed. Her name left unspoken. I realized that she had been erased upon her departure. She never came back to visit, nor did my father invite her to remain in his life. This was to be my fate, as well; I just hadn't seen it yet.

Despite our wounds, none of us are exempt from the results of our own behavior. I had my own portion of responsibility for having become so alienated. I replayed in my mind how selfish I had been. I questioned over and over again how it was that I had failed so miserably at securing my father's love.

Why didn't I work harder to fit in?

Why couldn't I have been a better daughter?

I am an awful human being and no good will ever come of me. I tried so hard, but it's no use. I am corrupt.

I felt powerless to fight against the doubts of my own worth; even my own father, for some reason, could not come to rescue me. I tried to soothe the savage voice inside me that urged me to put out the light and just give up. I didn't really know what to make of the world after such a crushing blow, but I needed something to kill the pain of it.

BY MOST STANDARDS, I had always been a pretty good kid. I kept good grades, minded my curfew, and generally achieved all that was expected of me. While the other high school kids were out testing the boundaries of their coming adulthood with the usual suspects of sex, drugs, and alcohol, I usually preferred to keep distant from the riskier adventures. My pride came from my accomplishments in school and in music. I had looked forward to my own future enough that I didn't care to challenge the odds of getting pregnant or dying in an alcohol-related car crash. There were times when I'd make my way to the clandestine parties that took place out by the river, have a couple of weak beers, then head home, but that was usually more than enough for me. Whenever I felt like I needed to blow off steam, I typically picked up my horn and let her rip, but as the gravity of my losses at home began to settle in, I was finding that I needed a stronger opiate to soothe my wounds.

In a lot of ways, I had always tried to be good for my dad, but I was starting to doubt the point of it. So far as I could see, the new gelding stood a better chance than I did of being cared for, so I decided to loosen up a little. Instead of spending my whole weekend delivering pizzas or breaking my face with trumpet practice, I decided to spend more time with my friends. Before I knew it, I'd be graduating and have to be a responsible adult without ever having had any fun.

It felt good to lose control. Come Saturday night, I'd head out with my friends to some dark, less traveled country road, park my car, and begin to tear through a flat of whatever beer we could afford. We'd let the alcohol take us through the paces. From the lip-tingling stages of getting buzzed to the syrupy world of unrestrained inebriation, I had finally found the trick to stop my mind from racing into darkness. I loved pushing through the alcoholic haze into the land of complete numbness. With enough booze, I could get to a place where I couldn't even remember my own name or how to go back home. My mind would fail, along with my limbs, and all I had left to do was sit there, swimming in dark nothingness. What bliss it was to have finally found a way to express all the pain I was feeling inside.

I wanted to feel like that all the time. I started to think that I was pretty clever. I was the so-called good kid that no one suspected was actually bringing my grog along with me to school and drinking every day in class. I found that if I added just enough schnapps and vodka to my ever-present bottle of orange juice, few realized that I had a constant supply of my numbing agent.

I got to where I was drinking myself to sleep each night, hoping that I wouldn't wake up the following morning in a home where I was not even noticed. When the alarm clock splintered through my head the next day, I'd go through the same motions as I had every other day. Drive to school, mix my cocktail out in my car in between classes, and nurse my woes through the day.

Just keep putting one buzzy foot in front of the other, I kept telling myself.

All the things that I had fueled my spirit with had seemed to lose their luster. I was struggling to see how music was going to get me out of my house, away from my parents, and out of my sleepy little town. I would grow sad when I would think of what my old friend Carol would have thought if she knew how low I had let myself sink, especially when it came time for my last performance at the Kansas All-State Band concert.

My senior year, I had won the first chair for trumpet again. After four years in a row, I was growing bored with the affair, not to mention that I failed to see the point of it when college now seemed improbable. Rather than spending the day aware of my surroundings, I did my now-usual routine, sipping my vodka-or-ange juice cocktail throughout the day's rehearsal. When it came time for the evening's performance, I suddenly realized just how drunk I was.

The lights flickered, the audience rustled in their seats, then the conductor took his place in front of the band. I looked over my horn, down to the sheet music in front of me where the black dotted notes swam across the page. I couldn't make sense of any of it. I didn't know how I was going to get through the perfor-mance.

The conductor raised his arms so quickly to start the piece that it left me feeling dizzy and seasick. The cymbals crashed. The band leapt into a march and there I was, stuck in the middle, try-ing to keep up.

I don't remember what we played, really. I faked my way through most of the night. That I even sat through the perfor-mance at all seemed my best achievement of the hour. My fin-gers, lips, and brain were barely under my control. At some point in the evening, I had a few bars of solo to perform. It should have been a moment of supreme achievement. My senior year—a step-out solo as a state-honored musician, and I was blowing it. It was a moment in which I could have celebrated all that I had worked for in recent years, but I was so intoxicated, I don't even remem-ber how well I played it, or if I even played it at all.

It could have been a wake-up call, but it was just the begin-ning. Somehow, I managed to avoid anyone detecting the fact that I developed a serious drinking problem. No one seemed to notice, so I figured that I had a pretty good handle on things and kept on drinking. I relied on the alcohol to get me through every stressful occasion. It gave me the courage to get through what remained to be lived out in school—through prom night, through SATs, through the last of my high school concerts, until at last I called upon it to numb the pain of leaving my childhood home.

For all the years that I had spent dreaming of getting out and away from home and moving on to college, graduation day came with more of a thud than a sense of relief. As I sat and listened to my old band play countless rounds of "Pomp and Circumstance," I waited for my name to be called so I could take the stage, have my tassel turned, grab my diploma, and walk off the stage into my new adult life. But, as I sat there, I realized that I was now officially adrift and alone.

While all the other students were greeted with loud pockets of cheers from their families in the audience, I walked up for my turn in relative silence. I scanned the crowd to see if my father had come, but he had not. I was devastated. I felt like I had reached a dead end rather than a new beginning. His absence confirmed that whatever I was to do now in life, it was going to be without his support.

That night, and for the several days that followed, I fell into an alcohol-induced abyss of self-pity. I spent my nights crashing on sofas or in the back seat of my car, convinced I had fallen down the wormhole of despair I deserved. I was stuck vacillating between complete rage and devastating suicidal depression. When I was high, I had the courage to be justifiably angry at my father's lack of visible support. When I was hung over, I fought to keep from sliding into the suicidal depression that was overwhelming me. I was at a crossroads, trying to weigh the options of whether I wanted to continue living. The dreams that I had, the joys of music, the deep love I had for experiencing life were still floating around somewhere in the chaos of my mind, but they were at war with the darkness of having lost the sense that I mattered. The anger inside me won out. I didn't have any earthly clue what I was going to do next, but I wasn't going to give into the idea that I should just quit living.

In a moment of brief sobriety, I returned home, packed a bag of what little I thought I could not live without—my trumpet, my papers, and a few clothes. A part of me hoped for a sign of resistance, hoping that my unexpected departure would start a fiery family brawl to mark my last rite of passage. Instead, my father sat frozen and silent in his Laz-Y-Boy, as I gathered my things.

"I can't live here anymore," I said, resting my bag beside the back door. I waited for him to speak, but there was nothing. I needed to go, but I was afraid. Outside, a friend was waiting in the driveway to take me to wherever I wanted to go next, but I had no clue where that was going to be. I would have taken help if I had known how to ask for it, but all I could do was stand there wishing my imaginations into life.

I wanted my father to say, "Just stay for a little while longer so we can figure out what comes next."

I stood next to him, frozen, waiting for a response. Unmoved, he sat with a stillness unlike any I had ever witnessed. I could hear the dogs barking outside. The mantle clock ticked away. I could hear him breathing. He took a deep intake of breath as if some kind of proper goodbye was about to escape his lips, but all that came out was a plaintive sigh.

At last, I opened the door, fully broken and in tears. "I love you, Dad," was all I said, and I was gone.

For the next few months I bounced between both sets of my grandparents' care. I spent my days fiendishly working minimum wage jobs and my nights drinking down my anger. As the summer came to a close, all of my grandparents were urging me to live up to the potential they had imagined for me. They loved me and wanted me to succeed, but I was going nowhere. I needed a plan other than nursing hangovers on their sofas.

It was early August, college should have been starting soon, and they were all wondering where I was going to go. After all, I was a smart, talented kid, and music had been my life. I had all but forgotten about the scholarship that was waiting for me at nearby Pittsburg State, but my grandparents urged me on. They weren't going to let me waste the opportunity. They did their best to lovingly kick me out of the nest and remind me what I had been working for. Together, we scrounged up enough money, and borrowed a car to get me started for at least the first semester. After that, I'd have to grow up and figure out how to make it work on my own.

six

I was glad to have finally made my way to college, but I didn't have the kind of enthusiasm I saw in my fellow students. While the other girls in my dorm were busy settling in, I felt lost in the blur of an experience that I had barely any time to prepare for. As usual, I dealt with the stress of it by getting lost in the boozy freshman party scene.

I had managed to enroll in my music education courses, but classes and performances were only the backdrop to the life I was truly living. I'd stumble through my days, but each night I went out to party. I didn't really have enough cash to keep up my habit, but soon enough I'd found a way to keep happily numb. With a little flirtation and promise of a good time, I could usually find an accommodating fellow who would gladly pay for my drinks. We'd party all night, eventually make our way back to his dorm room, car, or frat house, and the rest was predictable, if not absolutely shameful. Most of the time, I could scarcely remember what happened the night before or who I had been with. I often awoke in some strange place in the wee hours of the morning, woozy and used, unable to recognize or even recall the name of the man lying next to me. I'd manage to skulk my way back into the dorm, oftentimes to the visible and vocal horror of the girl who lived across the hall.

Ami and I met the first week in Tanner Hall. She was a soft-spoken and reserved girl who seemed marginally shocked by my rough demeanor. No doubt I spoke with a steady stream of obscenities during our first encounter. I was eager to get to know where the local nightlife was happening, while she was quick to let me know that she was a Christian.

I found her strange. I'd never really met anyone that was so particular about describing themselves in such a way. As I sat in her room, it was clear to me that she not only acted differently than most people I had known, she also had a peculiar and obvious interest in Jesus. The walls of her tiny room were covered in religious paraphernalia. Her room was littered with crosses, not to mention dozens of posters awash in pastel colors and ornately printed inspirational sayings.

In our odd little friendship, Ami would become the gatekeeper of my shame. As I cycled through an almost daily ritual of alcohol-fueled depression, sexual encounters, and hangovers, she seemed to keep a tally on my ignoble escapades. I rarely returned to my room undetected. It was as though she took on the role of a full-length mirror. As I struggled to put the key into my lock each morning, she'd open her door, both glad to see that I had made it home from whatever dangerous liaison I had had the night before, but also with a stern mixture of disgust and pity. In her face, I could see the emotion that I would feel later on when I had sobered up. I wasn't in any way happy with what I was doing, I honestly felt ashamed of myself, but more chilling was that I was scared of how out of control I was. Every new day that I opened my eyes came with a shuddering reality that I was playing a dangerous game of Russian roulette, risking pregnancy, disease, and potentially violent encounters. I would awake, depressed and aware of what was happening, but it seemed that I couldn't control myself. When was I going to get myself into a situation that I could not endure?

In the odds hours between drinks, I would confess my sins to Ami. She was the one friend to whom I told my truths, and I received some portion of truth in return. She spoke aloud what I already was starting to accept, that this behavior had the potential to kill me. I was starring in my own tragic drama. Like Nicolas Cage in *Leaving Las Vegas,* I was on the verge of drinking myself to death. I was no longer able to regulate the choices that I wanted to make. I'd vow to stop, succeeding in only a few odd days at a time, only to wake up in again in some strange place, with little recognition of how or what I had done to get there.

I was at such a desperate point that I needed outside help. I was no longer the master of my own choices. I wasn't entirely certain if I wanted to live, but I was stunned by how Ami continued to insist that I had a better life ahead of me than where I currently found myself. Day after day she continued to listen to my sob stories, often nursing my hangovers, so that I could make enough classes to avoid getting kicked out of school. Occasionally, she would rescue me from further injury by pulling me out of the local bars before I was too sloppy to move. She was a kind soul, but her patience was wearing thin. I relied on her like a backstop to keep me from completely destroying myself but, at some point, she insisted, I had to make a decision to help myself. I could see the truth of it, but I had gotten to the point where I felt powerless against my own will.

One night, in one of the most violent episodes of alcohol poisoning I had experienced, I had found myself immobilized on the dorm room floor of one of my dorm mates. I had become so ill I could no longer hold up my own head to avoid drowning in my own filth. The people I had been partying with had abandoned me. They had placed my head in a trash can and vacated the room. Word had gotten out, and soon Ami was standing in the doorway. I will never forget seeing her standing there, hands on hips. I was terrified. I don't know if I actually said the words aloud, but I pleaded with her, "Don't let me die like Elvis," and I meant it. I truly thought I was going to die there.

I don't remember what she said, but I will never forget the vision of her standing over me. Her expression was all I needed to know that she had had enough. And then she was gone. I closed my eyes for what I figured was probably the last time.

I was surprised to awake the next day. I got through the night, but it would take several days for my body to recover. Bedridden, dehydrated, and finally ready to admit that I was a fractured human being, I began reading some of the Scriptures that Ami had dared to share with me over the previous months. She'd written several pages of verses that called upon themes of redemption. I had always been skeptical about all her talk of Jesus, so I'm amazed as anyone that I engaged in any of it. I don't know why I bothered, except that I had no other earthly clue as to what to do next. I had to admit though, some of the words resonated with me.

By His wounds we are healed.
> *The Lord is my light and my salvation—*
>> *whom shall I fear?*
> *The Lord is the stronghold of my life—*
>> *of whom shall I be afraid?*

He will rescue them from oppression and violence,
for precious is their blood in his sight.

My ego may have cringed with cynicism, but the poetry touched me to the core. I wanted to have my life back, I wanted to be counted among the living again. I wanted to be loved. I wanted to find a way to respect myself again. I began to well up with the awareness that if I wanted to survive and stabilize my life I was going to have to make a serious attempt at change. Surely this wasn't *who* I was?

Part of my journey back was recognizing that I had developed a very serious alcohol problem. It may seem like it should go without saying, but I hadn't fully acknowledged that I had a dependency problem. I just thought that I was a slutty lush. Despite the fact that I wanted to stop drinking, I would find that I could only go a couple of days before I'd be beside myself with agitation, depression, and general anxiety. I didn't know how to manage my mind or my body. When I was sober I felt ill-equipped to manage even the most modest of my stresses and worries. The only way I knew to get relief was to have a few drinks. Despite my best efforts, I was really struggling with staying sober. It wasn't Ami's job to keep watch over me; besides, I had worn her out. It was pretty clear that I wasn't capable of doing this alone, so I decided I needed to get some help.

At first, I looked into the on-campus mental health options. I had no money to sink into what I imagined would be costly psychological support, so I stopped by the university health center and shyly leafed through the pamphlets on display. There were a few meetings for students who talked about how to adjust to college life, but mostly they were just social get-togethers. It wasn't enough. I was on the brink of death, and a few donuts and free coffee weren't going to cut it. One of the on-campus leaders suggested that I might be clinically depressed and in need of individualized care.

Fortunately, I discovered that there were income-based mental health services available through the county. State-funded therapists who were better equipped to deal with the significant problems I was having. I decided to invest in the services of a professional therapist.

One afternoon, I skipped classes and went to my first appointment. I had no idea what I needed or how I could be helped. I just knew I didn't want to be alone in my fight any more. When the receptionist handed me my first round of paperwork, I answered a whole host of intake questions as if I were in a life-dependent exam.

How much do you drink a day?

Do you ever think of suicide? How often?

I remember looking down at the million-dollar question on the page: *What is the reason for your wanting counseling?*

Sick to my stomach and shaking, I wrote: *I am afraid I am going to kill myself.*

There it was. My fear, finally written down in black and white.

It wasn't until I began meeting with my new therapist that I began to realize what a serious situation I had gotten myself into. I was in shock when, after the debrief of my first intake, she assessed that I was an alcoholic. I fought the diagnosis.

"Listen, I'm just really sad. I've got daddy issues and just need someone to talk to," I insisted. The thought that I was this dark thing, incapable of handling my drink, made me angry. I didn't understand that part of what was happening was that my body had become dependent on having alcohol in my system, and that I was using booze as a drug in an attempt to keep on an even keel. I had spent so long filling my body with alcohol that when I didn't have alcohol in my system, I developed withdrawal symptoms.

My counselor laid down the new world order. She insisted that I needed to be in therapy every week and strongly recommended that I attend AA meetings. I signed in thinking that she was going to help me with depression—I was willing to admit that alcohol was my method of coping with it—but I was looking for my therapist to be a neutral shoulder that I could lean on. I thought that if I spent some time talking about my horrible childhood and generally confessing the guilt of my sexual sins that that would be enough. Her assessment that I needed treatment for alcoholism angered me. I wanted help, but this was more than I had bargained for.

After a few sporadic sessions, I went back to self-medicating in a rebellion-fueled binge before I began to consider that she might be onto something. I wanted to get over this hump. I wanted to live. I found myself limping back to my therapist in defeat. At first all I could manage was sitting in her office for an hour unable to speak. Finally, one day, she leaned forward, looked me in the eye as seriously as any human being had ever dared, and laid it out.

"You want help?" she asked sternly. "Then here's what's going to happen. You get serious and start engaging in the options we've got that can help you. You have to start dealing with your problems. You can't just sit here and cry. You've got to start going to the AA meetings we've discussed. You have to start making some choices that are different from the ones you're making now."

The pit of my stomach began to burn with rage. I didn't want to be there anymore. But she had one more thing to say.

"Jennifer, I'm this close to intervening here and putting you in the hospital. You plug in, or what happens next is me filing to have you involuntarily committed."

I had no idea if that was possible, but I was eighteen years old and her words finally got through to me.

"You have a choice to make. Detox in AA or in the hospital. Either way, that's what's next."

I was humiliated, but she was right. I needed to put in the same time, energy, and effort into staying sober every day as I had done in the days of keeping numb. She reminded me that miserable was miserable for the time being, that as much as getting straight might hurt, there would be a better outcome to sobriety than the current path I was on. There is a kind of pain that leads to healing and a kind that leads to destruction. I had known the latter, but was I willing to try the former?

So it was that I spent the next several weeks camped out at local AA meetings. I don't remember much of it, mostly just feeling queasy, jittery, and pretty arrogant, convinced that I was nothing like what I imagine to be a sorry lot of ladies who had gathered together to bemoan their waning lives. Every one in my group was middle-aged, had fairly serious social problems, and other drug dependencies that were beyond my ability to empathize with. I probably could have used a group that had a demographic and experience similar to my own, but I suspect that most of the folks in this particular group were under the same kind of arrangement as I was, being somewhat mandated to attend rather than truly looking for change.

I didn't engage, but it was a safe place for me to stare into oblivion for an hour or so, and there was free coffee. In the end, upon getting past the detox phase, what became evident was that I had a brokenness in my spirit more than I had an addiction.

I didn't end up relating too much in the group setting, but I was finding ways to get in touch with my own reality. I found that I wasn't dying to get back to the bottle as much as I was eager to move on with my life. I stuck with my therapist for a year or so, but after detoxing, AA became more of a reminder of my old ways rather than a useful tool for moving on. I started to get it into my mind that in order to move forward, I needed a clean slate. I began to get restless and hungry for some way to eradicate the shame of the life I had been living and into a new life that was fresh, clean, and new.

One night, in an insomnia-fed rage of frenetic energy, I went to Ami, as I often did, and begged her to keep me company so I wouldn't go on a bender. I was pacing around the room, fully exhausted, but still sober. I didn't want to give up on myself, but I was losing the strength to be alone. I didn't want to drink, but I wanted to drink, and so on. I had all this nervous energy, uncertainty, and anxiety that I was going through, and I wanted someone to help me with the burden. While she continued to be appreciative and supportive of my journey to get clean, she was also very clear that there were just some burdens too great for a human being to manage. She pointed me to a Scripture that blew my mind:

> *Therefore, if anyone is in Christ, he is a new creation, the old has passed, the new has come.*
>
> *—2 Corinthians 5:17*

Part of me was frustrated that all she could ever do is point me to Jesus, give me this verse or that, but every time it stirred up a sense of possibility in me that I couldn't deny. Maybe I was a sucker; I didn't care. I needed to get my shit straight and I was running out of steam on my own. Other people were only going to be able to carry me so far. Maybe she was right; no one could save me but God.

"All right then, what do I need to do? How does this work?" I asked.

I couldn't believe what was coming out of my mouth. I was so scared. I was afraid I had finally been cracked by the Christian crazies, but my mouth kept going.

"How do I get saved?" popped out. *What? Who falls for this?*

It was like an out-of-body experience. I couldn't believe that I was falling for this crap, but I couldn't stop myself. I truly, deeply, and sincerely wanted to know. I needed to have faith again. I needed hope. I needed . . . I wanted . . . to be saved.

And so we prayed. Ami led me in a ritual prayer known among evangelicals as The Sinner's Prayer or The Prayer of Salvation. There's no specific script, but the basics must include acknowledging your sinful nature and repenting (that is, expressing remorse for your ungodly behavior). You must also recognize and name Jesus as the Lord of your life, recognizing that by the act of his sacrificial crucifixion, the Son of God took the punishment you would have otherwise deserved. It is through this confession and this recognition that you become saved, but you must also be willing to complete the pact by moving forward and living for God's purpose rather than your own.

I prayed my prayer, having no earthly clue what I was saying, but I prayed in earnest all the same. And whether it was real or imagined, all I can say is that I did truly feel as if my life began again that day. When I lifted my head and opened my eyes, it seemed I was filled with a joyous, almost electric, energy unlike anything I had ever experienced. My whole body felt unfamiliar and refreshed. My head was clear for the first time in a very long time. Everything looked as bright and vivid as a high-definition television. All of a sudden, I understood what it must have been like for Paul when the scales fell from his eyes (Acts 9). After that day, in the new language taught to me by my fellow friends of the faith, I was *reborn*.

DURING MY TIME at Pittsburg State University, there were a significant number of evangelically minded students that Ami had introduced me to. It is fair to say that the campus had a full-on subculture of Christians who were active, enthusiastic, and very public about their faith. While I had been living out my own Midwestern state school version of *Animal House*, Ami was part of a well-organized fellowship of Bible studies, prayer groups, and all-around clean living social network. Now that I had prayed my prayer and become a Christian, I was a new and welcome member.

Long before I felt comfortable enough to walk into a church, I started attending Fellowship of Christian Athletes meetings on campus. The weekly meetings were energetic, packed with young students, local adult clergy, and lay leaders. When I walked in for the first time, it seemed as though everyone knew who I was, even if I didn't know them. I saw a few people I already knew, but had written off as a little weird. I had no idea that it was their Christianity that made them stand out.

There are few things that get evangelical Christians more excited than new converts coming into the fold. It's like chum for sharks. My entrance into their world set off a kind of frenzy I had never experienced. It was practically a celebration to all who knew that I had "accepted Christ," as they put it.

It was like stepping into an alternate universe. These people were exaggeratedly happy and spoke in a language that I could barely understand. Their words sounded like English, but they were a strange creole of the common words and religious vernacular. I was being swarmed by a bunch of nut-jobs who were beaming from ear to ear, coming up and shaking my hand. They were saying things like, "I can't believe you made it! Praise the Lord!" and "I've been praying for you. I'm so glad you've finally made it!" and "Hallelujah! This is a miracle!"

I remember how one young man came up to me and declared in amazement, "Wow. If God can save you, God can save anybody!" *What the hell am I doing here?* I wondered to myself. "You've been praying for me?" I asked quizzically, both flattered and uncomfortable. "What does that even mean?"

Unbeknownst to me, Ami had been sharing her concern about my wayward exploits with her Christian friends for some time. Some had even been witness to my exploits through their own less than advertised backsliding. The fact that everyone around me seemed to be in on some kind of conspiracy to get me to know God was killing my salvation buzz. It felt like this whole thing had been planned. It just seemed so creepy and manipulative. Realizing that there were a group of strangers who I didn't know, but who knew me and were praying that my life would be spared by finding salvation through Jesus made me feel like a prize idiot. I was not only freaked out, I was a bit angry. It was hard not to feel that my privacy was being violated and judged. Like I was a bad person yesterday and thereby uncool when I wasn't a Christian, and that today I was good just because I prayed some weird little prayer.

I found myself at odds, balancing between the suspicion that Ami and my new Christian family truly valued me for myself or because I had become a member of their club. I have no doubt that their prayers for my life were sincere. Many of them had witnessed firsthand the dangerous results of my lost hope and now they were here to greet me with excitement. It was now up to me to suspend my criticism and find the merit in their joy.

For the many who prayed for my salvation, I was epitome of what debauched drinking and premarital sex does to the human spirit. I have to believe that my friends were truly horrified and scared, and equally hopeful that their God had the power to end my misery. They had joy and happiness in their lives and, though I might have been a stranger to them, I was a suffering stranger. In their witness of my suffering, they invited me to a space where I could share in their joy, comfort, and fellowship.

When I thought of it this way I grew astounded that anyone would even bother to take the time to hope on my behalf, when I was feeling that perhaps I had no hope for myself. After all the time I had spent in a pit of despair, convinced that I wasn't a person worthy of being loved by any human being on the planet, all of a sudden I was confronted with dozens of people who seemed overjoyed that I was still alive and safe.

It is this kind of juxtaposition that I find both oddly fascinating and maddening at the same time. Christianity can so eloquently remind me that we are all worthy of being loved. The Bible does well to illuminate and honor the selflessness and forgiveness required to keep love in motion, yet, at times, seems to suggest that God's love is reserved for only a chosen few. It's difficult to manage the idea that God only rewards those who do a certain measure of "right." It's mystifyingly complicated and alluring to me all the same. Before I became a Christian, and even now, I find myself readily angry that religion is rife with judgments born from facile assessments of good versus evil, but I cannot deny that if it were not for stumbling into this world, I might not be alive today.

It was such a relief to have hope, but there was more to it than just recognizing God. Now, I was supposed to act like Him. Inspired though I might have been to seek the promised peace of Jesus, there were things I needed to do to keep my membership current and valid. I needed to stop all my worldly ways of cursing and drinking, and of course, absolutely no sex. I needed to be baptized (by immersion was preferred), learn to pray, go to Bible studies, go to a so-called Bible-believing church every Sunday, and so on and so forth. According to all my lovely, well-meaning, sold-out-for-Jesus friends, I had to set about doing the work of becoming a new creation. If I was at all serious about the commitment I had made to Jesus, I had a lot of work to do.

seven

I had only been on the wagon for what amounted to a few shaky weeks before my freshman year of college came to an end. Summer meant that I had to move out of my dorm and head back to my hometown. My new Christian friends were headed back to their families as well, leaving me on my own without any witnesses, and little support to keep me on the straight and narrow. Many of my Christian friends were prayerful and openly concerned that I might backslide, fearing against fragile hope that away from their guardianship, I would return to my previous life of sin. Even my therapist implored me to stay in Pittsburg, where I could continue to work things out in a controlled setting, but I had no means to afford an apartment on my own. Back in Chanute, I had free rent and a job waiting for me. It would have to do. It really wasn't the best plan, but all I could do was put one foot in front of the other and pray for the best. Whether I had the strength or faith to manage was yet to be seen. I had no idea if I could or would succeed, but I was going to have to figure out a way to manage with what I had.

Going back to Chanute was the equivalent of heading straight into the proverbial lion's den. I was fortunate that my Grandma Knapp offered me her spare bedroom for the summer, but her home was far from neutral territory. Staying with her meant that I was only a few miles away from the childhood home that I had left under duress. It wasn't that I wanted to go back there; leaving had felt like a decision of survival. I was overwhelmed with crippling confusion. Every cell in my body was filled with dread at the thought of having to face my father again, yet, at the same time, I was devastated, convinced that he didn't miss me. It had been over a year since I had left home and I hadn't seen or heard from my father. Neither he nor I managed to find a way to close the distance between us.

My return meant that I had to come to terms with our shared failure to stay connected and, somehow, do so while remaining sober. Right or wrong, no matter how alone or abandoned I found myself, I was going to have to learn how to live with the prospect that we might never reconcile.

I found some solace by leaning into the idea of forgiveness I had been reading about in the Bible. Part of my own personal path to recovery was found in the words of Jesus. There wasn't a single soul he met—prostitute, adulterer, or murderer—that he could not forgive. While others mocked the fallen and demanded retribution, his way was to love at the moment of greatest need.

I saw my reflection in the story of the adulterous woman at the well (John 4:1-26) where on-lookers stood, stones at the ready, to punish her for her crime. I took comfort, learning that Jesus did not hesitate to come to her defense. I *was* the sinful woman who emptied her finest perfume on the feet of Christ, humbly grateful to have experienced his kindness. While others scoffed at her wastefulness, it was Jesus who encouraged her gift. (Matt. 26:6-13)

In some strange way, the full depth of that kind of compassion began to transform brokenness in me. I began to accept the fact I would never be able to go back and undo the things that led to this sorrow. It seemed that if there was any hope of comfort, I had to learn how to forgive. I had to stop beating myself up. Punishing myself for my every flaw by soaking my woes in alcohol had only made things worse.

No matter what I may have done wrong to create the gap between my father and me, or however cheaply I had given my body to strangers, I had to find a way to forgive myself. I had to open the door to the possibility that I could forgive those whom I felt had hurt me most. Holding on to all the sadness and rage I was carrying only seemed to keep me locked in a cycle impenetrable to love. I began to wonder: *What do I have to lose if I choose forgiveness?*

It didn't seem things could really get worse.

That summer I decided to keep myself as busy as I could. I took as many shifts delivering pizzas as I could physically handle. I'd lock myself in my bedroom, pouring over Scripture and directing my prayers of deliverance to God. I did my best to seek companionship among friends who didn't require social lubricants, and rocked myself to sleep praying that I might not fail. This too shall pass, it is said, and so all I had left were my prayers that it would.

I can't say that I got through the whole summer without a single drink, but I did manage to avoid any major mishaps. There were a few Sundays when I managed to make my way to a local United Methodist Church, getting comfortable with the idea of hanging out in a church as an actual believer.

I read the Bible every day. I started praying. I even branched out and read a few other faith-based books from authors like

Philip Yancey, Oswald Chambers, and C. S. Lewis. Someone had also given me a *Daily Devotional*, which was a daily planner of sorts, which gives you a portion of Scripture to read each day, as well as a pastoral message to let you know what it all was supposed to mean.

One of the many bits of instruction I had received from friends was that it would be helpful if I memorized verses. I was supposed to hide God's word in my heart so that I might not sin against Him (Psalm 119:11). On the days when I was struggling to keep on an even keel, this wasn't such a bad idea. Not that I dared utter any of it aloud in the presence of my old friends, but when I found myself having to make a choice between getting wasted or going home, repeating the phrase 'He is my light and my salvation whom have I to fear?' seemed to be a helpful reminder. Perhaps it was a different kind of drug. Instead of hitting the bottle, I'd curl up in my bedroom and immerse myself in the Word. I started journaling again, too. I returned to the pen and paper that had been my confidante in previous years, and found a place to rest all the chaos that was going on in my mind. After spending so long trying to disconnect from my own feelings, I found a way to face all that I had been running from and, all the while, growing in confidence that perhaps there was a knowing God who was listening.

I also remembered something that my friend Ami had mentioned to me as we parted ways for the summer. I had a nasty old guitar that I barely knew how to play. Occasionally, I would break it out and attempt a dreadful rendition of a Cowboy Junkies tune, or maybe some Tracy Chapman. I didn't really have any natural skill at the instrument, but I did enjoy the chance to close my eyes, use my hands and voice, and let the music carry me to some faraway place. I don't think Ami, or anyone else for that matter, found me entertaining in those early days, but she suggested that perhaps I could write a song about what God was teaching me. At the time, her encouragement seemed weird and out of the blue. Why she suggested such a thing, I couldn't imagine. Maybe she just wanted me to stop singing other people's worldy pop songs? Or maybe she just wanted to suggest a means of getting me to focus more on God? Either way, it seemed bizarre that it had never occurred to me to sit down and merge my poetry and love of music and write a song with my guitar in hand. Yet, in that one fateful suggestion, Ami planted a seed that would eventually take root and dramatically affect my life.

I didn't know the first thing about how to approach writing a song, but it seemed like a useful way to remember all the Bible verses that I had been studying. I started by taking a verse that spoke to me and crafting it into a song. I'd weave it into the story of my experience. If I doubted, I'd sing of it. If I was confused, I'd reach for clarity with abandon. For all my longing to start my life anew, I'd make a melody of the prayer. It was such a release to take everything swirling inside my head and heart and speak it aloud into the music. It made it easier to speak of my journey without the pressure of worrying whether I was praying correctly. It was a safe place for me to be honest and truthful without the insecurity of being judged or ridiculed for my weakness. It was as though I were writing my own Psalms, and through them, finding a way to manage my energy and anxiety, and moving toward a kind of healing. They were my own tunes, written between me and God. It never occurred to me to share them. What made it easy to write honestly was that no one would want to hear them, so I just wrote, unafraid of the outcome and eager to express my deepest longings.

When summer had ended, I made my way back to Pitt State, found a few wholesome roommates to share an off-campus house with, and started catching up with all the Christian students. Before I knew it, I was knee-deep in prayer circles and Bible studies and had even written a few songs about my experience. I think most of my friends were very surprised to see that I made it back in one piece. I was probably just as stunned as they were to discover that I was getting more and more at ease with the idea of identifying myself as a Christian. It really did seem quite improbable that I would truly adopt the faith, but there I was, spewing out verse after verse, rocking back and forth on my knees in fervent prayer, and rewriting my life story with the songs I had composed. It seemed like every time my friends and I got together, they'd ask me to pull out my guitar, play a few songs of my own, and encourage me to play some of their favorite praise and worship tunes as well.

I had finally jumped all in. It felt good to be surrounded by the safety of those who understood what I had been through. Everyone was on my side and wanted me to succeed. With God, we all knew that all things were possible. Whatever reservations and judgments I had previously had in regard to Christianity, I had put them out of my mind. Slowly but surely, all that prayer and Scripture were starting to sink in. These weren't just words on a page; it was as if the Bible were a living thing. The verses were instructional and helpful, to be sure, but it started to feel as though these words were written specifically for me and to me every single day. Always right on time and in rhythm with the very anxieties, needs, and lessons required in the very moment they presented themselves.

> *Trust in the lord with all your heart, lean not on your own*
>   *understanding.*
> *In all your ways acknowledge him and he will set your path*
>   *straight.*
>
> *—Proverbs 3:5*

It was such a relief that I could absolve myself from the worry of being responsible for knowing what I was supposed to do next. All I had to do was open my Bible, like reading tea leaves, or casting lots, and pray that God would show me what to do next, and there my leading would be. I no longer felt the pressure of having to make decisions on my own. God had a plan for me, and all I had to do was be faithful and follow exactly where He led me.

I didn't get to that understanding alone. I found that whenever I sought encouragement or support, or struggled to get on board with what my Christian leadership had hoped I would become, the push was always to return to the Word. I wasn't to lean on my own understanding; I needed to learn to listen for God's voice over my own. In some ways, it felt like I was being taught to mistrust my own voice. When I approached my elders for advice, I was encouraged to discern the difference between what I might desire and what God would have me desire. The idea was that whatever I could imagine or want, God might want to replace it with something better. If I intended to be serious about my faith, I needed to learn how to prioritize God's voice over my own.

After all I had been through, my task was now to pray and listen for God's calling in my life. He had saved me, for certain, but for what I had no idea.

DURING MY SOPHOMORE year of college, I was asked to play guitar in the Fellowship of Christian Athletes (FCA) worship group. I was nervous about the endeavor. It was not an activity I would have chosen on my own. If I were honest, I wasn't that into singing worship music, so the thought of leading other young adults in what seemed to me like childish vacation Bible-school songs wasn't exactly appealing. But when I responded that I wasn't interested, my friends encouraged me to pray about it and seek God in the same manner in which I was being taught, through prayer and daily Scripture reading. Ever earnest, I did as I was encouraged, when lo and behold, a verse seemed to jump right off the page and speak directly to me.

Sing unto the Lord a new song; play skillfully and shout for joy.
—Psalm 33:3

A serendipitous reading of the words "new song" and I at once had the answer. God was telling me that I was supposed to sing in the worship band. He was making a way for me, so now it was my job to be obedient to the call.

Month after month, I did my best to faithfully mine the pages of my Bible in order to discover what God had in store for me. A theme began to develop. Music had always been the gift that rose above all others in my life, but now it was starting to look like my calling had already been foreseen.

> *Whatever you do, work at it with all your heart, as working for the Lord, not for men, since you know that you will receive an inheritance from the Lord as a reward. It is the Lord Christ you are serving.*
>
> —*Colossians 3:23–24*

Everywhere I looked, I was constantly reminded and inspired to believe that I had been called to a higher purpose in life than I had ever imagined. He had picked me out of the mire and delivered me. It was hard for me to ignore the logic of it. I had read that *he who has been forgiven much, loves much (Luke 7:47)*. I felt I had, indeed, been forgiven of so very much, and was profoundly grateful. On that premise alone, I owed my entire life. As all these thoughts, words, prayers, and instruction swirled, I began to understand that music was my only true gift to offer.

Before I knew it, I was fully engaged. Everywhere there was music in the church, I was there. By the following year I was the FCA worship leader, responsible for learning the catalog of worship songs with which everyone expected to open the meetings. I was a member of the contemporary worship team at my local church, and had even been asked to join a Christian rock band.

eight

$\mathcal{I}$t seems like every guitar player I've ever met dreams of being in a band. One guy meets another guy who knows a drummer, who knows a bass player, who knows another guy who can sing or maybe write some decent lyrics. I suppose it makes sense that eventually you might want to join forces with other like-minded people who want to make some noise, but it was a bit of a foreign concept to me. I had always been rather reclusive with my guitar.

I never had any specific intentions when I bought my first guitar. I just figured that it was a good idea to have a concept of how string instruments worked, since I was going to be a music major in college. So, in the summer before my freshman year of college, I happened to see an old, barely functional acoustic guitar hanging in the rafters of a local flea market and decided that I'd give it a go.

For fifty bucks, I bought what I later learned was a classical guitar improperly strung. Her neck was bowed by the strain of the metal strings and could scarcely stay in tune. My little hands could barely reach across her broad classical frets enough to form the most basic chords, but I persisted. That guitar was a clunky beast that seemed better served to decorate the rafters of a flea market than inspire musical passion. How I learned to play guitar on such a ramshackle instrument, I have no idea.

I didn't have the kinds of aching lust that most guitar players eventually become infected with: I had yet to be charmed by the alluring craftsmanship of Martins, Gibsons, or Taylors. I had no idea about the sensual nature of exotic, resonating woods or comely mother of pearl in-lays. For all I knew, it was just a box with metal strings stretching across it that you could use to pluck out a couple of tunes, and that was good enough for me. I was after the education more than the seduction of being a rock star.

Like every other instrument I had picked up, I set out to learn in solitude. I grabbed a couple of books to learn some chords and jumped right into it. It wasn't until I had a few basic chords under my belt that it finally dawned on me that I could attempt to play some of my favorite songs. I figured out that I could play some Cowboy Junkies, R.E.M., and even a little Tracy Chapman. Along the way I wrote some songs of my own creation. I didn't think I was very good at it, but I enjoyed the private hours when I could close my eyes and sing away. It was like a secret therapy that I kept to myself. An instrument that didn't have all the pressures and demands of precise execution like those in my classical world of trumpet playing. I didn't have to share it with anyone, nor did I want to. It never occurred to me to want to perform with it until my friends from church learned of my secret musical skills.

It was a minor miracle that I ever agreed to start playing guitar in church. I barely knew how to keep my guitar tuned, let alone play through a catalog of praise and worship music, but the invitations to play in a group setting helped me become more confident in all the practice.

Before long I got asked to join a band that a few of my

friends had pieced together. They were a band of Christians from my college and church who wanted to write and perform Christian pop music. I had written a few songs of my own by then, but I didn't think they were good enough to be performed by an established rock group. But my friends were eager to have me join the fray. They had the idea of writing original music and dreamed of performing concerts like real rock stars do, and seemed convinced that I would fit in their plans nicely. It was novel and something to do for fun and, although I had no idea what I was in for, I said *yes*. With the enthusiastic backing of our local church, the band set out on a mission to be a good Christian version of so-called worldly music. We named ourselves Captured (as in captured for Jesus) and began seeking out opportunities to play local concerts for youth groups and summer camps.

Initially, we were rather disorganized. We had several eager members, three lead singers, a violinist, three guitar players, and a guy who was willing to play bongos to keep time. It wasn't until Byron, a bass player from our church, agreed to join us that we even stood a chance of taking the shape of a proper performance group.

We were all excited that Byron had agreed to jump in. He had the experience of performing in rock bands and touring the Christian music scene. To land his expertise gave us a chance to up our game. Byron not only knew what it took to rehearse pop music, he also had an idea as to what it took to deliver a performance that people would actually want to listen to. His talents and experience helped give Captured a cohesive vision, organizing us to the point where we were finding opportunities to play well beyond the polite invitations of our home church.

Thanks to Byron, we had a decent schedule of performances.

From time to time, we even got paid to play. It was an exciting day when we'd earned enough money to print our own band T-shirts! We finally felt like we were a legitimate rock group. All we had to do now was get a record deal!

The whole idea of becoming rock legends seemed fanciful to me. While it was all well and good to play about for a bunch of highly churched teenagers, it seemed another thing entirely to think that we had what it took to be professional musicians. I had little idea of what that actually meant anyway. Besides, I wasn't overly excited about using my musical talents solely for singing songs about Jesus, but I was working on my spiritual attitude. When the music we were playing left me feeling a bit cheesy or embarrassed, I comforted myself, figuring we were probably not going to make it to the big time anyway. It was all in good fun, but I wasn't looking at making a career of it.

Byron, on the other hand, saw something in me that he wanted to bring to the fore. Through his encouragement, I went from singing mostly backup to fronting a majority of songs. He encouraged me to write more music that I could contribute to the group, and pushed for me to play more guitar. I was having a good time for sure, but I didn't really have the vision for it like everyone else did. Byron went a step further and suggested that I consider the idea of doing some work on my own. He thought the music that I was writing was particularly good, and was sincere in thinking that I had the ability to do more. He started encouraging me to think about doing some solo concerts. I had enough music to do so, he said, and he could find me some places to play.

It felt like a dirty coup against the band, but Byron actually followed through with the idea of getting me solo gigs. I started to play just as many gigs with just me and my guitar as I was doing when I was playing with Captured. Essentially, he started managing me as a solo artist. For a while, I was happy to go where the wind blew me.

Captured had started by putting together a decent run of paying gigs while, at the same time, I was also getting an equal amount, if not more, solo dates on the side. Tensions were starting to mount as to where my and Byron's loyalties truly were.

One night, after one of the best-attended concerts, the members of the band called Byron and me over for a side meeting while we were packing up cables to go home. Our lead guitarist explained that everyone in the band (besides Byron and me) had voted and decided that they wanted to disband the group. Captured would be no more. As it turned out, Byron and I were being fired. The group would go on in another incarnation, but they would do so without us.

From then on, Byron and I set about starting what would be the beginning of my career as a solo artist. I had no idea what I was doing, but I kept showing up and singing wherever Byron got me a place to play. He started schooling me as to how to set things up so that I had enough money to travel, and even fund a recording or two.

Until I met Byron, it had never occurred to me that I could make a career out of writing and performing music. There were times when I had struggled to understand how my new-found Christian faith was supposed to be a functional lifestyle but, with music, everything started to come into focus. If being a Christian meant that everything that I did had to be motivated in a Godly direction, maybe it was possible that I could serve with music. I didn't see myself getting into ministry or being a stay-at-home mom, home-schooling her good little Christian children, but maybe I could sing my way through it?

Byron offered me the hope of direction. He saw potential in me and nurtured the idea that what I had to offer through my music could be meaningful to a lot of people. He helped me make sense of the strange and bewildering community of Christian culture. What started out as a lark was evolving into a pathway of finding my own longed-for significance. I had come upon Christianity at a time where I needed to rediscover my own value and strengths, but I also needed the guidance and encouragement of Byron to get a glimpse of the possibilities. I needed the structure of doing something that would build my faith, and music was starting to do that.

Byron's enthusiasm for making a difference with music dared me to dream in ways that I never had before. I couldn't imagine the idea of being a recording artist, it was too far down the road, but Byron kept paving the way, one gig at a time. Before I knew it, he had me booked with a steady stream of performances, introducing me to a genre of musical expression I had never known existed: Christian music. He helped me earn enough money to buy a halfway decent guitar, put some gas in the tank of my rusty little pickup truck, and sent me out onto the road.

nine

By 1995, the end of my junior year of college, I had now been living my life as a converted Christian for nearly three years. I focused all my attention on trying to absorb and adopt the lifestyle changes that were expected of me, so that I could be called a Godly woman. I really was an entirely new creation and was fully committed to being faithful to my calling. I was finally clean and sober but, more than that, I was starting to believe that I was capable of being a person worthy of being loved. That, in itself, seemed the greatest miracle of all.

I'd put the drink behind me, stopped sleeping around, and even managed to stop swearing (*mostly*). The fact that I had so many significant un-Christian behaviors to undo, and that I was making headway against them, made it clear to me that God was at work in my life. Just a short while ago, I had been at the brink of death, hopeless and desperate, but I had been saved by the grace of God. I was getting back to the spirit of who I had once been—an eager student, a hopeful musician, and now, finally, a worthwhile human being. I had a new lease on life and I was so grateful for it that I couldn't help but write and sing about it.

When I struggled with feeling like an alien inside the church culture that I had been grafted onto, I sang the prayer of who I hoped I could be. When I was ashamed of my past, I faced it head on. I wrote it down, looked it in the eye and sang it into submission.

Papa, I think I messed up again
Was it something I did, was it something I said
Didn't mean to do you wrong, it's just the way of human nature

It's time to get down on my knees and pray
Lord, undo me!
Put away my flesh and bone 'til you own this spirit through me
Lord, undo me!

—"Undo Me," *Kansas*

The things that had sustained me through the hard times—writing, music, and, now, faith—all of a sudden seemed to have come together to make perfect sense. I was relieved to fall into the comfort of them, compelled to follow their collective muse wherever it led. Whenever anyone asked me to play, I played. So far as my church, my friends, and I saw it, these sustaining gifts were from God, and the trials I had gone through were so that I would have a reason to sing of how God has sustained me through it all.

Thanks to the encouragement from Byron and the urging of my home church, I had finally began to fully embrace the idea of serving the church with my music.

Byron filled my summers with concerts to perform. Before I knew it, I found myself driving alone through hot, solitary plains of the Midwest. Up I-29 into Nebraska, I-80 over to Iowa, down I-35 through Missouri, and back again to Kansas. I saw more of

America in the span of a few months than I had ever imagined this small-town country girl would ever get to see.

Many days I would find myself in a simple little country church where I'd stay with the pastor's family, or with a youth group leader. I had no previous experience as to how to cope with being a travelling minstrel; always the stranger in a new place. All I had to go on was the comfort of knowing that we all shared the common bond of our faith. I took to heart the honor of being an invited guest, called there to share the testimony of how I came into the fold.

I played countless Sunday morning worship services, where I would sing my one special song, so that I could be introduced to the congregation, letting them know that I would be there later that night performing during the more relaxed evening service. In particular, the youth of the church were encouraged to join in the fun—the concert being a fun way to hang out at church and stay out of trouble.

As I traveled around to different churches, I began to notice how often people referred to my music as a great alternative to secular music. The comments were usually delivered with high praise and gratitude, but I found it difficult to receive them as a compliment. To me, *all* music came from a deeply spiritual place. It got even harder when a youth pastor once asked me what music inspired my own writing and I innocently answered, the Indigo Girls.

"Oh, no, no, no, no, no! You can't do *that!*" he practically screamed, "They're *gay!*"

It had never occurred to me that this was any kind of problem.

He thundered on, "You can't listen to that stuff any more. You're a new creation. You put that stuff into your head and it will *ruin* your heart. Honey, you best burn all of that devil music and start filling your ears with the music of the Lord!"

Mental note: Next time, only mention Christian music artists that you like and don't be gay—Okay, got it.

Well, I didn't burn my records, but I certainly learned to stop talking about them in public. As for the gay thing, I hadn't really considered it one way or the other, but at least now I knew what I was in for if it ever came up. And thus continued my immersion into the world of all things Christian.

Most of the time, I enjoyed the adventure. I was starting to get the knack of how to perform, and I was meeting plenty of interesting people along the way. Over the course of the summer I came to appreciate how diversely people approached their spiritual lives. I found myself in the company of Methodists, Episcopalians, and Baptists, even singing alongside charismatics, who spoke in tongues. Scattered among them all were those who claimed to know the *true* faith. If ever there was a time when I grew certain of what I thought Christianity was supposed to be, I'd find myself in yet another new church, surrounded by new people, practicing their faith in ways that were true to their own views of God but very different from my own or even the last church I had been to. When their ways were unfamiliar to my own experience, I did my best to look for the commonalities of our shared inspiration.

Because I had adopted my faith as a matter of choice, rather than inheriting it from my parents, as many of my peers had, I had a particular appreciation for what it felt like to be pressured to conform. There were times when I felt like I was the clumsy new member of some kind of exclusive club. For whatever part I had to play in being an ambassador for Jesus, I hoped I did so in such a way that helped people see how worthy they were of love and respect. The way I saw it, life wasn't always so clear cut as to call one thing a sin and another thing holy. Sometimes, you just had to give people enough space, time, and grace to find their way to safety. Despite whatever mistakes I had made in my own journey toward faith, I couldn't see how forcing the issue upon others did much to speed up the process. Still, it didn't seem to stop some folks from trying.

It certainly didn't stop one youth pastor I met in Missouri. I'll call him "Skip."

I met Skip during my junior year of college. When school was in session, I spent most of my time bouncing back and forth between Kansas City and my college home in Pittsburg. Skip was a Southern Baptist youth pastor who worked for a church in Kansas City. They had a healthy budget for their youth group activities, and he was always eager to give me a place to play. Skip wasn't my favorite kind of guy in the entire world. There were times when his idea of sharing his faith differed from my own, but, for the most part, we got along. I was grateful for church leaders like him, who were often kind enough to share their network of contacts. Their support not only helped me develop a great regional following as a performer, it also proved financially fruitful enough to help pay my way through college.

In my second summer of touring, Skip invited me to perform a special concert at his church's camp in the northern woods of Missouri. I wasn't a big fan of being part of youth retreats. I much preferred to come in, do my shows, and head on to the next church, but Skip insisted that I come as early as I could, so that I could enjoy the solitude of the place. Feeling the pressure to not disappoint him, I agreed to go.

I was to arrive the night before, hang out and connect with

the kids during the next day, then, the subsequent evening, perform. After a long hot day of driving, I was really looking forward to the solitude of the cabin in the woods he had promised me.

Back in the day, when we used maps and directions rather than GPS systems, I managed to find my way off the main roads, through the dark woods and into the remote Bible camp. In the late hours of the night, Skip greeted me warmly, then led me to my cabin, some distance from the main camping grounds. All was quiet. The kids were nestled in their bunks somewhere away in the darkness and I was set to enjoy my own private space. I had a hot shower, and, Skip assured me, eight hours of uninterrupted sleep to look forward to.

"There'll be breakfast in the morning if you want it, but don't worry about coming down for us," Skip said. "Get your rest. And when you're ready, come down to the main grounds and find me. I'll be on campus somewhere."

Exhausted, I changed into my pajamas and hit the sack.

I'm uncertain how long I had been asleep when, suddenly, I was startled awake by a banging at the door.

"Jennifer! Jennifer! Wake up!" It was the voice of one of Skip's minions. *"Jennifer!"* More banging. *"You're going to want to see this! You have to get up!"*

I was dazed and suddenly filled with adrenaline. I jumped out of bed and went to the door, where I was told that my assistance was immediately required.

"What's going on?" I asked. But Minion didn't give specifics. He hemmed and hawed, but bubbled with a wide-eyed enthusiasm. Whatever in the world was going on, he insisted that I come immediately and wouldn't close the door until I agreed.

Still in my bedclothes, I had to push him out of my doorway

so I could get some privacy to put some proper clothes on. "Gimme a minute," I said in groggy agitation. "Let me at least put a bra on and I'll meet you outside in a second."

Once outside, in the pitch dark of the night, I began to wake and realize that, indeed, something was afoot. In the distance, down the hill toward the main campus, there was a steady stream of what sounded like a frenzied crowd in chaos. Minion led me through the woods toward the ruckus and into a clearing where I could finally get a visual.

The scene was pandemonium. Flashlights were waving around in the dark. People were shouting. Children were on their knees crying. Someone was blowing a whistle. I stood there watching all this trying to figure out what in the hell was going on. Meanwhile, Minion was tugging at my sleeve trying to get me into the mix, but to what purpose I hadn't quite figured out.

I focused on a twenty-something male leader towering over a few young campers kneeling on the grass. He was shouting, "*What are you going to do?*" while pointing a flashlight at their faces. "*Who will you choose?*" He was screaming like he was the drill sergeant from *Full Metal Jacket*.

"*Jesus is here! He's here right now! The world is at an end! You must choose this instant!*"

I was so stunned that, for a few moments, I almost believed the end-of-days rapture was actually happening. I had to rub my eyes and slap myself to make sure I wasn't actually dreaming.

The children were scattered everywhere. Some fell at the crier's feet, weeping uncontrollably, but these supplicants were not in spiritual ecstasy. They were sobbing and trembling with terror. All around me, I began to hear the responses of the children in the dark. Many of them were begging for the onslaught to stop.

"Please, please. I choose Jesus," I heard one of them acquiesce.

This isn't salvation, I thought, *this was awful!* There was no spiritual revelation in their voices. Those kids were terrified and in distress! The poor things had been shouted out of their sleep with bullhorns and, now, the camp counselors were jeering at them.

Christ has returned and you are going to die. Choose you this day who you will serve. God or man? Satan or Christ? You will die tonight! Where do you want to spend eternity? Heaven or hell?

There were only two options for relief from the barrage: to make a confession for Jesus Christ, or collapse in exhausted dysfunction. It wasn't until a child made his or her proclamation that they would be released from the drill. Confessors were rewarded with celebratory hugs from the more compassionate counselors and escorted out of the terrifying darkness into the light of the camp sanctuary; all others were left trembling beneath the stars.

At one point during the affair, I caught sight of Skip marshaling the troops. Puffed up, sweaty, and excited, he kept watch over the exercise, interjecting the occasional command. When he saw me, he turned to me. Grinning wildly, he shouted over the chaos, "Isn't this fantastic?"

I found myself so angry that I became physically ill. I was stunned by what I was witnessing. It was utterly abusive and unholy. Somehow, I had managed to avoid any spiritual suspicion when I held back from participating, but I still felt guilty. By my silent witness, I felt complicit to a spiritual and psychological crime.

Skip, on the other hand, was proud. "We are literally scaring the *Hell* out of them!"

The kids weren't the only ones who were scared. I was

freaked out, too. I felt powerless to get any of this to stop. I was outraged, for certain, but I had no clue about what I was supposed to do. It felt like a trap. If I didn't find a way to agree with some part of what I was seeing, then it must have meant that something was wrong with *me*. Maybe I was spiritually weak? Surely if I were a faithful Christian, this would have made some kind of sense to me.

I tried to recall any verse of Scripture that could help me understand how God could find this exercise redemptive, but I just couldn't see it. Honestly, how could this be holy? I remembered back to the day when I first responded to the Gospel. It was nothing like this. It was a moment of rest, of peace. In those moments I felt relief that I had truly been lifted out of a pit of despair. It wasn't like this at all.

Thankfully, the camp eventually yielded to exhaustion. By the wee hours of the morning, all the youth had been rounded up and ushered into the chapel, where Skip took his proud and accomplished self to the front of the room.

Softly now, in his most tender and pastoral voice, he began to speak.

"What happened here tonight, kids, was a drop in the bucket compared to Judgment Day." His tone of comfort did little to quiet the sniffles and faint sobbing still coming from the crowd. "If you think you know fear," he gently warned, "think again. There's always hell."

At this point, I really had come to doubt whether I could find any portion of Skip's faith to empathize with. That kind of polluted message of grace was so far removed from the Gospel I had responded to. Through Christ, I heard the voice of compassion, not coercion. Skip seemed to disagree.

"For those of you who finally realized tonight that Christ is the only way? Welcome . . . to your new beginning."

While Skip's end-times exercise was an extreme example of evangelical altar calls, his wasn't an anomaly in terms of ideological practice. As I was discovering, my calling as a musician inside the church, especially within the evangelical community, came with the expectation that I was there not just to sing about my experiences with my faith, but to win souls for Jesus. I struggled, however, to find my footing in terms of such an evangelical mission. I didn't like the idea of putting people on the spot to make such an intimate, personal decision about their faith publicly. I thought there should be room for those of us who respond best to hours of quiet contemplation.

Throughout that long, hot summer, I had been asked countless times to participate in leading people to Jesus. Most churches called me a music minister, but I had no inclination to be anything other than a musician. I was happy to sing my songs and even say a little about my personal experience as a Christian but, when it came time for the invitation, I found myself making all manner of excuses to get out of the responsibility of telling people that they needed to accept Jesus then and there.

When I got back to my home church in Pittsburg, after weeks away, I would often be greeted by my pastor: "So, how's your ministry going? How many people did you lead to the Lord?"

The first time he said it, I thought he was joking.

"How many?" I asked quizzically in return, "I don't understand!"

"If God is working, you're bound to see the fruit of it in the souls of those you lead to Christ." He smiled, but it felt like a reprimand. In that instant, I felt as though I had failed to be honorable to my calling.

Not only did I have no numbers to report, but I'd stumbled into a profound theological quandary as to how to speak responsibly about my faith. Something inside me didn't agree with the idea that a person could only find their faith the way my pastor and my evangelical peers prescribed, but I hesitated to admit it aloud.

On the surface, I understood the premise, but had difficulty with executing the mandate. My home church, at that point, was of a Baptist denomination that taught that there was only *one* way to know you were a true Christian: *confess* (preferably with witnesses) that Jesus Christ is your personal Lord and Savior, be *baptized,* and *serve* Christ through all things in your daily life. I had come into Christianity this way and hoped to succeed by following the same standards, but it didn't stop me from being uncomfortable about insisting to others that they take the same path that I had taken. To me, it was *a* way, but I wondered, was it the *only* way?

Unlike many of my churched peers, I hadn't grown up believing all this. I wondered if my discomfort was more cultural than theological? Maybe they were just used to talking about God and Jesus all the time, while I was still getting used to such things.

It wasn't that church was completely alien to me. With few exceptions, my family made certain to attend Christmas and Easter services. It wasn't that my family rejected God, we just didn't use the same kind of language and style that my new evangelical friends did. Faith, however it came to us, was ultimately a private experience. Church was for Sundays and the Golden Rule (do unto others as you would have them do unto you) was the ideal we were encouraged to keep. We prayed together as a family at Thanksgiving meals, but we explored our doubts and human suffering, quietly, on our own.

I had taken deliberate steps in following Jesus, and that made sense for me. Still, I was nothing like the supposed good people that I had seen in church when I was growing up. I saw myself as broken and in need of serious renewal. There were times when my Christian peers described my past life as debauched, and I felt judged when my friends celebrated my new life by calling me a redeemed harlot. I knew how it felt to be called a sinner so fallen that only God had the power and mercy to love me, while those who called themselves my friends could not look past my weaknesses.

In the end, what moved me to continue on was the waiting grace that I finally saw in God. I was inspired by what Jesus had said and done, forgiving all, loving all. I not only wanted to be the beneficiary of that kind of grace, I wanted every person I met to know they were loved. I wanted to stand in front of the Skips of the world and sing of a different story. I wanted to tell a story of hope rather than that of shame. I wanted to sing a song of joy rather than that of anger. I wanted to join together with others who were willing to wade through the religion and look for something real and life changing. To me, *that* was the spirit of what sharing one's faith meant. To pay forward, in action, the essence of the love we know that we have received.

ten

My faith, along with my music, was evolving.

In 1992, I was an eager, yet fragile, convert, dependent on others to inform my faith. By 1995, I was starting to develop my own sense of responsibility and ownership of my individual spiritual identity. Although I didn't see myself necessarily out to convince people they should follow into Christianity as I had, I was developing a vision as to how I could contribute to the conversation of spirituality. Despite the times that I found the church and religion bewildering, I had also found incredible stability and comfort. I was going on three years sober, my grades in college had dramatically improved, and my head was starting to clear enough that I started dreaming about my future again.

My friend Byron had spent the previous couple of years trying to encourage me to consider a professional career as a performer. In 1994, he had the grand idea to make some home-studio recordings of my early songs.

On nights after class and weekends, when I wasn't traveling, I headed over to Byron's little farm house in Scammon, Kansas. He set up a four track reel-to-reel tape machine and a couple of old microphones through an old eight-channel Mackie console. I had never before considered recording my original songs, but we were off. I sang four original songs and one arrangement of the classic Sunday school tune "Jesus Love Me." Byron sent the master recording off to a vanity press, where the whole thing was packaged into a nifty shrink-wrapped little cassette tape, titled *Circle Back*.

Byron ordered hundreds of those cassettes, convinced that this was only the beginning of a career he thought was to be my certain destiny. Personally, I thought he was a little nuts. I couldn't imagine how in the world I was going to sell so many tapes in the short term, let alone see myself as having enough talent to make a career of it.

I was astounded however, when, only a few months later, Byron announced that we needed to order more copies. Now that I was performing on a regular basis, I was selling tons of them at shows. Byron had also been sending them to Christian coffee-houses, youth camps, and churches, so that he could give folks a sample of what I sounded like. Along with references from my church and other faith leaders I had worked for, he sent out packets and made cold-calls to every place he could think of, looking for places that would hire me to play.

Byron's efforts were paying off. I had practically spent the entire summer of 1995 traveling and the fall was starting to fill up as well.

The good news was that I was getting so much work that I had to start taking my minicareer seriously. Thankfully, I was earning enough with concert fees and selling my cassettes that a bit of the financial sting had been taken out of being a college student. The bad news was that I had so many gigs booked for the coming school year; it was going to be tricky to figure out how I could travel for work and continue to go to college.

Up until then, financing school had been a tight-rope act. When I had entered school in late 1992, I had done it on the back of music scholarships. The scholarships covered most of my direct school costs, but did little in terms of providing for my food and housing. There were times when all I could afford for groceries was a twenty-five-cent packet of knockoff mac'n'cheese. The rest of my funds went to sharing the rent with my roomies whom, I hoped, didn't notice or mind when I "borrowed" their butter and milk.

I worked as many part-time hours as I could, but keeping up with my school load made it difficult to make ends meet. For the last several years, I struggled to balance the demanding classroom and performance requirements of my music education major. Besides coursework, I was busy attending my own private lessons on trumpet, performing for multiple ensembles that included the symphony, marching band, and orchestra, not to mention the vocal choir that rounded out my obligations for keeping my scholarships. Between the demanding practice hours, performances, classes, then the part-time minimum wage job I had schlepping burgers at Hardee's, I was exhausted most of the time.

As I looked at the prospects for the coming 1995–96 school year, I admitted something had to give. Excitingly, it was already looking like Byron had many of my weekends booked with gigs, but I was going to have to choose whether to forego the scholarships by missing out on my required marching band performances or work singing my songs. I couldn't do both.

The truth was that I hadn't been the same trumpeter since entering college. From the moment I had haphazardly entered the Pitt State music program, I had always been two steps behind. I had spent the first year drunk, the second year sobering up, and the third year focusing on giving my life to Jesus. By year four, I was at a crossroad.

If I was to stay in school as a music education major, I was going to have to stress through another year of financial crisis and curtail my singing gigs. If I accepted the opportunities that were becoming available to me as a Christian artist, affording school would be easier, but I'd have to give up my music major and switch to something more compatible with my schedule.

I chose to take on Byron's challenge and get serious about my Christian music prospects. I changed my major to psychology, traveled on weekends to various gigs, and kept writing more music. Mondays through Fridays, I was a psychology undergrad and fast-food chef. Fridays through Sundays, I was a traveling troubadour.

Life, for me, was starting to become more vivid.

Gigging through the weekends, I enjoyed watching how music seemed to give people permission to express their own experiences. After shows, I talked for hours with my peers who were starting to become regular, supportive fans. We'd discuss our doubts, our faith, and our convictions, and compare how our individual experience might compare to the experiences of others. It felt good to have a growing audience, but more so, I enjoyed connecting with others about spirituality on an intellectual level.

If I were to be a Christian artist, I needed know more about its music as well. Before Captured and Byron's influence, I never knew it existed. Everybody called it contemporary Christian music (CCM). To my ears, most of it sounded like wanna-be knockoffs of mainstream music. Most styles sounded similar to rock-and-roll or pop, but with syrupy, trite lyrics, which, to my ear, often sounded like religious propaganda.

I cringed when I realized that my early songs didn't sound too different from that:

Shine on me!
Once a slave to sin but now Your blood has set me free!
If there's anything that I can do Lord, anything that I can say–
Anything that I can do to make you my way–
Then let it be . . . !

—"Shine," *Circle Back*

It wasn't that I was necessarily offended by the idea of faith-based music. I just wanted to reach for the kind of musical and poetic depth that I had come to admire as a listener. For all my years as a trumpeter, playing High Church music, I had no problem leaning into music that pointed toward the heavens. It was just that, when it came to music, I wanted to get lost in lyrics that were rich and deep with meaning. Even when it came to my choice in popular artists, I had never been a pop-radio junkie. I loved songwriters like Natalie Merchant and Joni Mitchell, whose poetry had a way of mysteriously connecting my earthbound soul with their divine muse.

I continued to be fascinated that I, of all people, had had an experience with faith so radical that it had altered my outlook on life. My life had literally been saved, but it sounds so cliché to me (even still) to say that Jesus saved me, when there is so much more to the story. My choice to be a Christian was important, so I didn't want to be trivial in my writing. I wanted to try to tell the truth of my new spiritual life and set it free to show up in the lyrics.

All the pennies I've wasted in my wishing well
I have thrown like stones to the sea.
I've cast my lots, dropped my guard, searched aimlessly
For a faith to be faithful to me.

—"Faithful to Me," *Kansas/Wishing Well*

It was all well and good to say that Jesus had saved me, but so too had a good therapist and some serious cognitive therapy. With my new pursuit as a psychology major, I wanted to explore more about how the human psyche develops and functions.

I was fascinated by how, even in secular, academic conversations, there always seemed to be a roving dialogue among the students about what is or isn't supposedly normal. To me, it was similar to the attitude that I encountered in the church, when we discussed whether who/what was or wasn't good.

On any given Sunday, I'd find myself immersed in a church culture obsessed with how imperfect or lacking we are as human spirits. The conversations always seemed to center around how broken humanity is, how distant from the perfection of Christ we all are, and how laborious and frightening it can be to continue to aspire to the seemingly unattainable sinlessness required of the Christian disciple. At times it left me wondering why I even bothered imagining that I could renew my life if all I could ever be was one misstep away from spiritual disaster.

On Monday morning, perhaps in a psychology of adjustment class, I would find myself confronted with how inescapable most human behavior actually is. None of us are immune from precariously trying to balance our primal and cognitive needs. We have sex drives and hunger, greed and compassion. Strangely, along the way we usually manage to mix our own experiences with shame and insecurity that threaten to overpower our sense of emotional well-being. If we're lucky, we will discover what it is within us that helps us press on.

Creatively, as a writer, and a person of faith, I became fascinated with human frailty. How do we cause it, respond to it, or endure it? I saw benefits in both psychology and faith. Between the rational and spiritual, I felt like I was finding my peaceable footing with my own peculiarities. In my own life, I was eager to move beyond the Christian idea of flawed humanity and get on with living life to the full. If we are what we are—that is, inescapably human—then part of my responsibility is to learn how to honor myself and others along the way. From a Christian perspective, if Christ's sacrifice was to represent how my sinful nature (read: *human nature*) is reconciled with God's perfect holiness, then why should I be afraid to acknowledge my true self?

I was free to be loved for who I was and wanted to live that way. I didn't want to live under a cloud of shame for being, as it turns out, only *human*. The best of what Christianity would ever teach me was that even on my darkest days, no matter what condition I was in, I was a person made to be loved. As a child, there were times when I never dreamed this could have possibly been true, but all that was changing for me.

There's a place in the darkness that I used to cling to
That presses harsh hope against time.

In the absence of martyrs there's a presence of thieves
Who only want to rob you blind.
They steal away any sense of peace.
Tho' I'm a king I'm a king on my knees.
And I know they are wrong when they say I am strong
As the darkness covers me.

So turn on the light and reveal all the glory.
I am not afraid.
To bear all my weakness, knowing in meekness,
I have a kingdom to gain.
Where there is peace and love in the light
In the light, I am not afraid
To let your light shine bright in my life, in my life

—"Martyrs & Thieves," *Kansas*

THE LYRICS STARTED taking the tone of self-examination and discovery, but I had yet to find a place where I could do so with abandon. Most of the work I found in the summertime was at youth camps or Sunday evening services, where I was expected to be bright and cheery, wholesome entertainment for the kids. When I launched into a pulsing, dramatic tune, singing "You in the mirror, staring back at me . . . Oh, conscience let me be," the children seemed bored and the pastors looked concerned.

For one thing, I didn't really look like the so-called good Christian girl most people were expecting. I usually dressed in jeans, some kind of T-shirt, and a pair of boots. It was a far cry from what most of the churchgoers expected to see.

Girls were supposed to wear dresses to church, play piano, and sing politely.

Me? I was pounding out rock songs on a guitar, sweating, breaking strings, and generally more than eager to talk about how hard it was to measure up to the high standards of Christian living. Usually, the soundtrack for elementary Sunday school was more genteel. Most folks were happy to support my love of music because I was singing about my faith, but weren't always in agreement that the church sanctuary was the best place for it.

Fortunately for musicians like me, Christian culture had embraced the idea of the live music coffeehouse. By the late 1990s, Kansas City was teeming with them. Whether it was a makeshift venue set up in the basement of a church or a strip-mall bookstore converted into a barista parlor for the night, there were finally places a good Christian kid could go to hear some music that expressed their own spiritual experience, rather than simply parroting the faith that they had inherited from their parents. It was a great environment for college students seeking an alternative to the alcohol-fueled club scene to have some good clean fun, but it also proved to be a safe place for many of us to explore and live out our own ideas about faith without the worry of upsetting the applecart of orthodoxy.

On the weekends, when I wasn't working in a church somewhere, I drove up from Pittsburg to Kansas City so I could hang out at my favorite venue, New Earth Coffeehouse. Hearing the kind of music that was being played there and chatting with different kinds of people, altered everything I thought I knew about what Christians were supposed to look and sound like. Preppies, virgins, druggies, Baptists, Pentecostals, skeptics, rich, poor—it didn't matter. We came. Hundreds were packed in like sardines and got lost in the sounds of artists like Dakoda Motor Company, Over The Rhine, Waterdeep, Dime Store Prophets, and Sixpence None the Richer. There were many nights when I stood, pressed in among the crowd, and wondered if I would ever be cool enough, potent, or talented enough to play there.

The sounds and the lyrics that came from those musicians blew my mind. Their music and personalities seemed subversive compared to the light of the sanctuary. Heavily tattooed young men took the stage, cranked up their amps, and let it rip. Solo acoustic guitarists sat center stage and bared their souls so freely that we were compelled into reverent silence.

The artists that left us speechless were those that dared listeners and performers alike to be brave and honest about their true selves. Ska bands, rock bands, songwriters, and poets—all of them young and set free on the stage to tell the story of their journeys. It was different because they shared about their experience as Christians, the good and the bad, the believers and the cynics alike without fear of judgment against their imperfections. A wide path was given to all to explore and stumble, if need be, toward a spiritual experience that called and united us. We just were, and the art we shared was what came out of it.

I will never forget the first time I got a chance to play at New Earth. It might as well have been Carnegie Hall, such was the level of admiration for all I had seen and heard there. Before I had been one of the many silhouetted heads floating behind the spotlights, clapping and hungry for inspiration. Now, I was the one, exposed and center-stage, being called upon for greatness.

I had a half-hour set to fill and perhaps only four songs in which I had any confidence. My knees shook like jelly. My hands cramped and sweated. Just me and my guitar, left alone in a room full of people who had never heard of me. Madness.

I don't remember playing the songs as much as I remember the rapid-fire thoughts that shot through my mind while I played.

Don't screw it up.

What am I doing here? How did I get myself into this mess?

Wow, this is so awesome! I'm killing it . . .! Oops.

This song is so cheesy; they hate it. I gotta *write something better.*

Is that an espresso? Man, I'd love an espresso right now.

Do they really like my songs that much or are they glad I'm finally finished. Is that good applause or bad? Oh, my God, what have I done? Thank God this is over.

My first gig there was a crucible of sorts. Resident pastor and founder of the little urban church/coffeehouse, Sheldon Kallevig, said I could give it a go but, in the end, it was the room that decided.

"There are no promises here. If they like you, you come back. If they don't, well . . ." He was candid, yet openhearted about it. He had the spirit of a man who wanted every contributor to succeed, but success wasn't necessarily about popularity at New Earth. The folks who came back tended to be those who tapped into the journeyman spirit of the community that was there. You could play any style you wanted to, talk as much or as little about Jesus as you needed, be holy or even a little unholy, but you had to come with an eye to love and making a way for others. Those coming to simply make a name for themselves or who just played for the sake of praise didn't seem to last long. At New Earth, you had to find a way to connect on an emotional level.

Through the blur of my first night, I must have done something right, because I ended up cutting my teeth in that coffeehouse. I think I played my first set there in 1994, and watched countless other artists perform, grow, fail, and succeed along the way. By 1996, I was in among them—an artist in my own right, headlining a few nights a year at New Earth and making fans that were urging me to continue.

eleven

Long before the Internet became the workhorse of the modern musician I was amassing a humble following. There was no digital social network. I didn't have a Web site. It was all about doing gigs, word of mouth, and miles of open road. And it was more than helpful if you had a CD.

The little *Circle Back* cassette tape Byron and I made did well for a while, but I was writing more music, outgrowing my older work, and gaining more regional fans familiar enough with me that they wanted to hear my latest work in the modern CD format. In between college classes and touring, Byron sat me down in the studio and helped me arrange and record my songs into a full-length project, titled *Wishing Well*.

Recording your music means that your songs can go to places you've never been. Besides selling CDs at shows, you can pop them in the mail and send them to a deejay, to a college events planner, or even to a record label in hopes that someone will actually listen to it, like it, then offer you a deal that will change your life. I didn't know it, but *Wishing Well* would be a project that would change my life.

Over the course of a year I had sold over three thousand copies of that CD. During my fourth year of college, Byron sent CDs to every Christian label in the market. He'd even managed to get a couple of well-known trade magazines to write reviews of my indie work.

From the early days of Captured, Byron had always had an unshakeable belief that I had what it takes to be a legitimate artist. I had been traveling along with the idea, enjoying getting to play, and loving that I was paying my bills doing something that I loved to do, but I figured the odds of making a lifelong career of it were long. However, by the spring of 1996, Byron started to get calls from Nashville.

For a while, it seemed as though Byron was fielding a steady stream of phone calls from CCM (contemporary Christian music) producers and A&R representatives. I didn't even know what an A&R guy was until Byron explained to me that it was short for artists and repertoire. (Those are the record company personnel in charge of discovering and signing new talent, along with managing the current roster of artists on the label.)

But, for all the phone calls, it didn't seem that I was what the big labels were looking for. There were only a few guitar-wielding chicks that I had ever heard of in CCM anyway, and I didn't look or sound anything like them. I was used to playing in grungy little Christian coffeehouses for college students. When I heard artists like Amy Grant, Twila Paris, and Sandi Patty, I thought there was no way that CCM would consider me. They seemed so clean cut. Me? I was a woman who grew up in the world. I had a dark past littered with sex and booze. I had a hard time imagining, despite my story of redemption, that I had been a Christian long enough to be considered trustworthy enough to be on a Christian label. I held out a little hope when I got hold of artists like Margaret Becker, Ashley Cleveland, or even Christine Dente of *Out of the Gray*. They wrote and sang like they'd actually lived out a few hard, unholy years in their lives, but had they really? Anyway, who was I compared to them? They all seemed so shiny, spiritually certain and . . . wearing *dresses!*

At times, I could be crass and unpolished with my onstage delivery, enough that some people wondered if I was polite enough to have a career that relied on a predominantly conservative church audience.

I remember one day, when I was sound checking at a church before a concert, one of the fellows running the PA system came over to give me a hand in setting up.

He'd heard me described as a rock-and-roll chick, but was confused when I showed up with just my guitar.

"You got a band? Where's your band?" he asked, looking me and my guitar up and down as if we were somehow unprepared.

"Nope. It's just me."

"Tracks? What about tracks then? Don't you have any cassette background tracks you're going to use? I gotta tape player wired to the system," he offered, still baffled.

"Nope. It's just me." I tried to keep my growing agitation to a minimum.

"Well, then, wha . . .who . . .?" Exasperated, he kept looking at me as if mystified at how I was to perform with no band and no backing tracks and only a guitar. I felt like I clearly wasn't the sweet little singing Christian girl he needed me to be. "Who do you play with then?"

I replied, "I play with myself." I giggled aloud at what I had insinuated, but he didn't seem to notice. Again, for my own pleasure and to see if he would cotton on. "Yep. I *play* with my*self.*"

The young sound guy turned beet red and walked away, and that was the end of our preproduction conversation.

I could get away with that kind of thing in the underground scene, or at some out-of-the-way church somewhere, but on a CCM label?

Byron got quite a few calls, but I never seemed to make it past the initial phone call. Well-respected labels like Sparrow, Ardent, and Forefront came and went in a flash, and I started to figure that was pretty much the lay of the land. I'd have my fun traveling around for a few years while I finished school, but that would pretty much be the end of it. I couldn't have been more wrong.

At around that time, a group called DC Talk was revolutionizing the face of CCM rock music with their double-platinum, Grammy-winning album "Jesus Freak." To say this album was a game-changer in the world of Christian music is an understatement. They eclipsed the CCM marketplace and spilled out into the mainstream world. Christian kids were flipping out. Almost overnight, DC Talk made being a young Christian a cool thing. Teenagers and young adults finally had a soundtrack that helped legitimize their Christian cultural experience. Every track on that album channeled the rumbling teenage angst of the late nineties, familiar to fans of Nirvana, Stone Temple Pilots, and Pearl Jam. The dark, warm, electric throbbing manifested itself at live concerts, where, at last, a hormonally raging Christian kid could cut loose and mosh his brains out. For nearly a decade, the wave of DC Talk's "Jesus Freak" took the social stigma out of being Christian.

The driving force behind DC Talk's vision was Toby McKeehan. Toby was one of the trio of front men for the group. Toby not only had a vision for what he hoped DC Talk could accomplish, but expanded his vision by starting his own label,

Gotee Records. Their early roster included a wide variety of acts. Among their early notable groups were R&B trio Out of Eden, grunge-rockers Johnny Q. Public, and the hip-hop duo GRITS.

They were a small company, with little staff and less money, but they were determined to offer music from Christian artists that reflected more of the faith culture than just middle-class, conservative, white folks who had grown up in the church. Toby and his crew had a heart for real people who had been through real life and wanted to offer more than clichéd music.

It was an electric ego boost when TobyMac called and said he'd listened to my old *Wishing Well* record and liked it. In April 1996, Gotee invited me to hang out with them at the Nashville Christian music event of the year, GMA (Gospel Music Association) Week. To go meant skipping a week of my college classes, but my grades were okay, so I decided that I could take the risk. It seemed ridiculous to pass up the opportunity to meet with a label that actually seemed interested in signing me.

When I got there, I met label president Joey Elwood and the small staff that worked in keeping Gotee up and running. The company attitude reminded me a little of the New Earth scene, with a bit more polish. Not too much, though. It seemed like a few of the people that worked there had lived a little, and I liked that.

The Gotee peeps took turns showing me Nashville and the behind-the-scenes world of the CCM industry. That week, I spent most of my time around the primary meeting place of the GMA crowd, the lobby of downtown Renaissance Hotel, and walking along Broadway, Nashville's Main Street.

Hanging out in the musically historic Nashville for the first time thrilled me. Walking past the storied Ryman Auditorium, the birthplace of the Grand Ole Opry, where legends like Hank Williams and Patsy Cline reached out to the world over live radio broadcasts filled me with awe. It was exciting to walk past the Broadway honky-tonks at midday and hear the live music spilling into the streets! I wondered if the players in the bars played all day in the hopes that the Music Row record executives would stroll through the scene looking for the next untapped talent. Even the buskers on the street turned the sidewalks into stages. I wondered if every hopeful country singer and songwriter in the world had landed here, vowing to sing nonstop until their dreams came true. That I had been flown in by a record label added to my sense of how rare this occasion was.

During GMA week the Christian music industry filled the streets of downtown Nashville. The artists that were the face of CCM could be seen passing through the lobby of the Renaissance nearly every second. I tried not to freak out at how intimidating it felt being around all the signed artists. It was hard not to be when cameras were going off everywhere. Everyone who was anyone in CCM, at some point, had to pass through the revolving doors into the lobby, braving the bustling crowd filled with fans, media, and Christian retailers. Even if I wasn't a fan of all the artists that were walking around, the truth was, these were people who I could only dream of equaling in terms of success. Heads turned and bulbs flashed when artists like Stephen Curtis Chapman came through. The crowds parted and stilled like the waters of the Red Sea when gospel sensation Kirk Franklin and his entourage of glitter and gold thundered through the mob. In my wildest dreams, I couldn't imagine how on earth I found myself in such a place.

One of the nights, Gotee was putting on a showcase concert with all their acts. Toby was interested in signing me, but few people in Nashville had ever heard me play. It was up to me, that night, to take the stage and prove that I could handle myself. I was terrified. It didn't matter that I had a hundred shows under my belt—compared to this crowd, I was a rookie to be sure.

Gotee had rented a vacant bar to serve as their venue for the week. On the night I was to play, it was packed with very serious fans buzzing about how excited they were that Johnny Q. was going to be rocking their faces off. The band had amps and drums and fans ready to mosh. I, on the other hand, was armed only with an acoustic guitar.

The crowd looked so cool that I felt out of place even in the audience. Backstage, the all-male Johnny Q. filled the room with their rock-star musk. I remember TobyMac calmly welcoming me into the green room while he casually picked at a box of sushi with a pair of chopsticks.

Sushi? Raw fish? Who on earth—I said to myself, completely grossed out. "Who would *ever* eat raw fish?

My subconscious answered me back in a jazz-cool voice, "Rock stars, babe. Rock stars eat sushi."

What was I doing here? I was definitely not in Kansas anymore.

Before I knew it, Joey Elwood had taken the stage to introduce me. The buzzy room stopped for a moment, a few lazy hands smacked together when he announced my name, and then it was my stage.

All I could do was take a deep breath, close my eyes, and play my heart out. I couldn't be anybody other than who I was, so I had nothing to lose.

Thirty minutes later, I looked up and it was all over. I don't remember much about the applause in the room, just that I automatically did what I always do when I leave the stage. I reached to pull the cable from the end of my guitar, gave a little thank-you wave, and turned to get off stage without further embarrassment.

As I walked off, one of the girls who squished up into the barrier in front of the stage asked, "What's your name?"

"Jennifer," I said off mic. "Hi!" I didn't know what else to do except smile and try to leave.

"No," the girl returned, "What's your *name* on your *record?*"

"Oh, uh—" it felt strange introducing myself to someone with my full name, but she wanted it all, "Jennifer . . . Knapp." Weird.

"Cool," she said, "I'll be looking out for you!" I heard her say, as I walked off.

AFTER GMA WEEK had ended, I returned back to Pittsburg for the last few weeks of the spring semester. I fought the remaining adrenaline and flattering buzz that still lingered, and tried to focus on the coming final exams when I got the call from Joey. Amazingly, Gotee wanted me on board and were offering me a five-record contract.

I was twenty-two, a new Christian with barely a dozen songs to my name, and I said yes.

I was still a semester or two away from completing my psychology degree, but it was going to have to wait. I finished my classes that spring in what would be my last term at Pittsburg State. I committed myself to being a full-time, signed, Christian recording artist.

twelve

*S*igning with Gotee Records was both exhilarating and nerve racking. On one hand, it was an incredible opportunity to have a job centered around music, yet, on the other, I doubted whether I had the goods to make it work. That I had the makings of a Christian rock star seemed almost laughable to me. I couldn't see myself as anything other than a country tomboy. If I was honest, I felt ugly, fat, and a little nerdy. That's to say nothing about my self-image as a Christian. Alone, and in private, I was being drawn further into a spiritual world that continued to shape, inspire, and strengthen my inner being, but outside? I was self-conscious of how different I was. Everything and everybody in Nashville was larger than life to me. The CCM industry looked to be filled with people who had grown up in the church and worked to stay there. To my eyes, everyone was fashionable and physically fit. Maybe that's because they ate sushi. I'd never eaten sushi. I'd never lived in a big town. I'd never . . . there was a lot I hadn't done, but all that was about to change very rapidly.

I moved from Pittsburg to Kansas City. Moving to KC got me closer to the airport, so that I could easily fly back and forth to Nashville without having to move so far from the Midwestern world I was comfortable with. Besides, there was no guarantee that my career was going to last long. As is often said to musicians, it's always good to have something to fall back on. I figured if this whole thing turned out to be a bust, at least I wouldn't be far from the safety net of my friends and family.

Thankfully, the staff at Gotee was small and down to earth, making my introduction to the music scene relatively smooth. They had a reasonably diverse core of personalities, ranging from executive accounting geeks and pop-culture hipsters, all of whom warmly welcomed me into their family. I was sure the vibe came from the merged influences of founders, Toby McKeehan (Toby-Mac) and Joey Elwood. Together, they represented, inspired, and encouraged Gotee's collective passion for creating music that was culturally and spiritually relevant to Christianity.

There was no doubt Toby was driven to keep his finger on the pulse of what was cool to young people. Though my interactions with Toby throughout my history at Gotee would be limited, his philosophy would leave a lasting mark on me.

What struck me about Toby was that he was confident in the person he wanted to be, both as an artist and as a Christian. It was hard not to respect that about him. "Jesus Freak" had changed the landscape of CCM, and it wasn't a joke or a money grab. Yes, the record was hugely successful, but behind the scenes, Toby was dead serious about integrity. He was serious about Jesus, and the lengths he went to to put out quality music and entertainment was his way of reflecting that.

Though we were completely different in terms of style, I took a lot in from Toby's peripheral leadership. Whether he intended to or not, he impressed upon me the importance of both spiritual and artistic integrity. As an observer, Toby appeared to have seamlessly merged the two.

I looked to Toby's example as the standard of what would ultimately be expected of any CCM rock star making a living in the spotlight. If I were to succeed, I had to be excellent at my craft, as well as be beyond reproach with Christian integrity and unabashed when speaking about my faith.

In the early days, sitting around a conference table discussing what my image would be, Toby was the one who shaped what my personality would look like to the outside world.

I credit Joey Elwood for keeping me grounded through the chaos of what was a strange new world to me. He wanted to run his company well, but never let that get in the way of our becoming friends. He kept me motivated to stay passionate about the joy of serving others through music. He and I would share many conversations over the years about the challenges we both felt in balancing our faith and having careers, when faith was our business.

He was one of the few people who seemed to understand that I wasn't just performing for the money. I wanted to do something meaningful with my life, and music was a way to make that a possibility. Music, for me, was about what it did when you told it your secrets. Music seemed to turn our inner longings into prayers. Played back, shared, and transmitted, the impossible happened. We knew that we were *known*. By someone, somewhere.

Through the music, with Gotee's help, I truly believed that I could share a vision of the God who made me *known*. The God of Love that I had found, through Christ, through music, through faith.

These things weren't easy to keep hold of when the world seemed to be spinning so fast. As soon as the ink had dried on the contracts, I was neck deep in planning meetings aimed at creating the storefront image that was to be my public life.

No stone was to be left unturned. It seemed like every note of every song was dissected, every hair on my body colored, cut, or plucked. I was now in the music *business* and I had to look like I was up to the task.

Apparently, I needed a head-to-toe makeover.

Now, from what I understand about girls who *aren't* tomboys, getting the opportunity to have a complete makeover at someone else's expense would be a dream come true. The idea of spending days with endless spa treatments is enough to make some giddy with delight. Me? I was mortified.

I had no idea how much work it took to prepare a woman for a photo shoot. My hair was cut and colored by a stylist (back in Kansas we just called the lady down at the Main Street beauty parlor a *hairdresser*). I was introduced to and trained in how to use things called *hair products*. Who knew you could put more into your hair care than hairspray and mousse?

When the hair on the top of my head was taken care of, the hair *on* my face was next. According to the lady at the spa, I needed two eyebrows, not one. And, of course, absolutely no mustache! *Ouch!*

It was exciting to come out the other side of the beauty mill feeling like a new woman, but it was unnerving as well. Until that point, I had taken for granted how important and private my life had been. My body, my clothes, my faith, and my music had always been mine to decide. Now, I was only at the beginning stages of learning what it would be like to have to share elements of my private domain with others.

In 1998, Gotee Records released *Kansas* and, that fall, put me out on the road for my first official tour with headliners Audio Adrenaline (Audio A, for short). Mark Stewart, the lead singer for

Audio A, had produced *Kansas*, so he was more than eager to do his part to help launch my career by giving me a spot to play on his *Some Kind of Zombie* tour. Outside of a little professional nepotism, there really wasn't much reason for me to have been on the tour. Musically, I didn't seem to fit into the night.

Audio A was a rock-and-roll band that catered to mostly young men, and supporting ska act, The O.C. Supertones, did even more so. To say this was a testosterone-fueled production is to put it mildly. I had no money to hire a band with which to sonically compete, so it was up to just me and my guitar to make it work.

Nearly every night for four months, I had to walk out onto a huge, dimly lit stage, alone, in front of over a thousand amped-up (mostly teenage) Christian music fans. All of them were there to have their heads blown off, not to be lulled to sleep by some chick with a guitar.

For the first few weeks of the tour, I was an absolute nobody. When I walked out on stage, the audience was either ambivalent or annoyed.

I could see it in the faces of the boys assembled in the mosh pit. While they excitedly tried to push and shove their way to the front, a few faces stared up at me in disbelief. As if to say, "What is a *girl* doing here? Girls don't rock."

Behind me, The O.C. Supertones backdrop towered and sparkled to remind everyone of who I was not. I was some unknown delaying the show they really came to see. My name was announced, a few outnumbered young girls clapped in feminine solidarity, the spotlight turned on . . .

I tried to think of it as my special honor to start the show. I had to be good. Better than good. The applause was feeble, but it was my job to change that. I wanted them all to know that the night had started and I meant business. I wanted to win them over. The cards looked stacked against me, but I tried to put it out of my mind.

I had three songs to do my thing. Without a single word, I laid into the most rockingest songs I had, hell bent on pounding my guitar into splinters. I sang harder than I should and louder than necessary. I sawed my guitar as hard as I could. I played this way every night, trying to swing attention my way, until one night—*Thwack!*—a string broke on my guitar. The room went silent as my miniset came to a screeching halt. Disaster. Without a word, I took off my guitar, reached for another, and picked up right where I had left off. All of a sudden, the crowd went nuts. Every night after that, I made it my mission to play until it broke or die trying.

After every show, I came out and sat, usually unnoticed, at the end of the autograph table while fans made their way past Audio A and the Supertones. Occasionally kids would hand me their tour posters to sign, more out of mercy than anything else, but, on the night of the broken string, things started to brighten.

One sweaty boy came up to me and asked if I had a pick that I could sign for him. While I signed, he added, "I don't really like chick music, but you rock!"

Meanwhile, Gotee had been doing their best to get Christian radio stations to start playing my songs. People started making the connection.

"Oh! You're that girl with the song I like on the radio!"

The boys kept walking by, fully decked out in their Audio A T-shirts and hats, but then the girls started coming by too. By the end of the tour I was signing more and more *Kansas* CDs.

It took the sting—or maybe I should say, stink—out of being on tour with all those guys. I was one of only two girls in the whole crew, the other being my road manager/merch girl. We were on the crew bus, which we shared with the ten guys who unpacked, set up, and packed the entire tour production each day. Twelve people crammed into what is basically a big RV, most of them stinky and tired. One toilet (no number twos allowed!) and two televisions to share among us. The only guaranteed privacy you got on tour was your assigned bunk. Seniority determined your allotment. Bunks were arranged six on each side, end to end, in two stacks of three. The lowest on the floor were hummed to sleep by the sounds of tire treads, the highest rocked to sleep by the gentle sway of riding more than ten feet off the ground. The middle was a perfect blend of both hum and roll. There was no one favorite bunk to sleep in, but most everyone develops their own strong preference. Getting the bunk you wanted versus the bunk you hated could be the difference between your tour simply being long or a crucible you would have to suffer. When every day for months on end is the cycle "Rinse. Wash. Repeat," a little thing like your bunk becomes a high priority.

Every day was the same: wake up, set up, sound check, and show. Pack up, get on the bus, and go to sleep while the driver heads to the next town. Wake up again, in a new place—it doesn't matter where. You have to do exactly the same thing today as you did yesterday. Just make sure that when you get on stage and shout to the crowd you remember where you are!

That tour was the first time I experienced the phenomenon of not knowing or even caring what city I was in. It all bled together. We played a lot of small arenas on tour. Arenas are either round or square boxes made of rebar and cement. The hallways all look the same. The dressing rooms (if you got one) are usually gray and musty, thanks to the showers. Often, they were locker rooms of whatever local sports team makes the venue their home. Getting use of the showers was a mixed blessing. It was great to be able to have a place to clean up, but bad when it came to staving off athlete's foot, and brutal when the water only ran cold.

It was hard going, but by the end of the tour I was finding my stride.

Unbelievably, my first album was selling well. Better, I think, than any of us expected. A few of my songs had made it to #1 on the CCM charts as my name became more recognizable across the country (for Christian music fans, anyway). In early 1999, *Kansas* had sold well enough to give TobyMac measured confidence in signing me as the opening act for DC Talk's spring leg of the *Supernatural* tour.

It would have been unthinkable to do the tour without a band. So, before the tour kicked off, I flew down to Nashville, auditioned and signed a guitar player, a drummer, and a bassist. The only one of them I actually knew was the drummer, who teched for the Supertones on the Audio A tour. I don't think anyone of us had done a tour as big as the Supernatural tour was going to be, and we would be lucky if we ever repeated it again. Joining in with us were ska up and comers, The W's. They would warm the crowd up, and I'd launch into the best of *Kansas* and pray that a riot didn't ensue before DC Talk took the stage.

We played every major city in America on that tour and then some. East coast, west coast, north, south, midwest to southwest. In the span of a few weeks, I had traveled through more states than some Americans would see in a lifetime.

In March, we took a small break from the tour and came back to Nashville. It was GMA week and the thirtieth Annual GMA Dove Awards (sometimes referred to as the Christian Grammys) were to take place. I'd barely been on the scene a year, so I was surprised to learn that I'd been nominated for a few Doves. The most shocking was New Artist of the Year.

It was certainly an honor to have been nominated, but I found myself shaken by the exposure the nominations seemed to generate. Out on the road, I was nestled safely in the cocoon of my bus. I did my shows; I hung out for autographs. I'd even made a few public appearances at malls for radio stations and bookstore signings. It was chaos, but it was controlled. Everything was on a schedule, at predictable times of the day. It was contained. I could walk the streets in obscurity as my face wasn't yet as familiar as my name. I was only famous when I was at work and I liked it that way. The frenzy of fans clamoring for autographs could be an affair that was entertaining and rewarding, but I'd only sign after shows with organized lines and security to keep things moving along. Plus, I had always hidden under the shadow of the headline acts. My popularity grew, but the pressure of it was nothing compared to what DC Talk faced. I was more than satisfied making a living sneaking through with just enough popularity to stay employed, keep the record company happy, and have a good time with it. The nominations were changing all that.

The week of GMA was insane. Now, when I walked through the lobby of the Renaissance, I was being recognized, stopped, quizzed, and photographed. It wasn't excessive, but it was jarring. I couldn't relax. I felt like I was always being watched and I wasn't prepared for it.

One of the reasons I dared to sign with Gotee was because they were a small label. It was a place where I hoped I could be a small fish in a big pond, in a way. But the success of *Kansas* changed all that.

All of a sudden I felt thrown into the deep end of CCM. It may sound crazy, but part of me was terrified about having to go to the Dove Awards because I didn't know what to wear. I'd gone to the Doves the last two years, and I knew that I didn't look anything like the other women in CCM. They were so feminine. They wore gowns. They wore high-heeled shoes. They had ankles. More than anything in my life, I truly feared the prospect of having my name called and having to take the stage. I had no idea what to do on a stage if I weren't standing behind a guitar. It all seemed so exposed.

I hoped that my name wouldn't be called, but the awards were being broadcast, so I had to wear something halfway fitting for a celebrity for when the cameras panned to my face when my nomination was announced. I chose a black leather suit, threw on one of my sparkly gig shirts underneath, and prayed that this was enough to get me through unembarrassed.

When my mother found out that I had been nominated, she flew down to give her support. Her being there was the one sure reminder in a storm of uncertainty that I was a normal, real-life person. Immersion into the circus of flashing lights, awards, and ball gowns was the stuff of celebrity. *Was I really a celebrity now?* Whatever happened, I could rely on being able to look to my family for seeing me as the ordinary person I reckoned myself to be. Knowing that, underneath it all, my mom knew me as "just Jennifer" was comforting.

When my name was called for New Artist of the Year, my

skin went numb and my brain went static. Inside, I tried not to panic. I could tell that the Bridgestone Arena was filled with music and applause, but it came into my ears only as muffled white noise. The only distinguishable sound that I heard was my mother, yelling from the darkness, "That's my daughter!"

Whatever words came into my brain and out of my mouth at the podium felt like gibberish. I hadn't truly prepared and even if I had, I still don't think I would have been ready for the flood of emotion that came pouring over me that moment. Something deep inside me had changed, but I didn't yet know what. I found myself distracted, pushing through a wave of memories that came flooding in, demanding my attention. However, I still had to get through the rest of the night.

I took home my first two Dove Awards and experienced my first press conference. I fielded tons of questions about what it was like to be crowned that year's best new CCM star. It all seemed so trivial compared to what was going on inside me. All I wanted was to get to a place of quiet, so that I could process it all. The moment had been significant for me, but it wasn't about all the pundits swirling around me seemed to think.

Something inside me locked into place. A steadiness of spirit is the only way I know how to describe it. It started when I heard my mother's voice. My mind began to race through a thousand painful quotes I had held onto from the stepmother, who said I would grow up to be nothing. Mental pictures of my early college days, of my body broken and inebriated, came clicking through like a rapid-fire slideshow. The nights of shame and the days where I felt so lost and out of control. A dark voice inside me said I didn't deserve to be here and pointed to the past.

Yet, that day, with a surprising new store of strength, I pushed it back.

I had the power to stop being afraid of failure. I had failed in the past, I might fail in the future, but I didn't have to waste energy on being embarrassed about the outcome, good or bad. Even if things were hard or confusing to navigate, I'd be okay, no matter what.

thirteen

The transition from my independent days into the corporate Christian music industry would be both welcome and challenging. Initiation into the professional ranks made it possible for me to spend more time simply being an entertainer, rather than being obligated to act as a so-called minister.

Rather than continuing to be the special musical guest for church services and youth camps, I was now entering a world where the Christian rock concert was *the* high point of the night. As a signed artist, I was being asked to perform exclusively as an entertainer, a legitimate Christian rock star in the making. (Look out Amy Grant, here I come!)

There was no doubt that I was still responsible for presenting music that engaged my Christian faith, but now, I hoped, I was free to leave the preaching to the preachers and the altar calls to the evangelical visionaries. I hoped I could be a good, wholesome entertainer who, like every other Christian, was doing their best to be like Jesus. The only difference I could see was that my journey was going to be very, very public.

The idea that all performers are extroverted attention seekers couldn't be further from the truth. Songwriters, especially, are quite often introverts. We often spend hours of scribbling lyrics alone in some quiet corner somewhere or losing track of time, eyes closed and singing with abandon, until the waking birds tell us that morning has arrived. The passionate music we make for others to enjoy is usually created in solitude. Alone and uninterrupted, we plumb the depths of our memories and emotions, until we emerge from the quiet abyss back into the illuminated world with a song to tell of our adventures.

It would take me years to learn to understand my own self in this way, as an introvert. At the time, all I knew was that I was being led into public life by God as a matter of service. My Christian peers and mentors explained to me that it was my role as an obedient Christian to follow and, at all times, be like Jesus as much as humanly possible. If I was uncomfortable for any reason, if I felt pushed or worn out, it was evidence that I was being used by God. If it felt as if I was living beyond my emotional or physical means, it was an indication that I needed to submit more fully to God's will as opposed to my own. Without nuance or appreciation of my own personal limitations, this idea was a seed that would eventually sprout into confusion and disillusionment.

It was first planted in the early days of my independent career, when I was traveling alone from gig to gig. Both inexperienced as a Christian and as a perpetual guest, I often stayed in the private homes of my hosting religious community. It didn't take long for me to realize that, after a long night of commanding the stage, signing autographs, and generally hanging out with folks afterwards, I needed time alone. I needed to retreat to my own space somewhere, so that I could refuel and reboot to be at my best for the next lengthy round of social demands. It seemed to make sense that, after a long day, heading to the quiet retreat of my own hotel room might be in order.

On this, my friend cum manager, Byron, and I always seemed to disagree. Part of what came with my role as a leader in the church, he explained, was to be open to accountability. The idea being that, in avoiding the appearance of evil out on the road, I was to always be surrounded by witnesses to testify on my behalf that I was indeed on my best behavior. Going to a hotel was not only ignoring the gracious hospitality offered by my hosts, but also meant that I wasn't observed or protected.

Explained to me this way, it seemed that something was wrong with how I was growing as a Christian. Being grumpy or momentarily antisocial was grounds for having the validity of my faith criticized, never mind that I might just simply be tired. If ever I was short on niceties after driving endless miles, living out of a bag for a few weeks, or allergically swollen and puffy from sharing my bedroom with my host families' cats, I might receive a letter of complaint or phone call of concerned accountability from one of my hosts.

They might say, "We're really concerned about Jennifer's walk with the Lord. When we asked her to spend the day of her concert whitewater rafting, she declined. It's not a very good witness for Jesus if she doesn't hang out with us."

At the end of the day, I knew that it was up to me to be well-rested and prepared to perform my concerts. What mattered most was preserving my energy for the time I was called to use it. Whenever I am out sharing, it's an honor to give every ounce that I have in connecting with others. The point for me was that I *wanted* to share, but for that, I need to be prepared and well-rested to do my best.

Early on, I became accustomed to how people in the church can have a tendency to complain about others by judging someone's likeness to Christ by their own perceptions of what a Christian should or shouldn't look like, do, or not do.

The trivial criticisms were easy enough to handle. It took a lot more to dent my sense of spiritual integrity than to call me un-Christlike for not having energy for, or want to risk death over, rafting. It didn't matter to me that anyone would judge my character by such a thing because nothing in true depth of character could be revealed in such a choice. That I was here, everyday, persisting in striving to follow God, understand God, and serve God—that was the best evidence I had to offer.

Being a dedicated entertainer seemed to fix all that for a while. I was cloistered away on tour buses, in backstage dressing rooms, and in controlled autograph settings. I still played at the odd church or two, but it was under the umbrella of the tour machine. For a while, I thought that I had found a way in which I could navigate living in a world where my decision to be a person of faith walked in the room ahead of me.

But, after the Dove Awards, my world seemed to contract instead of expand.

What I was going to have to understand was that in signing on to be a Christian artist, I wasn't just an ordinary Christian anymore. Now, I was going to be a model example for the Christian life. From the trivial to the theologically defined expectations of everything a Christian is supposed to be and represent, I was now responsible for representing Jesus.

It doesn't take long to figure out that in the Christian subculture, the biggest criticism to throw at someone is to question their integrity as a believer. To survive it, I was going to have to learn how to function while having my every perceived misdemeanor scrutinized under the high expectations of what it means to be, act, and speak as a Christian. I had to learn to roll with the punches. If I failed to make the proper eye contact with a fan while signing an autograph, or if they were asked to move forward in the line too quickly, bam!: "You're not a very good Christian."

If I wore a tank top in a one-hundred-degree heat, boom!: "A skin-revealing harlot!"

Such trivial matters are relatively easy to move past, but it fosters a kind of risk/reward relationship between public Christian figures and those who look upon them. Regardless of the gravity of the slight or imperfection, every Christian artist's career rests in the hands of those who measure the integrity of their spiritual journey against their own idea of what a Christian is, or should, be. Fail to represent that standard to the right people and your CD could sit on the shelf collecting dust, career over.

For those unfamiliar with the contemporary Christian music industry, I like to describe it this way: Music made by Christians, for Christians, and for the intent of making more Christians. While it is a genre unto itself, it is unique in that the style of music is not the primary identifier. The musical styles run the gamut from inspirational worship to rap but, as a genre, CCM is beholden to a lyrical content and intent that must speak specifically to Christ as the Redeeming Son of God.

This is also a mandate for the personal, private religious life of an artist in the industry: Each must be a credible, self-professed Christian. There was a time, and perhaps it still exists, when a new artist would have to be observed by the label for a year or so before they were allowed to sign a contract. It needs to be evident that the artist is the proper kind of Christian in order to proceed. It's not unusual to have morality clauses woven into recording contracts that encourage the artist to stay on the straight and narrow.

Some artists have been required to sign legal documents that attest that they will abstain from sex if unmarried, avoid drunkenness, and, occasionally, declare that they are not gay. The principle obligations for every artist, writer, preacher, or leader of any kind are to be the embodiment of the Christian lifestyle, to illuminate Christianity as *the* way to God, and to encourage others to follow with you. In terms of observable religious practice, this is pretty much the standard definition of traditional Evangelical Christianity. It is in this way that those who participate in the genre of CCM are ultimately expected to appreciate, endorse, and maintain that same evangelical standard or look for another job.

I understood that for listeners to trust Christian music as a genre, consumers had to be confident in the artist's faith. (This is generally true through all the inner workings of the CCM industry, from whoever answers the desk at reception, to the cashier at the local Christian bookstore, to the decision makers, like label presidents. Each must generally be comfortable defining their status a follower of Christ.) However, what happens to those who have chosen Christianity as their religion and language of spiritual expression but are not, by nature or reason, theologically evangelical?

I had given my life to God and was more than willing to acknowledge how much that decision had positively affected my life. I had vowed to serve Him with my music and relied upon that commitment to sustain me. Yet, in doing so, I began to realize that I had stumbled into a curious predicament that befalls so many people of faith. So long as my personal commitment to Jesus was deemed worthy by my fellow Christians, I would have a place at the table. I would be welcome in church. Welcome to sing. But, if I stumbled, and committed too great a sin (however such things are variably measured), if I doubted too much, or was *too* liberal in my thinking, or theology, not only would my faith be criticized, but my entire livelihood also stood to be affected as well.

It may seem strange, but the worry about losing my career didn't matter to me as much as the constant adjudication of my spiritual character. A career as an entertainer, Christian or otherwise, is ultimately an unreliable field of employment. The fact that I had a career at all was remarkably humbling. The odds are never in favor of a career of any sort, let alone longevity.

No, I liked my job, but it wasn't what made me get up in the morning. Above all, I sought to be a person of integrity. I wanted to honor God with my life and spent every day living, breathing, and working to that end, but what never ceased to wear away at my endurance was the constant assessment of everything I did, funneled through but one narrow view of Christianity.

In my travels, and all the people I had ever met and been inspired by, what moved me was the diversity of how we all came to see a common thing. *That* is a conversation I can contribute to. I've known what it is to be inspired and moved by God's grace, the frailty of humanity, the power of forgiveness, and boundless love. This, *this*, is what kept me talking about my experiences. This is what I wanted to write about. If I had a choice as to what kind of Christianity I hoped to represent, it was not that there was only *one* way, but rather, *a* way, that had given me hope. I wasn't taking the stage to endorse a particular brand of theology, but rather to inspire, connect, and rejoice in the revelation that we can all love and be loved.

For my own part in CCM, I did my very best to remain faithful to presenting the best virtues of Christianity but, as my star continued to rise, and the expectation that I would be a Christian role model came to the fore, my theologies and spirit were being tested.

One day, in the chaos of an autograph line, a young, tomboyish girl pushed her way forward and handed me a CD to sign. With tears in her eyes, she leaned toward my ear and whispered, "I have to thank you. Your music has saved me from a life of homosexuality." She seemed shaky and unconvinced, almost coerced.

I was gob smacked. This was far from what I had signed up for. I wanted to ask, "What on earth gave you the idea that *I* thought being gay was wrong?" But I said nothing to alter her course. I'd like to think that I gave her a resounding affirmation of whoever she felt herself to be, but I probably just offered a trite spiritual cliché, signed her CD, and moved on to the next person. Instead of hugging her and telling her that she was beautiful just the way she was, I kept my views to myself. I knew better. I kept my mouth closed and my fingers tightly wrapped around my Sharpie. I had read my Bible cover to cover, and again in multiple translations. I was aware that there were verses that didn't look favorably on homosexuality. I had even been pulled to the side a time or two myself and rebuked for having the appearance of being gay—being judged to be too friendly with this girl or that. But, then again, that had happened with my male friends as well.

Still though, even after I had read the Bible, what seemed important was the heart of a person, anyway, not so much the body.

While the body did matter in some part, everything that I read seemed to point to taking care with our bodies so as to reflect respect for our own physical person and that of others. Love, above all else, however, *must* rule, even if we debated about how to use the plumbing involved.

My church taught, and most people in CCM believed, that homosexuality was definitely a no-go. That I didn't necessarily agree was a matter that I learned to keep to myself for fear of being labeled supposedly un-Christian. I didn't want to unnecessarily rock the boat. It wasn't until I met this young woman that I took into account what being a representative of that style of religion actually said about my own character and beliefs.

WALKING AWAY FROM the night, I replayed the incident over and again in my head. The encounter left me physically sick to my stomach and questioning whether I wanted to be associated with encouraging this kind of Christianity. My faith had been teaching me to be at peace with who I was, and to not be humiliated by imperfection. If anything, I had hoped that what I brought with my music was a sense of valuing ourselves just as we are presently found, accepting the grace that we must surely need in order to move forward in our journeys positively.

Foolishly, I thought I was doing an incredible job at subtly distancing myself from the fire and brimstone kinds of Christians that viewed gays as *less than* in the eyes of God, but clearly, I had not. She thought I was one of them and I had done nothing to tell her any differently.

It was one thing to hold a different theological position privately, but now I was being credited with supporting this potentially spiritually and psychologically damaging tradition. I could have stood up and taken responsibility for my part in this tragedy but, in my silence, I gave consent. Rather than take the risk of being compassionate, I chose to not inconvenience myself. I chose to protect my career first and hoped that the young woman could survive in a world that said it was wrong for her to be herself.

Egotistically, I was ashamed that she could have viewed me as the sort of person who would have such an idea. In a more global view, I was reeling at the thought that I was perpetuating such a limited brand of Christianity. I don't know why it surprised me so much, when I knew that I was a part of a religion that had a history of calling such things a sin. I had in the back of my mind a vague recollection of Anita Bryant's gay witch hunt through Kansas in the late seventies. I found it comical that Jerry Falwell's favorite scapegoat for disastrous earthquakes was homosexuality and not a natural shifting of tectonic plates. The lunacy and demonization that they preached didn't seem to add up with the gay people I had met in my own life.

I'd known a few girls who liked girls and boys who liked boys in college. I came from a small town, but there were a few gay folks there, too. I knew better than to speak of it, but there were a couple of times when I had felt drawn to kiss a girl friend or two myself. When I bothered to think of it, my own sexual experiences with men weren't really all that appealing. As it was turning out, celibacy was a great safety net for my private, internal questioning.

Maybe, I wondered, *human sexuality is a little more diverse than just being attracted to the opposite sex?*

I learned to keep my thoughts to myself. I'd seen the effect of whispers behind the backs of my unmarried, middle-aged friends. I'd watched as my own Christian friends ostracized those whom they suspected to be gay.

In my own life, I found celibacy the best way to avoid any spiritual judgment regarding sex. After I became a Christian, I had experienced the harsh sting of having my natural hormones and sexual past pointed out as failure. There were times when my sexuality came into question, but I was eager to move past any shaming. I didn't realize it at the time, but I handled any potential conflict by shutting down my entire sexual identity. To not have sex or talk about having sex was the best way I figured I could keep the peace. If I was to ever have sex again, it was a long way off. I had too much learning to do in figuring out how to be a good Christian woman first.

In meeting this young girl, I knew her pressure to conform both socially and spiritually, and, now, I was conscious that I was perpetuating a religious prejudice, thanks to my own silence.

That episode would be one of many in a growing stockpile of experiences that began to chip away at my faith. The pressure for me conform to a world that dictated what a Christian looked like, believed, and endorsed, was increasing. Everywhere I turned, I was either being praised for representing the conservative ideals of Christian culture by simply showing up and singing or I was being accused of being a charlatan for not supporting specific causes.

Eyebrows were raised and my faith questioned when I turned down the honor of having one of my songs used in support of a True Love Waits campaign. (This was the name given to a religious campaign that hoped to inspire teenagers to remain virgins until marriage.) In all honesty, I just couldn't do it. It wasn't my style, nor of any benefit, to my thinking, to tell a young girl that God loved virgins most. Whatever came out of my mouth, I wanted it to be: *God loves you. Period.*

The ironic thing was, though I didn't necessarily want to be the kind of evangelical that led people in prayers to accept Jesus, I was truly moved to be an ambassador for the best parts of the joys I had experienced in becoming a Christian. For kids who had grown up in the church, I wanted to be the person who helped inspire them to keep exploring Christianity, even when it seemed the church made it seem as though they couldn't measure up. I wanted to take away the stigma out of doubt for believers and skeptics alike. Sure, the church and its people could be challenging, but what was that compared to the joys of tapping into Divine Mystery? I truly believed that one of the reasons that I was defying odds (that I was alive and healthy, a role model for faith, and getting the opportunity to make a life out of the music that I loved so dearly) was that I could honor the very faith that made it all possible. To suggest that I failed that mission, or was motivated otherwise, was to strike at the very foundation at what gave my life meaning.

I could hardly believe it, when, in 1999, I got an invitation to spend a week on tour with Sarah McLachlan's Lilith Fair. It's not often that Christian artists are given much credence in mainstream environments, so I took it as a high compliment on both a personal and an artistic level. First, that the Lilith gang didn't think I was so far gone in religious overtones that I would be a distraction to the proceedings, but even more so, it was flattering to be considered artistically worthy of being allowed to rub elbows with some of music's most inspiring female artists. If I had any career at all as an artist, it was via the legacy of such artists as Sarah, The Indigo Girls, Sheryl Crow, and Chrissie Hynde. From Emmy Lou Harris to Suzanne Vega, there's not a chick on this planet who plays a guitar without being driven by their inspiration and talent.

I jumped at the chance to play a few stops on their tour and didn't think twice about it.

As we chased the tour through Ohio and Michigan in a packed Ford Econoline, we happened upon a Christian radio station that was hosting a heated talk-show debate. I could hardly believe what I was hearing. The emcee was going on and on about how *I* had embarrassed the church by playing at Lilith Fair. By chance, I found myself eavesdropping on a conversation over the airwaves about how I was lacking true Christian character by engaging with a group where there were known lesbians performing, as well as certain alcohol and drug use. How, in my right mind, did I not have the decency to see that this was a crime to the Christian witness to play in such a place? Through his rabble-rousing, he gave the number of the station and encouraged listeners to call in to add their thoughts.

I grabbed my cell phone and called. To my surprise, the host picked up the phone directly.

"Hi. I'm Jennifer Knapp, the singer," I didn't expect him to believe me. "I thought maybe you'd like a chance to talk with me directly rather than postulating on why I'm playing Lilith?"

The other end was quiet for a moment. "Uh, really . . .? You're the *real* Jennifer Knapp?"

I explained that I was in the van, cruising to the next show, and happened upon his lively one-sided debate. Rather than talking about me, maybe he'd like to talk *with* me instead, I challenged. Surprisingly, he put me on the air for the better part of the hour, peppering me with all manner of suppositions, the grandest and most presumptive of all being that good Christians don't associate with the likes of what Lilith represents.

"Why wouldn't I aspire to be excellent in my craft?" I asked. "I'm not changing the lyrics to any of my songs. I'll be singing them as they were written. Why shouldn't I celebrate wherever I get the chance?"

I am dubious that I changed his opinion of my exploits in any way. I recall we ended at an impasse. The chink in my armor had been found, however, and the criticism of my faith started pouring in from all sides. Bee in my bonnet, I wanted to answer them all, both in defense of my own integrity and for honest criticism of Christianity. For one short summer, I let it rip.

What on earth makes one Christian better *than another? Aren't we all on a spiritual journey together?* I dared wonder aloud.

I was single, in my mid-twenties, and hanging out at Lilith Fair. Internet forums were filling up with accusations and judgments. Some speculated that I must be a lesbian, since I had yet to marry and had no children, so advanced in years as I was at twenty-five! Like a fool, I thought I could engage the crazy and make some kind of sense. At one point, I posted this response:

"I've never been arrested, shot up with heroin, and I'm not gay. (*At least I assumed I was straight at the time.*) Besides those things, the answer to anything you could possibly accuse me of is *yes*. So what then? Does my faith mean nothing? And what if I were or had done any one thing that you think makes my experience with God invalid? Who of any of us gets to decide or judge? I am doing my very best, beyond that, it's your choice to listen to my music or not."

It was so dispiriting to have to continually defend the value of my faith and the methodology and places where I chose to share it. To me, Christianity was more than a lifestyle club, where all the good kids wore WWJD (What Would Jesus Do?) bracelets and sang only Christian music. Beyond the culture, there was an opportunity to discover inner peace and divine consideration. Yet, with increasing regularity, I seemed to be running into Christians devaluing the path of the journeyman.

Every day, I met young, beautiful, and inspired people who, like me, tripped along in their faith until they were disillusioned and fearing moral failure rather than living in the freedom that their faith promised. Whether I was tucked into a dark corner on campus at Liberty University digging into the confounding questions of Christianity with an eager student or consoling a teenager who had just been kicked out of her youth group for having sex, I couldn't bring myself to believe that we were all engaged in a pass/fail religion. I couldn't stomach the thought of witnessing yet another teen evangelical event where the raging sex drives of teenagers were held up as evidence of evil. I didn't want my music to be the backdrop to this kind of insanity. Everything seemed to be about what you looked like, while in the background, we were all living double lives. We'd put on our best faces for the crowds, sing our ditties, go to church on Sunday morning, then drive twenty miles away to nurse our sorrows in a thirst-quenching beer, while we tried to reason our way out of being complicit in whatever we were a part of.

These were the thoughts that occupied my mind as tour after tour passed. In 2000, I recorded my sophomore record *Lay It Down*. I let my growing frustrations out in the title track.

Seeing as I found a rock in my pocket.
Seeing as I found a glitch in my soul.
Make-believe won't hide the truth
When judgment falls, it falls on you
Bend a knee my friend, bend a knee . . .

Lay it down, say it's "all my fault"
Say, "I believe! I believe!"
Lay it down.
It's the hour of my healing.

—"Lay It Down," *Lay It Down* (2000)

I wrote about the forgiveness I knew I had experienced and the building pressures of having to defend that faith. Many understood that defense of faith as being sung to an un-Christian world, but I was singing it to Christians. The sophomore release got a Grammy nomination and was said to have been critically acclaimed, which is to say that it didn't sell as well as some thought it should have, but a lot of people had heard enough of it to be critical. It "only" sold 250,000 copies. It was a disappointment at the time, considering *Kansas* would go on to sell more than twice that.

Professionally, I had no right to complain. I had success and could bank on it more than most. Still, I found myself pushing through an inner turmoil no amount of professional success could quiet. The way I saw it, I had worked so hard, pushed past my introverted nature and into the outside world so that I could engage with those who embraced the mystery of grace.

I was still in the middle of touring *Lay It Down* when Gotee came calling for another record. I needed to take time to process the spiritual quandaries I was facing, but instead I wrestled them in dark, lonely dressing rooms in between shows.

Gotee wanted a record and I barely cared. I was tired. I struggled to find joy in my faith. All I could see was an endless uphill climb.

The only thing I knew how to do was confront the conflict growing within me.

In sitting down to write the songs for *The Way I Am*, I decided to go back to the story of the Jesus that started it all. I wanted, desperately, to return to the wellspring of my adventure. I needed reminding that my faith was more than a religious cult, but practical, relevant, and not just for the elect few.

Whether anyone liked it or not, I was growing up, graduating from the religion that I had been handed, and wrestling with the reality of what being a Christian was going to mean for my life in the long term. I looked to the Passion of the Cross, the flesh and blood, the humanized body that took the punishment for all our sins, and used that as inspiration for my third record *The Way I Am*.

I took my frustration and put it into what I thought was obvious satire. I wanted to paint a picture of what humanity remained if we literally did as the Bible implored—to pluck out every sinful eye, cut off every thieving hand.

Blind these eyes who never tried to lose temptation
I'm so scared, where's the hesitation?
You so easily proved that you could save a man,
Well I am that man.

It's better off this way, to be deaf, dumb and lame
Than to be the Way I Am

It's better off this way, to be searching for the grave
Than to be the way I am.

PRETTY GRIM STUFF, considering the saccharine cheer from the standard CCM offerings. It was meant to lead to an aha moment, to consider grace when we are a little less than perfect, to insist that we are all still worthy of being loved, as we were found by God. That to go to the extremes of punishing ourselves was more damaging than it was fruitful. More limited than freeing. That we missed so much of the good, destroying any hope of the future, by cutting ourselves off for one sin, one flaw, one weakness, at the expense of the full measure of life in front of us.

One night, I shared my growing frustration with my audience. "If I chopped off every part of my body that has ever caused offense, there would be nothing left of me. Nothing!" Some shook their heads in sympathy, but most seemed annoyed that I was talking.

When I pushed the audience in front of me to contemplate their faith and not just dance to it, all that came back was confusion. "I thought the point of all this was that none of us were without fault. We're all in this together. 'That while we were yet sinners, Christ died for us.' Isn't that what it says?"

The response was an entertainer's worst nightmare . . . *silence.* There were two thousand people in front of me, and there wasn't even a teenage girl giggling about boys in the distance.

I was missing the connective thread that allowed others to

join in my wandering, but had no strength left to find it. I felt hung out to dry and alone, an alien in a world that I had never fully ceased to test. Night after night, I failed to find community through the music that had so often supplied it. *Maybe*, I wondered, *I'm not really family after all?*

This wasn't like the early days of my faith, when I had the cover of anonymity to guard my personal odyssey. The demands of my career afforded me little privacy and rest to hash out my troubles in solitude. My internal thermostat was reaching a boiling point and I knew it. I needed to get off the road, recuperate, and try to make sense of all that was swimming in my head, but the train was going at full speed, showing no signs of stopping. I was a business now. If my person wasn't working, nobody in my camp was making money. And that was a big problem.

One day, in exasperation, my defeat tumbled out onto the public stage. In my usually uplifting between-song banter, I wondered aloud, "If I need to be theologically perfect with whatever it is everyone thinks makes a Christian a Christian, maybe I *am* lost?"

Nothing. Silence. Blank white-faced stares blinked back at me.

After that, I honestly felt like I had nothing left to contribute to the scene. I didn't want to stand in the crowd and feel so alone anymore. I didn't want to cause other people to doubt their faith. I didn't want . . . a lot of things. That day, I decided I needed out.

fourteen

The irony of my career as a Christian music artist was that I had a passion for the stage and, at the same time, always struggled to see myself as destined for it. Perhaps it was because the vision to perform Christian music had not been initiated from my own desire?

From the moment I had become a Christian, it seemed there was always a *believer* encouraging me to view what talents I had through the lens of God's anointing. Such things, at the start, didn't necessarily mirror my way of thinking. I had been, and continue to be, thankful for the gift of music, yet the idea that I was given that gift by God for the sole purpose of serving the church for the rest of my life was a seed that had to be planted and nurtured by others.

It was Ami who introduced me to the idea of channeling my faith experience into music. It was Byron who laid the ground-work for my burgeoning career. My home church was full of prayer warriors, leaders, and mentors who backed my every step, convinced that I was in the center of God's good will for my life, while I did my best not to squirm too much. I loved being on the stage, I loved connecting with people, and talking about my faith, but I seemed to always be getting pushed uphill by some-thing other than my own ambitions.

Byron and I had parted ways early in my professional career. He had been a good friend and mentor, but we never fully came to agreement on the mission statement my career was to have. He had a mindset for intimate, hands-on work in and amongst those I was called to perform with, while I was more comfortable keeping my zone of responsibility strictly within the boundaries of the stage. Byron and I parted ways when I signed on with Gotee, and I found a new manager to fill his shoes.

I was fortunate that, while Byron had kept me focused and motivated on a life serving the church, my new manager Steve quickly stepped in to bring me up to speed on life inside CCM. A Christian with his own history of working inside Christian culture, he shared my own idea to serve the church well, but also understood the nuances of making a profession in a faith-based industry. Together, we shared an understanding that some artists were simply meant to be artists and not ministers. We agreed that musicians were called, at times, to be the mirror of experience. We hoped that, rather than solely being exemplars of the homogenized Christian lifestyle, there could be a place reserved for artists in CCM to present the diversity of the lived Christian experience. So, around 1998, Steve and I bypassed a standard manager/artist agreement, and instead established our jointly owned artist management agency, Alabaster Arts.

Our hope for Alabaster was to professionally manage, support, and mentor Christian artists who were culturally relevant both in, and apart from, the church. For my part, I wanted to help artists professionally navigate the CCM industry while encouraging them to be artistically daring in expressing their true faith experience. Within a few years of setting up camp in Nashville, we began managing CCM veterans like The OC Supertones, newbies Relient K, as well as a few never-before-heard-of artists whom we would work to break out.

Part of setting up a management company was so that I had a job after I had had my day in the spotlight. While I loved my own work out on the road, I didn't see myself being on the road forever. The work was tiring, with little chance for rest, as well as being philosophically grinding. I was fortunate throughout my career to have fans, a label, and management that supported my efforts to be honest about my faith experience. Yet, for what it cost me in personal energy, the results coming out of the other side of the sausage factory seemed to be a rendered-down version of what I had imagined. There was no way I was going to be able to keep doing this forever, and I had known it since the beginning.

My plan in establishing and investing my experience and financial resources into Alabaster Arts was to continue with the passion that I had to affect Christian culture while not having it come directly out of my backside.

I never kept my intention of leaving the public eye a secret. I was quick to remind those closest to me that I didn't imagine that I would be acting out my role as a performer for the rest of my days. I had often had conversations with Joey Elwood, Gotee Record's president, about how I was putting every ounce of my heart into what I was being called to do, but that I did not hope to make a life of this particular kind of work.

Alabaster Arts was my distant finish line. My touring schedule and album releases had my body committed to being a Christian rock star for the next two years, while I filled my energy reserves to survive it with the dream of retiring behind the scenes to be a mentor.

My rigorous schedule had its benefits. The money I was earning as a performer went primarily into Alabaster Arts. I completely expected that this would eventually lead to my own job security, and preserve the opportunity to do work that was personally meaningful. Things were going well. We employed a handful of full-time staff, signed a range of veteran and developing artists, and had even extended into buying a small booking agency to build our empire.

From the time I had signed on with Gotee records and made my commitment to being a professional artist, every waking minute of every day had been all about my career. If I wasn't in the studio, I was on a bus. If I wasn't on a bus, I was on stage. If not there, I was tucked into a dingy dressing room somewhere trying to write more music for the next record. On and on it went.

I was so busy that, when I moved to Nashville in 1999, I had to hire a moving company to make it happen. I had to let strangers touch and pack every single thing that I owned into boxes, shove them on a semi, and trust that I'd have a home to go to when I walked off the tour bus.

I bought a modest home in the quiet, rolling hills, thirty minutes west of Nashville, in a little hamlet called Kingston Springs. I had walked through it once, maybe twice, signed the papers, then got back to touring. It took over a year to unpack the few boxes I had, as all I really needed was already on the road with me.

To the outside world, this was success. I had gigs booked, money rolling in, and record sales as far as the eye could see. My career was flourishing but, inside, I was growing weary.

There were no boundaries between my life and my career. They had merged to the point that my body was merely the host for industry. It didn't matter that inside my little body was a person who needed a vacation. The body that I inhabited had a business to run. Gotee relied upon it, concert promoters had tickets to sell, and Alabaster Arts had mouths to feed. My career didn't feel like it belonged to me so much as I belonged to it.

I had spent the better part of 2000 requesting that Steve devise a plan to get me off the treadmill for a while. My sophomore release, *Lay It Down,* had done very well. I'd shared a fruitful tour with CCM rockers Third Day. The record received a Grammy nomination, and had several radio hits. There was no question that I had a long future ahead of me in CCM if I wanted it.

"We've worked really hard and things have gone well, but if I don't get a break soon, I'm gonna lose it," I would say. Every chance I got I steered the conversation to easing up on the throttle, "You gotta stop booking shows and give me some time off."

"WE GOTTA STRIKE while the iron's hot," Steve would counter. His fear was that if you weren't in the spotlight, you were out. It was a risk I was willing to take, but Steve insisted, "If only you could push on just a little further, one more record, drive on for a while more . . . Just one more tour and Alabaster will have an office ready and waiting for you."

I found myself trapped in a cycle that seemed unending. Every time I would agree to one more push, the finish line kept moving one more step further. When was it going to stop? When was Alabaster going to be prepared for my retirement?

I was losing my grip out on the road, getting more and more agitated. I was a shell of a human being, walking about in a coma, mindlessly doing what was scheduled for my body, but completely empty in spirit; all I could think of was not being obligated to work one minute longer. For every minute that passed, it felt like a march against my own will.

To cope, I'd lock myself in the bus for hours on end, unable to find the energy to overcome my introverted nature. Even trips to sound check and back could zap what little conversational energies I had squirreled away.

Keeping enough energy to get through a night's performance was daunting enough, without having to run the crucible of Christian kids that were scattered in the hallways between the bus and the stage. It got to where I truly hated the sight of anyone who might be trolling for a backstage autograph. Something was very wrong inside me.

Normally I loved my fans. I loved them so much that I hated calling them *fans*. It belied the fact that I had always been so honored by their support and was always glad to spend as much time as humanly possible saying, "Thanks." But now the sight of a bright eager face sent chills down my spine.

"Miss Knapp! Miss Knapp!"

I saw a young, pretty college girl coming down a backstage corridor toward me. *Jesus,* I thought to myself, *why can't people just leave me alone?* A person would have to have been blind and deaf to not notice her, but I tried to get away with ignoring her.

Undaunted, she followed me down the hall, "Miss Knapp! Miss Knapp?"

"Who let you in here?" I turned and questioned with obvious disdain.

Caught off guard, her cheery face paled from the shock. "I—I . . ."

"What can I help you with?" I interrupted, pushing for her to get on with it.

"I only wanted to say 'Hi'." She mumbled, her chin dipping into her chest. She managed to go on, despite my ungracious demeanor, "Your music has meant a lot to me . . ." her words trailed off, unwilling to say anything more. She made herself vulnerable, sharing her appreciation to a stranger, only to be treated with ambivalence.

I gave her an autograph and said, "Thanks," but little more. I went back to the dressing room and cried from shame.

From 1999 until I would call it quits in 2002, things would move so fast, I would work almost nonstop, that I would call them my "heroin years" as I found that trying to remember the specifics of those years so hazy. If I want to remember what I did in any given year, I search Google instead of trusting my own memory. If I want to remember what was going on in my life during that time I have to use my discography and tours as a guide to my own and world events. And, still, what comes back is a loose recollection.

Despite my pleading with Steve for more than a year, demands on me seemed to only increase rather than decrease. I was not only plugging away on the road, now I had the growing needs of Alabaster Arts calling as well.

We had signed a talented and raw new artist, whom we hoped to develop, in a young girl from California named Katy Hudson. She was seventeen years old when her eager Christian parents brought her to us, hoping that we could help her have a career similar to my own. They wanted her to sing Christian songs on a Christian label, and had come to us to help her make it possible. Katy definitely had the *it* factor, she just needed a plan. She had a femininely styled Taylor guitar, a decent set of songs she had written, and a great voice, and it was exciting to watch her perform. She was young and unpolished for sure, but she had a huge, fresh voice, and seemed bound for the stage with a little direction.

In house, the idea was to put her out on the road with me, so that I could act as a sort of mentor. In theory, it was a great idea to give Katy some experience in touring but, by this time, I was hardly fit to be, nor selfless enough to be, a proper mentor. I was threadbare and the last example of Christian female artist virtue she needed to see. I was barely getting by, bitter, and in need of rest. In my role as manager, I was excited to help her on her journey, but out on the road I was cracking up. I hardly thought it was a good idea to send a minor out on tour with a supposed mentor who was in such a poor psychological and spiritual state. I barely had the integrity to take care of myself, let alone be trusted to be the chaperone of a beautiful, busty, flirtatious teenager.

Nonetheless, onto my tour bus she came. I took a run of shows in the Northeast, through New York City, then up to an exclusive youth retreat in New England. The idea was to give Katy an insight into the breadth of the kind of gigs that she might experience as a Christian artist at Alabaster. Some of the shows would have a secular feel, while others would be in a more intimate Christian setting. The whole thing was a disaster.

I had landed a gig at the storied Mercury Lounge in New York. The band and I were all excited to have a show away from the stuffy church scene, where we could have a few beers, relax, and put on a rock show free from the obligations to push Jesus. I was starting to get more shows that suited my desire to perform music as a so-called normal artist, and was making an effort to build my credibility as a marketable artist beyond the CCM scene. The following day we were taking a less desirable role as entertainment for a youth retreat, but today we were celebrating what felt like a hope for the future. Katy opened the show.

Steve came to Manhattan, as well, to talk with some contacts about expanding my career beyond CCM. After the show I joined him to wheel and deal for a bit, but quickly found myself angered by his approach. When all I could do was think about the rest I needed in the near future, he was trying to make more immediate plans for work. My input was causing the conversation to deteriorate to the point where he pulled me aside, gave me what for, and asked that I go back to the bus to babysit Katy. I was angry for that and let him have it. I erupted in a tirade of abuse. It became clear that I had reached my breaking point. Yes, I was encouraged by the thought of performing outside of CCM, but I needed him to stop pushing so hard. He told me that I needed to "get right with God" and I told him to go f#@k himself.

I went back to the bus, told Katy to stay there like a good pet, left her some food and water, then took off to whatever bar my band was hanging out in.

I wasn't alone in my low Christian morale. All of us in the band were struggling. Years later, when we would reconnect, many of us would confess to one another the turmoil we felt in ourselves. We were serious about our faith, yet we were also aware that we didn't want to act out the prescribed model of what we were supposed to be. That night, we drank heavily in our rebellion.

It was scary. Harkening back to my old ways of drunken debauchery, I tied it on like it was my last night of freedom. I let my despair pour freely from my mouth and chased it with more shots of tequila than my little body could handle. I garnished my night with salt and lime, forgetting about all my responsibilities. Screw CCM. F#@k Steve. I wanted no further part of any of it.

In the wee hours of the morning we all managed to make our way back to the bus, only to realize that innocent little Katy would be there. I slurred my instructions to the crew to get themselves together so that we might not be accused of being the disastrous Christian witness to Katy that we most unavoidably were.

Fortunately, Katy was safely where I had left her, and she greeted us with her usual perky personality. "Hey guys! Where ya been?"

One by one, we wafted past her in a haze of smoke and booze and tried to pass off just how irresponsibly drunk we all were. I thought we were all making a pretty good show of it until our old Senator tour bus reached the mountains of New Hampshire, or wherever it was were headed. Our driver laughed and did his best to keep the bus from pitching and rolling through the night, but one by one, we succumbed to inevitable seasickness. One bathroom, nearly a dozen drunk riders, all trapped in a rolling metal washtub. The idea that we put anything over on Katy was laughable. I was mortified at how I had behaved and had nowhere to hide my shame.

The next morning, our bus was parked in the heart of a Christian kid's camp. Our trusty road manager peeled herself out of bed and tried to keep a quiet perimeter around the coach so we could sleep off the previous night's bender. The excited campers had been looking forward to the idea of taking us horseback riding, swimming at the lake, and integrating us into one of their many afternoon Bible study sessions, but I was hardly fit for public consumption. Hung over and thoroughly ill, we barely managed to make the stage for sound checks that night. I didn't care what the fallout was. I didn't care how much saving and planning that camp had to do to get us there. We played our show. Picked up the check. I had done my job, but had little concern for much else.

This was not who I wanted to be.

At that point, I didn't know who or what I perceived I was failing, but I wasn't happy. I was depressed. I recognized it, but I had to stop the machine to get my bearings.

I went to Steve, to Joey at Gotee. I told everyone within earshot that I needed a break. I had decided that enough was enough and that my schedule was not going to extend one single booking beyond what was already there. At every interview, I conveyed my message: I wasn't going to be here much longer. I had hinted at such ideas before, but now my aim was clear. I was done.

Steve accused me of having a breakdown. Maybe I was having one, but with good reason, which should have prompted him to take my cries for a reprieve seriously. Instead, he pushed for me to get my head on straight and get back to work. Work was the last thing I needed. I needed rest.

"Let's finish off my schedule and start integrating me into the daily operations of Alabaster," I hoped aloud. "I really want to be a part of Katy's journey, but I can't do both the road and the office."

We couldn't get on the same page. Worse than that, our personal relationship had fractured and we no longer trusted in one another. In our negotiations, it was clear that Steve had a limited view of my ability to take on the professional workings at Alabaster, and thought it best for me to go on my way by supporting the organization solely as an artist. That revelation crushed me. For the final time, he moved the finish line, and I had no strength left to carry on.

At a time when I needed to call on our friendship for utter support and care, Steve retreated to attacking my character on an almost daily basis. He accused me of failing my Christian witness. He took the line that if I took a break from music that my career would be over, the general idea being that if an entertainer isn't out actively entertaining, they risk falling off the treadmill and never getting up to the same speed again. According to Steve, the marketplace wouldn't wait for me to get my head on straight. If I didn't serve God the way He intended, I would lose my voice.

He wasn't alone. Just about every mentor and Christian friend I spoke to about trying to resolve my discord with Steve, with Christian music, and my own vision of my future seemed to come back at me with the same ideas. That I was giving up. That I was failing because I wasn't in harmony with God's plan for my life.

"What is your spiritual life like? Are you praying enough?" were among the many comments.

"Lean on Jesus. Go to God with all this. Pray. Read your Bible. Listen to your elders . . ." And so on and so forth. But it all seemed so facile and incomplete.

"Isn't anybody listening? I can't do this anymore." I had to bail. I wanted out, effective immediately.

When I broke the news to Steve, tempers flared.

The whole thing was awful. I realized that I was not only saying goodbye to my business, but it was clear that I had lost a friend in Steve as well. After a year of haggling between lawyers, all my shares in Alabaster were reverted to Steve. You might say that he got everything in the divorce, and alimony to boot. My financial investment in the company was disregarded and the balance of what was left of my career in CCM was spent paying commissions from income back to the company I had created and lost.

Now, I was on my own. I had no manager, another year of concerts on the books, and a deep desire to jump off a bridge. The fallout with Steve and Alabaster had left me in a very dark place. I was beside myself with sorrow. I wept uncontrollably during the following months. *The Way I Am* was soon to be released and I didn't care. I felt obliged to follow through with the commitments I had scheduled, but there would be no more.

I sat down with my record company president Joey Elwood over sweet tea and broke the news.

"I'm done, Joey. I just can't do this anymore." I shook at the insanity of it all. What was I doing? A CCM artist couldn't ask for a better career than the one I had and now, I was going to just walk away? I was committing career suicide.

"I know I've got two more records on my contract and I want to honor it however I can, but after September 2002, I'm out."

We talked at length. I offered to do whatever work he asked of me in the time frame I had given; he countered with his soft voice of compassion.

"You'll be okay," he said, but in a manner unlike so many others who offered their opinions. He was sincere, loving, and fatherly. Professionally, he had every cause to hold me to my promise of fulfilling my contract, but he approached me, instead, as a much needed, trusted friend. He reminded me of all the good that came from the giving of my heart. That what I saw as personal failure wasn't a waste. He saw that I was battle weary, as any mortal might expect to be. He didn't go on about what my Christian duties were or what demands from CCM that I needed to honor, he tried to encourage me to not give up faith in the music that I clearly had a gift for.

However, at the time, there was no difference between my faith, my music, or my profession. They were all inexorably fused together. Freeing myself from one meant freeing myself from all of it. I was terrified at the thought of what my future was to be, and could say nothing but, "I'm tired. I'm tired."

Of all the people in the world, I could have told Joey the deepest fears of my heart, but I didn't know how to say them aloud. I thought what was happening was that I'd lost the favor of God. That I was a purely evil, awful, unworthy human being, and that no part of my attempts to be a Christian could change any of it. Surely, if Joey knew who I really was, he wouldn't be so kind.

To add to the string of misery, my behavior on the road was coming under fire and causing rumors. Not only was I not bringing the expected bubbly joy and light to my Christian fans, rumors were afoot that I was gay. (I had always traveled with a female road manager and was accustomed to such rumors. However, due to the obvious close friendship I was developing with my latest road manager, Karen, this time the rumors appeared to have legs.)

Joey dared touch on the taboo subject, "You know, you're not the first artist that's been accused of being gay. . . ."

I'm being *accused*?

"You know, people are always going to talk. . . ." He tried to sound sympathetic.

I wanted to throw up as blood came rushing into my head. I was embarrassed and feeling defensive, with no good reason to. Nothing had happened between Karen and me. Nothing yet anyway. I did have strong feelings for her, but I couldn't dream of defining them as *gay*. What did any of it matter anymore anyway? I was getting out.

"I'm not well enough to keep fighting these kinds of battles. I shouldn't have to. Besides which, I haven't had enough space in years to consider falling in love anyway."

Of all the dramas on my plate, contemplating the truth of my sexual orientation was far from the top. For now, I needed to make good my escape.

"There are just too many voices in my head, Joey. I'm gonna need some time to sort them out."

Of all those voices, Joey's was the one of only a handful that offered unquestionable support for me to find my way.

The other would be that of my trusted friend and blooming love, Karen.

fifteen

I met Karen working in the Christian music scene. As an artist, I'd played many festivals and youth conferences that featured multiple acts. These festivals might go on for several days, with each day having a single stage host a cavalcade of the latest and greatest Christian stars, and I was fortunate enough to be one of them.

Festivals are basically an exercise in controlling chaos, and Karen was a standout when it came to managing it. In a world that was often filled with part-time or volunteer production staff, Karen was a first-rate professional production manager. Her excellent skills were so rare, and so greatly appreciated whenever we would cross paths, it didn't take many meetings before I decided to get on her good side. Getting in rhythm with the way she managed her stage always meant having an excellent performance. With so many artists running around, each accustomed to having their own equipment, production crew, and staging, it can be a nightmare getting multiple acts adequately prepared to perform back to back and on schedule. On a normal day on tour with your own production staff and staging, a sound check can take a leisurely hour or so but, at some festivals, you may only get fifteen minutes. In these fast-paced settings, each player in the group has a very limited amount of time to make certain their equipment is set up properly, and that they can adequately hear the other players. Failure to get these things right can be the difference between a successful and a catastrophic performance. It can be a very stressful experience for everyone involved without a skilled person to coordinate all that needs to happen behind the scenes, but whenever we realized that Karen was working the event, everyone in the band would take a deep breath and know that we were going to have a relatively easy day.

She was definitely good at her job, which I appreciated professionally, but I found her memorable in many other ways as well. Her Australian accent was the first thing I noticed and found intriguing, but it was her personality as well. I loved that she walked across a room exactly the way that she spoke—direct and energetic. She never seemed to waste time in letting you know what she wanted to say. I didn't realize it at the time, but she fascinated me. She didn't clamor to be my friend by gushing on about how great an artist she thought I was. She didn't do what so many in the entertainment industry seem to do, which is measure the value of an artist by their perceived popularity. She treated each musician with respect regardless of their commercial status or self-perceived stardom. She spoke to me with candor and never treated me as though I was different from any other human being. Talking with her seemed to put my crazy artist life into a state of restful suspension, where I could be a normal human being for a moment. I didn't feel like I had to impress her with how great a Christian I was or hoped to be. We could just have a normal conversation, then get on with the job. When and if she ever offered a compliment after I made my way from the stage, it was a shock to my system. You could tell she didn't suffer fools, nor hand out gratuitous flattery. In fact, if I'd had a rough set, it was more than likely she'd offer a wry smile and say, "Well, that was interesting," and we'd find ourselves chuckling. I really liked her.

As the years working in the Christian music industry went on, I usually wanted to do nothing but hide on my tour bus until I had to perform, but whenever I learned that Karen was on the scene, I was eager to take a walk to see if she had a moment or two to hang out and chat. I tried to play it cool, but I would be so keen to catch her attention that I would get butterflies in my stomach. I felt like a little kid who wanted to be noticed by someone they admired. I might only be around for a few hours before I'd have to travel on to the next show, but I would always want to get a moment to connect with her. We might only see each other when it came time for my sound check, then perhaps a few minutes around show time, but they would be moments of peaceful delight. Being around her did something to soothe my spirit. Personally, I felt alive and refreshed, but I was also pleasantly surprised that I wanted to know more about her. I wanted to know that she was doing well. I was motivated to hear about what was going on in her life.

It would take years before I would realize that these are the kinds of feelings that happen when you find the person you will fall in love with. Maybe it was because I had been celibate for so long, and had essentially shut down the part of my heart that longed for companionship, that it had never occurred to me in those times that I might actually be attracted to a woman. All I knew is that when we met, she was a cool hang and a consummate professional.

On every occasion I found myself on *her* stage, I wanted to please her. If my set was to be finished by 10:00 P.M., I'd plan my set list to end at 9:59:30. If her stage was running behind schedule because other bands went over, I'd offer to buy the time back and cut my set, so that she could get back on course. I wanted her to think I was the bee's knees. Getting her to smile and offer her praise at how I made her job easier made me swell with happiness. There were days when I hated tripping in and out for the Christian festival scene but, when Karen was in the mix, I discovered reserves of joy that I didn't know I had.

After I had been acquainted with Karen for a couple of years it came about that I needed to hire a new road manager. As a solo female Christian artist, this is a hard spot to fill. For reasons that I will explain in moment, the position of road manager in my staff had to be a female, and Karen was by far and away the most qualified candidate I had ever come across. It was clear that she could be a reliable road manager capable to act as a body man for me as an artist, as well as excel in the day-to-day operations of a professional entertainment production. I can't speak for the mainstream entertainment industry as much as I can for CCM, but there aren't many female roadies.

To understand the importance of my traveling specifically with a female road manager, one has to appreciate the significance of sexual purity in Christian culture. At the most fundamentalist level, there should be *no* sex outside of marriage. *None.*

The most faithful of Christians are virgins until their wedding night, and die having only known their one partner. Any missteps along the way and problems can arise. For the most conservative religious communities, sexual impurity of any kind can lead to social stigma and scandal. (We all remember what happened to Jimmy Swaggart!)

Whether it's a teenager falling into temptation or a wandering spouse, sexual misconduct is not tolerated. For those in leadership positions in faith community, any discovered or confessed sin in this arena almost always ruins careers. Adultery and promiscuity are among the absolute integrity killers for Christians. If you want to stay out of trouble, you have to be willing to honor the most conservative common denominators.

From the beginning, I chose to reveal my sexual experience to the church. It was common knowledge that I was not a virgin and, on those grounds alone, there was cause for many to be openly suspicious of my moral code.

Once, while attending a behind-the-scenes industry convention full of CCM music buyers, I was approached by a man responsible for filling the music shelves of an entire national chain. He had discovered that I was not a virgin and openly expressed his concern. "I don't know if I can put your music in my store. Girls need good Christian role models."

I tried not to take his comments personally, but they stung. "Sir, where I've been and what I've done in my life . . . I can't take any of it back." I tried my best to speak in his language. "Jesus has forgiven me, so maybe you could too?"

Christianity is no different from the rest of the world, and sex-fueled gossip is titilating. The only difference in CCM is that religious missteps quite often prove socially devastating.

Remarkably, I learned early on to manage those trolling for juicy tidbits by closing up shop. I stopped dating entirely and tried to keep from developing any relationships beyond my trusted friends. I attempted to keep a safe distance between my male friends and me on the road, and always made certain I was accompanied by a woman who could act as witness to my whereabouts. I did my best not to give the seeds of wickedness any fertile soil from which to grow.

None of this ever silenced the scuttlebutt, however. There was always a rumor floating about. One day it would be about a guy on the crew, the next it would be that I was too sweet on the merch girl. No friendship, male or female, was immune to scrutiny. To me, it was the price of being a Christian working in the public realm.

In 1992, when I first became a Christian, I made the choice to abstain from sex. That included with it any idea of establishing a relationship that might lead to sex. I put my head down and did my very best to be as asexual as I possibly could. Over the years, it had all worked according to plan. I was alone and celibate. To make things easier, there had never really been any person that tempted me to act otherwise. So far as I could see, hiring and working with Karen wasn't going to be an exception. There was a role to fill, and she seemed the most qualified candidate.

Karen signed on for the summer of 2000 at a time when our entire crew needed her most. We had been touring extensively throughout the previous year and were showing no signs of stopping. I had released *Lay It Down* in February, and had just completed a grueling fifty-city tour with Third Day. Fifty dates wasn't much by our usual standard but, despite appearances, the tour was operating on a shoestring budget. Third Day and I had agreed to jointly share their acting road manager for the duration of the tour, but this proved disastrous. It was a move that basically left my crew without a primary advocate for our daily needs. Little things like needing to find places to do laundry consistently turned into major dramas, to say nothing of the fact that we had a borderline narcoleptic bus driver that nobody seemed to believe needed to be relieved of duty. We spent much of the tour terrified of going to sleep out of fear that the bus driver was going to pass out at the wheel. Eventually, members of the band decided to take turns sitting up front with our driver to keep him company. It was an exhausting, sleep-deprived, stressful three months, without a single champion for our cause. With the chaos of the summer festival season on the horizon, my band was threatening mutiny if I didn't put a decent road manager at the helm. Personally, I was starting to wear thin as well. I had been on the road for hundreds of days in the last year and couldn't remember the last time that I'd spent more than a few nights in my own bed. I was starting to question whether I needed to take a decent break from the touring business or if hiring some professional staff would ease the pressure.

Karen was a godsend for all of us. We were a mess. Before her, we were so strapped for time, organization, and quality communication that we were barely recognizable as human beings. We were a malnourished, pale, and mentally fatigued band of punks but, by the end of the summer, we were turning into a well-oiled machine. Our performances improved as well as our spirits, which was a good thing. For a while, thanks to Karen, I thought maybe I was going to survive. Though she had only signed on for the one summer, I practically begged her to stay. The months that were ahead looked terrifying.

When Gotee came to me saying they wanted to put out my third release, *The Way I Am,* in 2001, the task looked positively impossible to achieve. I was signed on for yet another tour in the fall of 2000, with Christian phenoms Jars of Clay, Steve and I were on the verge of imploding, and the only person in the world that seemed capable of keeping my head in the game was Karen.

If I had any chance of writing songs while I was touring, recording another record, *and* surviving yet another season without a break, it was going to take someone with Karen's skill set to get me through.

She had me by the scruff of the neck and she knew it. Ever her direct and confident self, she named her salary, twice that of any road manager I had paid before. I didn't know if I could actually afford to pay her what I agreed to, but I somehow knew that if the coming year was as busy as it looked to be and I continued on without adequate professional help, I had no chance to survive unscathed.

In the exposed, shared world of the confined space of a tour bus, it was evident that I was struggling to keep up. Through all of the chaos, Karen became more than a professional advocate. I found a friend.

As time blurred past, and I continued to limp forward, it seemed that only Karen understood how near the breaking point I was. She was there, every day.

She witnessed the countless hours during which I locked myself in the tour bus, attempting to shut out the rest of the world. She protected my privacy when I was nothing but a ball of nerves and tears, huddled up in whatever windowless dressing room was serving as my studio for the day.

She was the only person inside my career that encouraged me to look at my career as a choice rather than an obligation.

"You don't have to do anything you don't want to do, Jennifer. It's your choice to be whoever you need to be." It seemed an impossible thing to believe at the time. Almost heresy. All I had ever been was God's. The only reason I was on this earth was to do what I was doing. If I had my own voice, it had been a long time since I had allowed myself to listen to it.

"Do you even want to do Christian music anymore?" Her

question didn't come with an ulterior motive. She was genuinely open to helping find my truth regardless of whether or not she would have a job at the end of it.

I was afraid to answer it. The pain that loomed inside me curled my entire body in the fetal position and I began to weep uncontrollably. How could I say what I wanted aloud? If I did I would be destroying everything.

"Jen, what do you want?" she placed her hand on mine. Her gentle touch calmed me for a moment so I could say the words "I can't do this anymore. I just can't."

"All right, then." She patted my back and returned to her matter-of-fact voice. "You're gonna need a plan. I'll help!"

I leaned on Karen heavily when I decided to close up shop. For all the ugliness, rumors, and tears, she stood by me when few did. Without judgment or self-serving calculations, she encouraged me to follow my heart.

The more time we spent together, the more my affection for her intensified. If ever I had found her infatuating before, my fondness for her was moving on from giddiness into a deeper complexity. Our hugs went from casual greetings to lingering expressions of profound companionship. In her confidence and support I had the feeling of finding a soul mate, but I didn't dare release my mind to where it seemed to lead.

We were just good friends. *Very good* friends.

sixteen

$\mathcal{J}$n the last year of my time in CCM, I took the reins and managed the balance of my remaining career on my own. Karen agreed to lend her support on the business side of things to help me wind down but, in her spare time, when she wasn't working on the road with me, she returned to subcontracting jobs with her usual cast of large-event productions.

On one rare weekend that I didn't have a gig, Karen had decided to take a job down in Texas working for Youth Specialties. (YS is a popular national Christian youth organization that specializes in multiday youth conventions.)

I had performed on many occasions for the organization and had established a great working rapport with much of the staff. In fact, YS is where Karen and I became better acquainted. She always seemed to be stage managing when I was scheduled to play the latest YS convention, so we struck up a friendship as we worked. We knew many of the same people, enjoyed getting to hang out after all the work was done, so I thought, even though I wasn't invited to perform at that particular event, nothing much would be made of my showing up just to hang out.

Over the years, I had also developed a mentorlike relationship with a married couple, Rolly and Sandy. I had met them many years earlier through our mutual friend, Byron, and grew to welcome their wisdom and advice as the pressures of my public life increased.

That same weekend, Rolly was working as an event producer for the same Youth Specialties event. I had hoped that I could also find some time to catch up with him, as Rolly had been a key figure in planning major youth ministry events for decades. For years, he had seen many Christian artists come and go. I had gone to him for advice when I began considering leaving CCM. I figured if anyone could come up with a suggestion as to how to manage my crisis of faith in the spotlight, he or Sandy would.

They had listened supportively for months about how I was struggling, but we had landed at an impasse. They insisted that I needed to remain faithful to God's call in my life, but we disagreed that my calling continued to be CCM. When I told them of my decision to leave, they received it with heavy hearts. They loved me, they were quick to affirm, but continued to pray that I would realign myself with God's will above my own.

I was naive to think that Rolly and Sandy, of all people, wouldn't read anything into my presence at the conference. Whatever measure I had yet to admit the truth to myself, they saw straight through me and took aim at my budding relationship with Karen.

They weren't the only ones. Everyone was shocked to see me there unannounced.

Usually artists were at these events working or angling for work. As an otherwise uninvited guest, I used my relationship with the organization, with Karen, and Rolly and Sandy as an excuse to hang out backstage at the massive conference. However, the truth was that I was eager to share in every free moment Karen had to spare.

When I got there, Sandy was busy in her usual role, managing the backstage hospitality area. Rather than a smile of surprise, her face drooped with concern. When I explained that I came to just generally hang out, and that I was sharing a hotel room with Karen, her face went pale. Instead of her familiar warmth, she grew distant and shuffled quickly away.

An ache lodged itself in my gut. I had hoped she wouldn't read too much into my presence, but nothing I said seemed to ease the tension between us.

Sandy wasn't the only one acting weirdly. It seemed that all my friends were a tad uneasy, and straining to comprehend my presence. I wanted to chalk it up to my surprise drop-in, but it was clear that it was more than that.

It didn't take long under those circumstances before I felt exposed. When I caught up with Rolly, it was very clear that I was under suspicion. He, too, was less than his predictable, jolly self. He smiled weakly, gave me a side hug, and asked if I would come up to his and Sandy's room for some tea later that evening.

No way! They wouldn't call me out for being attracted to Karen, I thought. I protested to myself, *I'm only here to hang out. Why wouldn't anyone believe me?*

Apprehension began to creep in. My insides turned to sludge. I grew thick and anxious with an overwhelming terror that Rolly and Sandy were going to accuse me of being gay. I didn't know what I would do if they called me out on it. I had had people sit me down and warn me to not be gay before, but this was different. This time it was actually true. I was madly, deeply in love with Karen. I liked her . . . *like that.*

I had been such a fool to think that I could hide the depth of my feelings. The only person who didn't think I was there to chase Karen romantically was me. I hadn't been willing to admit it to myself. I thought I was playing it cool. I thought I was doing well at simply acting as a close friend, but it was evident to everyone who saw us together that there was something more. And now, I feared, I was going to have to answer for it.

I spent the balance of the day locked away in our hotel room, fighting a rising tide of panic. I grew afraid that everyone there was thinking that I was a fallen woman. I did my best to be positive, but I wouldn't know just how deep a mess I was in until the evening.

At the end of the day, Karen was getting together with much of the YS staff for their ritual after-show cigars and brandy, and she had invited me along. Karen had spoken fondly of how much fun their wind-downs could be. I was genuinely eager to join Karen and her friends but, I told her, Rolly and Sandy had called me to a meeting. She urged me to blow them off, but I couldn't help myself. I couldn't live with the mystery of what they were thinking. I had to go.

I had spent many nights hanging out in various hotel suites with Rolly and Sandy, sipping coffee and hashing through the adventures of Christian life, but tonight's script seemed decided before the door thudded behind me. I knew exactly what this was going to be as soon as I spied the seating arrangements. This was a tribunal.

Two chairs of adjudication faced a small sofa that would act as the witness stand. Sandy had taken up her seat in one of the chairs, leaving Rolly to the other, and thus assigning me to sofa. Obediently, I took my seat.

The best part of the whole night was the lack of small talk. They jumped right into it.

"Jennifer, we're concerned about your relationship with Karen," Sandy leaned forward, elbows on knees, holding her own hands.

Boom! There it is!

It's the kind of opening volley typical of a Christian smackdown. Anytime someone in the church doesn't like what you're doing or isn't of the opinion that you are acting Christian enough, this is the standard language. It's not an outright accusation, but it sets the tone for the inquisition that is to come.

"People have been asking us about you two for some time now and we've been praying about what to do about this."

Ding! That's another one. The old *I've prayed about it and God told me to tell you* gambit. It's not that, at the very least, you can't appreciate your accuser putting some level of contemplation into the matter, but the frequency of which prayer is used as the impetus for confrontation is uncanny. I've never sat through one of these kinds of meetings when someone simply claims responsibility for their own opinion or disapproval. Rather than saying *I disagree with what you are doing and here is why,* then going on to discuss the religious grounds and inspirations that support your position, it becomes a message from God. It becomes *I don't want to be the bad guy here, but God is leading me to help you.*

I thought I knew Rolly and Sandy well enough to peg them as conservative in their religious theologies, but the approach to this conversation was turning out to be startlingly cliché.

There was no doubt in my mind that if I *did* confess to being gay that they would be obliged to instruct me to turn away from it. It was happening now. But I never pegged them as distancing themselves from me and treating me as coolly as they were now.

It was like they were speaking to me as an object of ruin rather than a human being.

It went on. Blunt and to the point at least.

"Are you gay?" Sandy continued to lead.

"No!" I blurted out, "Of course not!"

On the edge of her seat, Sandy asked suspiciously, "You do believe in the Bible, don't you?"

I honestly didn't know how to answer that question. No one had ever point-blank asked me to describe the role the Bible held for me. I had learned long ago to just repeat what I was told it was: The Infallible Word of God. Beyond that, I didn't have a pat answer. It was complicated. I didn't want to be a smartass, but my thoughts on the matter were far more complex and nuanced than saying that a collection of writings was something to *believe in.*

What does that even mean? To believe in the Bible? I've read it cover to cover. From those pages I've found healing in my life. Strength and encouragement. Comfort and instruction. But it also says that every living animal got on one boat built by one old man and the world was saved from the cleansing flood of God's wrath. I'm not sure that I can believe *that.* I could go along with the moral of the story. I got the vibe of the thing.

What about more subjective, less scientifically challengeable things like women not being allowed to speak in church? (Cor 1 13:14) I spoke in churches all the time and was praised for it by many. And, as for homosexuality? The truth was I struggled to fall in line with the conservative Christian position that says gay is wrong. Like so many things, when I failed to agree with what was being taught and preached, I learned to keep my mouth shut. I always assumed that something was wrong with me and that perhaps I would get in line eventually. But, now, I was being called to answer.

I suppose it was a lie then when I responded, "Of course I believe what the Bible says." Yet, at the same time, I felt indignant. When did my failure to agree with every weird and confusing thing the Bible says disqualify me from being a Christian?

I could see their faces were awash with sorrow. To them, I was a friend—a good Christian woman on the verge of losing a very meaningful life by way of sin. I credit them for not taking out a Bible and reading it to me as if I was clueless. I wasn't, and they respected me for that, at least. Rolly and Sandy had witnessed how seriously I had dedicated my life to learning, following, and honoring Christianity. They knew that I was no fool. Knowing this made it worse.

They knew that I had a solid grasp of The Word. They had been witness to the role it had played in my life, in my art, and work. They knew that I had a sacred view of it; they just didn't know that I didn't always agree with everything that it said. I assumed that if they did they would discredit my entire life, my entire faith experience. It was happening now. I could see their esteem for me draining from their eyes as we spoke.

Our conversation swirled around the implications of what must be happening in my spiritual life for this kind of temptation to befall me. An hour or more centered around the necessity of prayer and the idea that if I did, in fact, ever engage in sexual acts outside of marriage, that I would be lacking in some measure of my faith. That, in essence, something was wrong with me if I was not being the kind of Christian that they or God expected me to be. In no uncertain terms they spelled it out for me—I was to be celibate, straight, and waiting for God to send me the perfect man.

I had been celibate for ten years but, if God was sending me anyone, it was a woman.

The longer this went on, I slipped further into what felt like a moral coma with every lie I told. I felt swallowed up by the sofa, as if my edges were bleeding into the background, stagnant and thick.

Of all the people in the world that I could lie to, Rolly and Sandy were the most undeserving. I deeply respected them to the point of admiration. If I had reason to label any couple my Christian parents, they were.

I wanted them to love me. I wanted to tell them the truth. I wanted them to rise to the occasion to deal with the reality of the human condition. I wanted them to be the kind of Christian that I had searched the world for: comfortable with life's mysteries and unfazed by religious contradictions. I wanted their kinship and affirmation, that I was loved and made, just as God wanted me to be. I wanted them to be what they were not.

They failed me, as I failed them. I could have started a genuine and open dialogue, but I didn't know how. I had spent years trying to craft myself into the kind of Christian people like Rolly and Sandy thought was the evidence of God's spiritual work. I worked to make them proud of me. I wanted to succeed at becoming a woman they could admire. Never, until that day, had I spoken one untruth about my faith. I had always been genuine, but I didn't believe everything that was being sold to me either.

Our conversation was leading me right to the doorway that I had longed to open for years, but had kept padlocked. I never dared open it for fear of how acknowledging my own religious uncertainties might damage my reputation in the church. I was losing the fight. The hinges were bulging and behind it came everything I had ever wanted to criticize and question about Christianity.

I don't think that it's as simple as "God made everyone heterosexual!"

I don't think that drinking is a sin!

I don't think that sex outside marriage is instantaneously sinful!

If I say fuck *a thousand times a day; I think God's got better things to hang me for!*

I don't think God torches every soul that doesn't pray to receive Christ!

A thousand thoughts swirled in my head. I wanted to have a *real* conversation. I longed to talk about faith in a way that got at the heart of my humanity. I wanted to share in the marrow of living. To celebrate, to fail, to aspire, and to proceed with abandon to the one true thing that the Gospel had ever taught me that I do believe in . . . *love!*

Yet, here I was, clearly facing an opportunity to talk about where my life had led me. With my deepest spirit, I loved Karen. It seemed shocking to say it out loud. *God taught me to love—and I love her!* But I couldn't find the courage to speak it.

The door couldn't have been opened any wider for me to have a substantial and direct conversation, but I was blowing it.

Up to this point, no one had actually asked me to clarify my true feelings for Karen. Our conversation that night continued to dance around the theological implications of what I was projecting and how I should remedy my observable behavior. Showing up at this conference unannounced was certainly a bad witness if I was to avoid the appearance of evil. I was both offended that I was assumed to be sexually attracted to her by suspicion rather than confession, but at the same time I was more than grateful I hadn't been put to task.

Suddenly, there it was. Sandy asked the one question I had thus far avoided, "Do you have sexual feelings for her?"

With unflinching eye contact, I gave my answer without hesitation, "No. I do not."

For the first and the last time, I lied about what I knew to be true.

I went on to spin a yarn so long and deceitful that, to this day, I am marked by the shame of it. I explained how my feelings for her were friendly, and framed my esteem for Karen as merely superficial. I made it seem as though I viewed her role in my life as a kind, feminine Christian mentor. That, yes, while I would admit that I loved her very much, it was like a sister or a dear friend. I tried to weave the truth into my lie, that I very much cared for her and, at the same time, not at all.

I felt like I was having an out-of-body experience. It felt similar to how people who die briefly talk about floating above the room and watching the world react to their lifeless bodies. I found myself somehow hovering over the room like a ghost, watching the drama unfold beneath me. I watched as I prattled on and on about just how unimportant my relationship with Karen was. I watched from overhead as Rolly and Sandy appeared to evaporate into nothingness. From that distance, I could see the damage my lies were inflicting. There were bodies everywhere. Mine, Karen's, Rolly's, and Sandy's.

If there was a positive to come from all my lying, it was that now I recognized that I wasn't just friends with Karen. I could no longer deny that I wanted something much more substantial than casual friendship. Regardless of what I was willing to confess, my mentors made it clear that I had to choose.

If I were a true Christian, I would sever ties with Karen, and thereby willingly eliminate any sexual temptation. For them, being gay was a deniable impulse that God, if I allowed Him, would help me to overcome. I was to choose my faith over my sexual orientation. I would be ruined otherwise.

I left that room feeling as though my life had spiraled out of control. I had walked into that hotel room in denial of my own feelings for Karen and left no longer unaware of my true longing. Regardless of their hopes, my mentors had forced me to confront the questions I had regarding faith and homosexuality. I was accountable now, and no longer able to ignore the theological questions. I didn't know if I had the courage to follow my convictions and confess that I didn't believe that being gay was a sin. I was unprepared for a single-Scripture-hurling war of words to defend what I believed. What I believed had nothing to do with sexual identity or gender. I believed that no matter who we are, who we love, it is *how* we love that matters. I had made that premise the backbone of my public message. I believed it to be divine inspiration. Now I was on the hot seat, my faith in question, my reputation at stake, and it appeared that I was crumbling.

Regardless of my own sexuality, I had sullied the whole affair with my lies. Maybe Rolly and Sandy were right in saying that these temptations came to me due to my lack of Christian virtue. After all, I was a liar.

I was devastated. In the years that followed, I would replay the night over and again in my mind, still regretting my behavior. My fear of uncertainty led me down a path that was unnatural to my character. I might not have had a say in being gay, but I could choose *not* to be a liar. So far as I could see, my integrity had nothing to do with my sexual orientation but, rather, could only be measured by how I responded to truth.

It would take me years of revisiting our conversation to unravel the life lessons from it. There seemed like a crack in the universe that I was responsible for, but it was widened by something more than my being gay.

I had broken the trust between myself and my mentors. I dishonored and disrespected them on the deepest level by not telling them the truth. It took me years of mulling over my regrets of that night to comprehend the tragedy of what had happened. I judged them as being incapable of nurturing who I truly was. I assumed that they could not grow beyond their current understanding of homosexuality as a sin. I assumed that all they wanted to do was change me. In my lies, I assumed that they could not love me as I was. I had assaulted their deepest faith by devaluing their ability to love.

To my thinking, I had betrayed Karen as well. In a strange twist, I realized that I was marginalizing the value and importance that Karen had in my heart. I didn't yet know what, if anything, our lives would look like together, but I had a fondness for her that went beyond sexual attraction.

By minimizing my relationship with Karen, I saw my actions as betraying my true respect and admiration for her as a friend. From my vantage point, my lies implied that Karen was a person of little value to me. Shamefully, I took a line that said that I didn't care enough about her feelings for me to tell the truth about how I really felt about her.

If I truly loved her, loved her in such a way that is beyond the surface of physical attraction or lust, surely I would have defended her worth to others? If she mattered to me, surely I would speak truthfully and without reservation? Karen had found her way into the marrow of my being. I loved her. I wanted her to love me back.

In the end, my dishonesty said more about my character than it did of any circumstances that I would use to justify myself. Christianity had reminded and inspired in me a deep desire to be judged for what was accurate and true about my nature. Being gay wasn't a moral problem to me, but how I was handling it with others was. Whatever my sexual orientation turned out to be, I had to get back to that place of honesty. I vowed never again to manufacture anything to the contrary. If I was to be judged, it would be for what *is* rather than lie for what I hope to be.

Sadly, cancer would take both Rolly and Sandy before I found the courage to take responsibility for my actions. We will never again have the chance to visit and share with each other the value of our uniquely lived experiences. I cannot share with them the positive impact of their confrontation and how it has shaped me into the woman who still reaches to live with integrity. Nor did I get the chance to criticize their approach.

Perhaps the latter is best left untested. What is done is done, but our estranged relationship is a reminder to me that I cannot write the stories of others. Had I the courage to be forthright in the beginning, I might have discovered that they could have taken a journey alongside me and come to be a part of my partner and my celebration of love—a relationship that, in the future, would turn out to be just as rich, meaningful, and life-giving as I hoped for when I looked to Rolly and Sandy's marriage as an example.

Were they here today, I would thank them for sharing joys of their union, as I would hope to share my own.

$\mathcal{I}$ left the confrontation with my mentors feeling dejected and muddled. The few confidants I held dear in my personal life had failed me as much as I had failed them. Many had offered their opinions, prayers, and counsel, yet nearly all seemed to have only one idea, that I was duty-bound to function as a musician for God alone, that anything less would be a betrayal of the blessing that was so graciously afforded me in my second life. But what life did I have, I wondered?

Was it a *Christian* life? I didn't call myself a Christian just for the sake of it. It wasn't a word I used lightly. To use the term indicated that I had experienced a specific spiritual paradigm shift in my life. I wanted more from the experience than simply blending into, and profiting from, Christian culture.

I wanted a meaningful life. I could remember a time when I truly wanted to give, serve, and bring other people to the kind of joy I had once known. Maybe I had given too much? Maybe I had nothing of merit to give? I seriously questioned whether I had done any good while in CCM. At the end, I only felt weak and deceitful.

I had invested my future in Alabaster and that was in ruins. And, now, it was starting to look like I was gay. Everyone around me seemed to travel in only one direction, toward a conservative school of religious thought, hyperfocused on Jesus. It was a world

I could only see as punishing for those, like me, who found the path too constrictive for personal growth.

I was stuck in a loop of contradiction. I deeply respected and had been moved to be a part of the positive impact Christian music could have in the lives of those on a spiritual journey, so much so that I put every ounce of my passion into the songs that shared in that experience.

I found hope when I shared the doubts and fears that had accumulated in my travels with faith. It was an honor to be given invitations to listen to stories from fans about their journeys. It was such a surprising blessing to know that I had, inside me, a gift that, when freely given, could help another person feel a little bit better about themselves.

Music is such a fascinating thing. It's amazing how a single song can so strongly teleport us to a place and a time in our lives that we thought we had forgotten. For those of us drawn in by music, there is a soundtrack that plays through the movie of our lives. It's as if all we have to do is turn up the volume, close our eyes, and we are there, capable of remembering and reliving what had been only a hazy recollection.

How incredible that I got to be a part of that! I was grateful, humbled to the core, astonished, even, that I had ever been asked to play a single note. I respected the privilege and always sought to live up to the task of offering my very best.

I was devastated when I realized that I had nothing more to give.

All I could think about was the kind of humiliation awaiting me if my private spiritual crisis became known to the Christian public. I was more than aware how intolerant the Christian industry can be of those who fall short of their standards.

When I attended my first Dove Awards in 1996, CCM scuttlebutt was atwitter about Michael English and his supposed fall from grace. Michael was a highly decorated CCM artist who had been crowned both Dove's Male Artist and Male Vocalist of the Year. After news of his extramarital affair had surfaced, English willingly forfeited his honors and returned his Dove Award to the Gospel Music Association. For further punishment, his records were pulled from the shelves and his songs removed from radio station playlists.

While his personal tragedy did not ultimately end his career, he seemed to be wearing a scarlet letter. The gossip and disdain I heard from the mouths of Christian music aficionados and industry gatekeepers was clear. CCM artists must forever remain above reproach.

I would see it again in the late nineties when, following a divorce, the queen of Christian pop, Amy Grant, was put through her own crucible of Christian judgment. Like English, retailers attempted to rebuke her by pulling her records from the shelves. Apparently her character was so flawed as to render her music flawed as well. Every news piece, every editorial, every Christian press item pointed to the shame of her spiritual failings.

I didn't want to find myself the centerpiece of another public shaming, but I also found the general principle completely nauseating. Believe it or not, Christian artists are not immune to the normal circumstances of life. There have been many who have found themselves navigating their own private challenges of divorce, drug or alcohol abuse, extramarital affairs, or even rumors of being gay.

That's not to say that any of these qualities makes any one

person inherently bad, or even un-Christian. It simply makes them human. If maintaining the highest perceived standards of lived Christian excellence was required for being a CCM artist, then I had to admit, I was not it. I didn't want to be responsible for pursuing a career in that environment, when I knew myself to be incapable of perfectly maintaining such standards. The only good thing I felt I had left to achieve was to leave quietly and, as much as possible, leave without adding yet another scar to the image of Christianity.

For the last year of my CCM career, I attempted to put a gag on my personal sufferings, and go about my business as if nothing were wrong. Whoever Karen and I were going to be, or not be, had to wait. Whether I was a going to be a Christian any more, only God knew. I couldn't even see my way to keep music as a meaningful experience in my life. I was walking through a wasteland of loss and despair. I put my own needs on hold, waiting for the final show where I could, at last, lock my guitar in its case and walk away.

On September 10, 2002, in Abilene, Texas, I did just that. I played my set, waved to the crowd, walked off the stage, and put my guitar in the case for the last time.

All my demons were latched securely in my guitar case. That day I vowed that I would never play again. I gave up on music, Christianity, and my career. I was nothing, again, and I welcomed it. I was exhausted and faithless.

Whatever came next had to be out of the public eye. I wasn't fit for consumption. I needed solitude in order to rebuild. I needed to find my own voice again, if I had one.

The tour bus deposited me in Nashville for the last time. With nothing to do, no concerts on the horizon, and no plans to speak of, I secluded myself in my Kingston Springs home, severing all communication with the outside world.

The exception was Karen. She had moved in earlier that year to help me get across the finish line. Well, I had made it, but to what end? I was spent. Lord only knows what damage I might have done to myself without her watchful eye.

"It's all in how you look at it," Karen tried to be positive. "It's not the end. It's a beginning."

Having Karen around was a mixed blessing. I loved that she was there every day. She helped me feel safe. However, I was embarrassed to be so vulnerable and needy.

I was unkempt, sleepless, and despondent. The silence I had imposed on myself seemed to be hurting more than it was helping. Normally, at times like this, I'd grab my guitar or a pencil and paper, anything to release the thoughts and emotions in my head, but this time, I couldn't. I trapped them all inside, afraid to let them out for fear they would destroy me.

As the weeks progressed I became more and more depressed, and at times, I contemplated suicide. It wasn't that I didn't want to live, I just couldn't see what I had to live for. Everything that I had put my heart into had left me barren. It didn't help that I had nothing constructive to do. In the past, I might have picked up my guitar and played through the pain or scratched away for hours in my journal. I had cut myself off from all of the support mechanisms and joys that had sustained me through hard times. There was a lot to process.

Karen and I had begun openly to explore the potential of our relationship, which was exciting, but with the specter of shame looming in being discovered as a fallen gay Christian, I was scared. Every part of me wanted to hide and keep our growing love a secret, especially to the Nashville CCM world. At home alone, or outside the 'Ville, my feelings for her were without equivocation. I loved her, and there wasn't much more to say. Yet if we so much as stood too close together while shopping at the local grocery store, I'd find myself trembling in fear. Every admonishing, antigay, Christian conversation replayed itself in my head, telling me that there was something wrong with me. One minute I would be fully present, loving and kind, the next, distant, making hope-killing comments.

My head was a tangled mess of passion, admiration, uncertainty, and fear. Fear of failure, fear of love, fear of God. What if I were wrong? What if my love for Karen was unholy? How could any love be unholy? Was what was in my heart for Karen really *love*? How was I to know if I didn't follow it until the end?

I had so many questions, and all I knew to do was to face them one by one. I had never given my heart to anybody the way I wanted to share it with Karen. I had only given my body, but knew that I wanted more than just sex now. I had been celibate for over a decade and I was hopeful that Christianity had taught me something about what it meant to love another person.

If it was true that no Christian could choose to be gay, then something had to give. Maybe people were right—maybe I wasn't a Christian anymore? If being gay invalidated my faith, if not wanting to be in CCM anymore was a sign of my moral failure, then what was there to argue? I only had the energy left for truth. I needed to move forward. I wanted to love. I was a liar when I said otherwise. I wanted to love Karen and that was the truth of it. I knew it. God knew it.

Together, Karen and I took a much-needed vacation to the Bahamas. We bathed our souls in the warm waters of the Caribbean. The distant horizon of the sea evaporated into the infinite clear blue sky. The local rum was sweet and relaxing, greeting us each morning in some cocktail that stole away my worries in ways that seem only socially acceptable on holiday. I fished, jet skied, snorkeled, and skinny-dipped my anxieties into oblivion. I began to dream of what life with Karen might look like, if we could make it. I fell asleep in her arms every night, released to dream of our future. She loved me, she said so, and it was a healing elixir to my weary soul. It was all so romantic and the possibilities limitless; I didn't want it to end.

Flying back to Nashville was excruciating. Going back to Kingston Springs was akin to shacking up in a haunted house. I locked myself away from the voices that I knew would curse the love I had for Karen. In the privacy of what was becoming our home, I was alive and caring, but outside it, I felt edgy and two-faced. I wasn't lying about my life, but I didn't let the cat out of the bag either. As our relationship deepened, it was obvious that Karen was becoming a major part of my life. Attempting to be stealthy, I began to use the genderless *we*.

On the phone with my mother, I would talk about what *we* had been doing. *We* took a trip to the Bahamas. *We* were living together. *We* were thinking about taking a long trip across the country.

Finally, Mom had had enough, "Who is this *we* you keep talking about? Is the *we* a she?"

I went quiet. The familiar shock wave worked its way through my whole body.

"Jennifer, are you and Karen in love with each other?"

Oh, man . . .

"Jennifer, are you gay?"

For the first time in my life I found the courage to share aloud to another human being the joy bursting from my heart: "Yes, Mom. We are a *thing*."

I waited for any uneasiness to subside, but Mom jumped right in there, as if the universe had failed to shift in any remarkable way for her, as it had for me. Shaking, I shared with her a glimmer of the fear, as I awaited her response, but she reassured me there was nothing of the kind. Without pomp or circumstance, she simply said, "I'm just happy that you are happy. That is all I've ever wanted for you kids, to be happy."

There was no nightmare yelling match. No discrediting of our love for one another, only the support of our union that only a mother can give. I hadn't, to that point, had much time to think about what I was going to do when telling her the truth of my love; she was there as the first person in my life to wholeheartedly, openly, and without judgment celebrate my joy. I never had to lie. There was no room for it; she outed me.

Mom's gentle nudge toward honesty was exactly what Karen had been trying to encourage in me for months. Through our many conversations of just how out I could be in Nashville, we had found a significant point of conflict we needed to work through. One of the admirable qualities that attracted me to Karen in the first place was her courage to be herself at all times. No matter where she was or who she was with, she never was a chameleon, putting on one personality for the room and another for the next. She was solid in accepting herself as she came. She seemed to take this all in stride and encouraged me to do the same.

"It's easy for you. You don't have anything to lose by coming out," I tested.

"Is that how you see us? Like you're losing something? You're not gaining anything here?" she pressed.

Of course, I loved her, but it wasn't as easy as she made it seem. The people that were talking about us outside the safety of my home weren't exactly saying nice things about me.

"So, what? It's your choice to figure out what you need to do here. Maybe you can and maybe you can't be out to the whole world." She wasn't judging or pressuring me, just making sure that I was aware of the consequences of staying in the closet. "Whatever you choose to do, I'll support you, but what I *do* know is this: I don't think I can hide a part of my life that means as much to me as you. You're not my secret; you are a part of what I hope will be my shared life. I won't lie about it. To anyone."

She made it clear to me that what she was offering wasn't so much an ultimatum, as fair warning. She was simply being honest, in her strong character, aware that rocky times might be ahead if I didn't find some way to resolve my response to those who didn't like my being gay. Christian or not, I was going to have to come to unabashed terms with my own sexual orientation. She spoke to the part of me that had become handcuffed by attempting to please all the people all the time. It was the same splinter that had lodged itself into my public life as much as it had my private one. I didn't want to be two people anymore. I wanted to find a way to be my honest self.

I knew I wasn't going to do that well in Nashville, so we began scheming about where we would move. Where could I find a place to figure all this stuff out? Maybe I would never figure it out. Maybe we would together. Maybe Karen and I wouldn't be long lived, but I would never know the truth of it here. I needed a clean slate, a place where I wouldn't be tempted to be what others asked of me, but rather to find a way to stand in my own skin, my own character and personality. But where?

I imagined all the cities in America that I had ever traveled to and enjoyed. Seattle, San Francisco, New York, Portland? They made the list, but they had one fatal flaw. I stood a chance of being recognized. I jokingly talked about changing my name and adopting an English accent, erasing my past life as a Christian rock star, but Karen was swift to remind me that that was just an avoidance tactic.

"Okay, then what?" I felt like I was running out of options. Never in my life had I had such a limitless scope of possibilities before me. I could do anything, go anywhere, be anything. What, then, did I want? I didn't know. My entire adult life had been all about pleasing other people, all about jumping onto the next lily pad that God seemed to put in front of me. It seemed like a thousand years since I had a dream of my own. Now, there was nothing and everything all at the same time.

"What cities do you love in Europe? You could start over there," she mused. It seemed ridiculous.

"There are a lot of intriguing places in Europe, but I've never been in any one city or country long enough to know if I really like any of it. It's always been fly in, work, fly out. I have no idea if I like Europe at all."

"Let's go then."

What? The notion seemed extravagant and far too adventurous. How on earth was that even a possibility? I asked.

"Easy. We buy a plane ticket and an RV and drive around until we find a place to stay. Who knows what will happen? We don't even know if we can be *we*, but we could set out and see if we can make a go of life together. You and I are no strangers to travel. You want out of Nashville, so let's do it. Let's travel!"

I thought she was nuts. I had heard of people backpacking through Europe and traveling the world in hopes of finding themselves but this hardly seemed like me. Surely such things were reserved for interesting folks, not frumpy country girls from Kansas? Music had taken me to many fascinating places over the years, and I had relished all of it, but my destination had always been assigned. Never in my life, except for our trip to the Bahamas, had I chosen to set out on an adventure without a plan. I needed a plan.

"How's this for a plan. Let's start in New England and work our way south until we run out of road. We can camp our way through all the national parks, eat, drink, and be merry. If we get through that together, then let's do the same in Europe. Who knows, maybe along the way we'll find our nesting place and never leave."

I had nothing in Nashville tying me down. I had no debt, a bank account full of money, and royalties that continued to fill the coffers. I wasn't wealthy by any means, but I had enough money for Karen and I to circle the globe a couple of times, get to know one another along the way, and leave the rat race behind us for a while.

Before I knew it, the once capable Ford Econoline van I used for touring was repurposed for the American leg of our honeymoon travels. Karen kitted it out with all the supplies we would ever need: a tent, stove, dry goods, fishing gear, road maps and more. We knew only where we were to start—springtime in New England—and end, perhaps waiting out the winter in the Florida Keys. Beyond that was anybody's guess.

Now, let me say this: If you ever want to know just how good your relationship is with another person, go camping. There's nothing like losing all your creature comforts, getting exposed to the elements and having to problem solve at three in the morning, ankle deep in rising floodwaters, to sort out your character flaws! Whether you're hot or cold, tired, hungry or stinky, if you've got somebody who still manages to love you, and you them? Well, things may just pan out, but it takes work.

Through flat tires, freezing nights, and innumerable conflicts about how best to pack the van, we found our stride. I learned to compromise and encourage Karen's boundless need for physical exertion by learning to appreciate our grueling treks to the top of whatever mountain we were visiting, to see what was usually a dripping trough, hardly a waterfall. She came to accommodate my need for lazy afternoons, nestled under the shade of trees, doing nothing but being alone with my thoughts. There were times where she wished that I had brought a guitar to entertain us through the quiet, dark nights, but I was happy to say there was no room in the van for such a luxury.

"Still, I miss you singing," she would say.

"I don't," I'd say, trying to be confident in my reply. I couldn't speak about my past life. I felt music was the most painful casualty of my spiritual breakdown. *I wasn't God's anymore. He won't let a homo sing. Not this one, anyway.* I spoke nothing of it, not wanting Karen to think that my professional demise had anything to do with her. It didn't. I just didn't believe that I had a right to music any more.

"I believe in you, you know," she said, breaking the silence. Her compassion reached into the depths I lacked the strength to explore.

"I know you do."

With every new stretch of road, I put another mile between me and my past life. Through Virginia, the Carolinas, Georgia, and into Florida, the ache made its way into my bones. As long as I was moving, I was alright. As long as we didn't turn on the radio, and avoided scanning through the stations, so as not to hear a single Christian broadcast—or worse, one of my own songs—I'd be okay. *You'll be okay. You'll be okay,* became my only prayer. Upon occasion I would look down to the calluses on my left hand, poke at them with whatever sharp object I could find, and wonder when, if ever, they would disappear. If I wasn't going to play anymore, I needed no reminders the music that had, for so long, been my companion, but it was still hard. How long, I wondered, until there would be no trace of them?

eighteen

Eventually, we reached a dead end at Key West. With winter approaching, we reluctantly decided to return to the only home I had, in Nashville. Like bears tucked away in a cave, we hibernated through the cold spell, using the long dark days to plan our next adventure. I despised being back in Nashville. I was too afraid to socialize and did my best to stay out of whatever harm's way I thought might be lurking in the real world. Coming home left me bound up in insecurities and obsessing about my supposed failures. I needed to keep moving.

Traveling kept me distracted and disconnected. These were the days before smart phones kept you tethered to the instant demand to communicate. There was no 4G network and usually, only patchy cell-phone coverage. On the road, I'd pop into an Internet café once in a while, to make sure the world wasn't about to implode, or that my house hadn't burned down, but that was about it. It was the ultimate expression of rebellion, to refuse to connect with anyone whom I didn't initiate a conversation with. Returning home, my computer only taunted me. It sat on my desk like a relic of the past, mocking my once busy and meaningful life. When I did bother to turn it on and tend to my affairs, I'd often find emails from my booking agent, attempting to send through offers for concerts on the off chance I would say *yes*. It had been over a year since I had walked away and still, it seemed that few of my professional associates were taking my departure seriously. As long as I had to walk by my home office every day, I would be reminded that I had imposed this exile on myself. All I had to do was say *yes* to any number of the opportunities that still came my way, but the mere thought of it reduced me into a fetal position. *Stop calling! I quit already!* I'd scream, half angry, half miserable and near tears. Every moment I remained in Tennessee fueled my bitterness.

"Let's do it. Let's go to Europe," I finally resolved. "I can't be in this place and survive it."

In June 2003, Karen and I took off for London. There, we bought a used diesel Fiat RV equipped with all we would ever need. It was a rolling home on four wheels, complete with a working kitchen, refrigerator, bathroom, and sleeping quarters. Compared to traveling in the van back in America, it was supreme luxury. Though it barely reached a top speed of fifty-five miles per hour, we were in no hurry. Once again, we set out with little plan, except to keep going until we didn't want to go anymore. Perhaps, I thought, we won't ever go back.

We made our way through the south of England, making sure to stop by Stonehenge, and some of the more interesting historical remnants of Roman occupation. On into Ireland, to the Ring of Kerry, Dublin, Belfast, and points further north. We'd make our way through Scotland, Denmark, Germany, the Czech Republic, Hungary, and more. We did our best to leave no stone unturned. From the famed natural wonders like the Giant's Causeway of Scotland to the Athenian ruins of ancient Greece, we immersed ourselves in all there was to see, hear, and taste.

There would be times where we'd travel to a different city or village every day, then weeks where we would find ourselves exploring every nook and cranny of a single destination. We reminded ourselves to be patient during our adventure. To take time to appreciate all that we laid eyes on.

I was beside myself with delight over the romance of it all. There was never a day when I opened my eyes untouched by the excitement of the possibilities.

I remembered the days back in Kansas, when I used to sit in my Grandma Knapp's house, leafing through her *Encyclopedia Britannica*, in awe of all the fantastic sights, history, and culture of other worlds. The Eiffel Tower might be a world away, the Roman Coliseum, the stuff of legend, but it was all there in those books. I would lose myself to imagination the way only a child can, daydreaming black-and-white picture into Technicolor, like Dorothy after the tornado, waking to the vibrant Land of Oz. Better still, I could peer into the magnificent 3D world of my favorite View-Master discs and stand on the very banks of Loch Ness, straining for a glimpse of Old Nessie herself. The delightful treats of postcards, history books, and educational toys inspired me to think of the expanse of the world beyond my own, yet often left me sullen, never believing that I would see such things with my own eyes. But now, *now!* I was standing atop Buda Castle, watching the Danube snake its way through Hungary!

There was more to the journey than seeing with my eyes. I began to reconnect with my passion for living. I had the privilege of getting to stand for hours in front of a single Picasso, searching every brush stroke for signs of his own artistic evolution. Whether he toyed with the impressionists, got lost in the monochromatic schemes of his Blue Period, or fractured the world through Cubism, seeing his creations helped the pilot light inside my wandering heart keep a glowing vigil. I may have lost sight of my own calling to create, but I couldn't keep denying that I yearned to be divinely moved.

It wasn't just Picasso that inspired me. There would be cathedrals, tombs of knights, ruins once built for the mystic glory of ancient gods, and many stunning creations of mankind that continue to speak to the legacy of our human dreaming. Even the alien landscapes spoke to me. From the lush emerald rolling hills of Ireland to the arid Mediterranean landscape of Greece, I saw with new eyes a world I had been taking for granted.

I began to appreciate how one culture's people were shaped by their surroundings. The landlocked toiled on the land; those born to the coast braved the seas. The monuments to the gods illuminated how each people saw their human experience. The Romans made their empire through war and enslavement, their ingenuity, philosophies, and legends reaching out into all of Europe to scar the world with their shrines to human strength. Modern postwar Croatia was still nursing its national psyche while patiently waiting for renewed strength to rebuild yet again, contemplating just how many of the genocidal machine-gunned bullet holes to repair, knowing that it is the history that reminds us of who we are today.

Slowly, I began to appreciate that I couldn't erase my past, but I could learn from it.

When I stood in line for what seemed hours waiting for my chance to take a look at the Book of Kells, I complained the entire time about how my feet ached. Yet, when I finally laid eyes on the painstaking years of dedicated effort it took to finish, I had to step back, and became aware of the reverence that made it all possible. I recognized the impulse of that kind of spirituality. It was my own once. Over a thousand years of theological evolution between us, but it was startlingly familiar. I began to wonder what had happened between then and now. Knowing loosely that the pagans were consumed by the Christians, the Christians bisected into the Protestants and the Catholics, the Americas religiously birthed from the radical offshoots of unrestrained spirituality. Europe's religious history wasn't just an isolated happening; its history was my own. The conservative, shiny, commercial success of the American megachurch wasn't born the way it was. It evolved. I both suffered by it and found benefit in it. It was hard to make sense of it. For every time I had wondered how in the world I had come to be so entrenched, so tangled by the theological tyranny of the religion that I had inherited, it never occurred to me that it hadn't always been this way. Maybe it wouldn't always be?

I began to read everything I could get my hands on. From modern religious historians like Karen Armstrong to Diarmaid McCullouch. Like an eager student, I poured over the early sermons of pre-Revolutionary America. I wanted to learn more about the religion that had affected my life so dramatically. Parts of me wanted to debunk it all; other parts hoped to find some ground to feel as though I wasn't the only fool moved by it. Rather than leaning on my own experience, I began combing through the highs and lows, looking for how others had made their way.

I read (and ate) my way through the Old World. America was a distant memory and I began to feel like a real person again. Our wanderings had led us by ferry from the port of Bari, Italy, to Peloponnese, Greece. We had tired of the months of touring the more familiar parts of Europe and longed for more exotic flavors. It was a welcome respite from the Christian lands. Though Greek Orthodoxy is the modern religion, the mythological past is seamlessly celebrated without irony or disdain. We did our dutiful best to make our way through the muscular history of Olympus and Sparta, eventually making camp on the temperate shores of the Mediterranean Sea. After many miles, we were ready to relax and stay in one place for a while. Gone were the heavy meals of goulash and potatoes. The standard fare was a welcome bounty of fresh octopus, stunning feta, and the most savory lamb you can imagine. I practically bathed myself in the plentiful Greek olive oil.

The Greek attitude is infectious, not jarring, but gradual, like a soothing glass of red wine, lulling you into a sense of ease. Outside Athens, the pace is so much slower than my accustomed American freneticism. I had to learn to quiet my sense of urgency and take life as it so slowly came. A simple lunch could take hours, even longer, if we found ourselves, as we so often did, sidled up beside a local restaurant owner sharing the tales of our travels over copious amounts of regional wine. Occasionally, we would gather ourselves from the pebbled beach and venture to the odd tourist trap, but mostly we just watched the sun rise and set. The only clock we needed was our stomachs.

Finally, we were lost. It seemed a thousand years since I had been forced to stand in a line or suffer the honks of an angry horn. Longer still since I had read an email, or even so much as looked at a calendar. Complete, quiet, soul-soothing bliss. We hadn't realized it, but we had been in the same place for nearly eight weeks!

It was October and the days were shortening. We still wanted to make our way back to the yet-to-be-explored Spain, so we pulled up our tent pegs, shooed the stray cats out from under the Fiat, and quickly worked our way through what remained of Greece.

I had acquired a sincere affection for the country, and leaving was like saying goodbye to an old friend. I loved it, but Greece wasn't the home I was searching for. It was time to make our way back across the Adriatic, catch up on Italy, and start considering how we were going to spend the winter. Christmas in Morocco, perhaps? We figured we had a few more weeks to travel through Italy and Spain before we would have to decide.

Reinvigorated, we planned on disembarking from the ferry in Bari, Italy, with plans of taking on the rest of Italy and Spain. Unfortunately, my back had other ideas. As I awoke from the rolling night's sleep aboard the ferry, pain suddenly shot through my entire body. I couldn't move a single inch without agony. I had struggled with a niggling back for many years, but this was another level of pain. Karen watched as the other passengers poured off the boat, encouraging me to get up, as I had so many times before. It wasn't happening. I was immobilized. If I was to make it to land, it was going to take a couple of sturdy paramedics and some narcotics to get me there.

In what I can only describe as the misadventures akin to the Keystone Kops, two orange overall-clad Italian boys unsympathetically loaded my shrieking person into a rickety wheelchair and haphazardly toted me through the endless stairwells of the ship and into a rusty white van marked *Ambulanza*. White-hot pain splintered its way down my legs and up into my skull on what seemed like an interminable journey through every cobblestone street of Bari. I moaned, wishing I knew the Italian for "Drugs please!" In my best broken Italian, I begged for anyone who could speak English only to be replied with a universally understood *no*, dashing any hopes I had for a quieting opiate.

When we got to the hospital, the medics parked the van and crawled into the back. No mad dash into the ER. They just sat there. One of the young men smiled, fiddled with his fingers and questioned, "Americana?"

"Si," I gurgled coolly. I wanted drugs, not chitchat. *Gimme the hard stuff*, I wanted to say. Instead, I got a cigarette. I attempted to smoke it, but such was my discomfort that I could barely lift my hand to my mouth. It smoldered down to the filter, my shaking hand littering ash into the back of the *ambulanza*, before I was finally taken inside.

Scans, more scans. Dark-haired men in aging white coats rolled me this way and that with enough English to make out the words *stay, hospital*, and *surgery*.

It would be nearly five days before I managed to make contact with a doctor who spoke enough English to help me understand that my back had three bulging discs pressing into the nerves that fed into my legs. They insisted that I stay bedridden; offering me little more than ibuprofen to ease the pain, and informed me that surgery was in order. After looking around my dilapidated room and watching the other patients moan through their postsurgical afflictions, I knew there was no way I was going to let this lot cut me open! The resident orthopedic surgeon didn't exactly inspire confidence when he grimaced, leaned to my ear and whispered "No here. Go America. Is better."

Yikes!

It was a horrifying experience, but Karen was beside me through every minute of the ordeal. She suffered her own test of physical endurance, spending every night sleeping on the floor next to my bed, determined to help me get back onto my feet. For two long, grueling weeks, she helped as we determined to force movement through my broken body until I was mobile enough to make my emergency flight back home. There would be no Christmas in Morocco. It was back to Nashville for another long winter.

nineteen

$\mathcal{I}$ had had enough with the on again, off again, internments in Nashville. As long as the anchor of my house in Kingston Springs kept acting as a safety net for my travel adventures, I would never be released from moving on with my life. Like a mismatched lover who is no good for you, it seemed every time I reached the end of one road, I'd end up coming back in an attempt to start yet another journey.

After making my way through countless cities, countries, and cultures, I had yet to find the new home that I longed for. In between the surgery avoidance tactics of physical therapy and steroid injections meant to remedy my back problems, I decided to cut the cord once and for all. I wanted to make a definitive move to get as far away as geographically possible, officially severing ties with Music City, USA. This time, we downsized what we owned, packed what remained into a shipping container, and made our voyage to Karen's native country, Australia.

If you're searching for a truly cathartic experience in your life, try purging your life of the material possessions that encumber you. In preparing for our relocation Down Under, we were limited to the given cubic space of a small shipping container. For me, it proved to be just what the doctor ordered.

In the throes of my own pagan ritual, I set about offloading every last reminder of my musical life by selling all I could on eBay. Had it not been for Karen, I probably would have burned my *Kansas* Gold Record plaque and chucked my Dove Awards into the Cumberland. Upon her insistence, I left it to Karen to seal them away in boxes and to keep them out of my sight. Just looking at them was enough to send me into a spiral of depression. My life in Nashville was over.

I was unsentimentally relentless. As much as possible needed to go. Along with sofas, cars, and office equipment, I purposed to jettison every guitar I owned, all my recording equipment, and even the trumpet that had so faithfully served as my gateway drug into music. One by one I polished, photographed, and priced my once darling little children, putting them to the auction block in hopes of never being reminded of them and the life they offered.

Karen was aghast.

"Surely you don't want to do this!" she said, confounded. "Maybe you aren't going to do Christian music anymore, but this is extreme. You've played music your whole life. Giving up on one doesn't mean you have to throw the babies out with the bathwater."

I didn't care. As long as these pieces were around, I felt taunted by the life I had lost. Even going through them now was a pain almost too debilitating to bear.

"They're just *thing*s," I insisted. "They don't mean anything special." I did my best to downplay the significance of the bloodletting.

"Hon, you'll play again. It's part of you." She gently grabbed my arm, looked into my eyes, pleading for me to not go through with it. "I just don't want you to do something you will regret later."

"Trust me, I won't." I reassured her. "I'm ready to wash my hands of the whole thing." I was fully convinced that whatever pangs of remorse that were moving through me were those of guilt over the life that I was denying God any access to. I didn't want to play CCM anymore, and in doing so, reckoned I was in no way honoring God.

The logic played itself out in my twisted mind:

No Christian music, no God.

You don't serve God, so there is no point to playing music.

To top it off, you're gay, and that definitely means you've fallen.

The thoughts echoed through me, muddled and yet certain. Every time I opened the door to even considering the deep sorrow of how I had come to this place, I was greeted by all the voices of Christian dissent that had written themselves in my psyche. They went on to say:

You are not worthy of singing.

If you dare sing again, God will smite you.

By not using your voice for God, you are ruining the good works for which you were purposed.

God will not bless the life of a depraved homosexual. You might sing again, but no good will come of it.

God will never allow you to sing again.

I LACKED THE courage and the confidence to test their certainty. No. Getting rid of all this stuff was the only solution. This chapter of my life had surely ended, so carrying it across the globe wasn't necessary anymore.

Avoid! Purge! Destroy!

Karen had had enough of my shenanigans. "I won't let you do it!" She stood between me and the instruments like a protector against my evil deeds. "You will play again. I can't help but believe it. Let's pack the most valuable guitars and take them to Australia with us. Give time a chance. Later on, if you still feel this strongly, you can sell them there." She appealed to my appreciation of value: "You'll get more money for them in Oz if you decide to sell them anyway."

With that, she took possession of what I seemed to so easily discard. She took the guitars and piled them into corner of all that we aimed to take with us. If it seemed I had given up, she had not. "They are part of you and they're coming with us." And that was that. Safely tucked away in their armored cases, they rested, gathering dust, awaiting the day that Karen's vision might come true.

I HAD VISITED Australia a few times, so landing in Sydney wasn't altogether unfamiliar. Along the way, I had picked up a few friends and had become a welcome, adopted new member of my partner's family. After a few months of settling in, my new community had gone back to their daily lives, leaving Karen and I to construct our new world together.

We found our groove on the leafy northern suburbs of Sydney. My new friends set out to initiate me in all things Australian. Backyard barbecues, long hours of casual beer-laden get-togethers, and sport. Lots and lots of sport. Aussie Rules Football, rugby league, rugby union, cricket, competitive swimming, tennis, you name it—if Australia has a national religion, its church is the arena of sport.

I had a lot to learn. Everything here was fresh and alien to me. While everyone spoke English, their accents made conversation challenging. The simplest and most casual conversations were adventures in themselves. Early on, I struggled to understand most of what was being said unless I focused hard, and paid attention to every word that was spoken. I couldn't half-listen to what people were saying, as I was so accustomed to back in America. The phrasing, sentence structures, and vocabulary were often very different to my Yankee ears. Their charming colloquialisms and lilting dialect often left me brutishly grunting, "What?" At times, I felt as foreign in conversations as I did nestled in the rugged landscape. Everything was different.

A carefree stroll atop Sydney Harbour North Head easily turned into an adventure all its own. At first, I floundered, trying to appreciate the beauty of the many spindly, yet sturdy shrubs Australians call *flora*. So much more romantic and inspiring a term than just to call these desperate things *bushes*. There wasn't a single leaf I could take for granted. It was all so unusual.

Upon closer inspection, I began to see the wonderment unfold. What at first only looked like a barren and godforsaken land started to bloom in front of my eyes when I stopped to notice. Bottle brush trees, with their bright red and yellow succulent flowers, blossomed and came alive, as vibrant black-and-gold honeyeater birds darted and flitted about. Each bird, danced about and through the branches in an effort to get a taste of the delicious, sweet nectar on offer. The wattle trees opened their tiny, pungent flowers and dusted the parched ground beneath with their yellow-green pollen.

Like a curious child, I was exploding with questions: "What bird is that? What is that tree? I want to see a wombat in the wild! Can I feed a kangaroo?" Karen was a city girl and, for the most part, had never been called upon to describe her native land in such detail, but she was more than game to help me out.

"You know what, we should go bush," she said. Her eyes lit up with a scheme on the brew.

"What are you talking about?" I had become familiar with how Australians referred to its wild nature as *bush*, but I had yet to understand the true essence of the term. "You mean camping. Okay." I was naive as to what she was playing it at.

"Not just camping, I mean, let's really get into the bush. Let's get a four-wheel drive and take a real adventure. Let's *go bush*. Let's go live rough. Let's go live in the mountains, the outback. Or, what about a trek through the desert?"

"You're crazy," I replied. I didn't know the first thing about the kind of off-road, sparsely mapped, isolated type of excursion she was suggesting, and neither did she, I was more than happy to point out.

Karen persisted. How hard could it be? All we had to do was educate ourselves about what we didn't know. We were already mad outdoor enthusiasts and Karen wanted more, urging, "Let's take it to the next level."

I had to admit, the allure of Australia's wild land spoke to me. I had more than enjoyed the mild-mannered exploring we'd already done. We had taken several road trips along the southern, rugged coast of Victoria's Great Ocean Road. We'd spent a few weekends tucked away in the tamed state parks of New

South Wales' Blue Mountains, but what she was talking about required more skill than merely setting up a camp stove and a tent.

Before I had a chance to entertain the idea, she was plying me with all manner of books, photographs, and maps. This wasn't just a nifty idea; she was dead serious. More than that, she explained, she had dreamed of the day where one day she could explore all that Australia had to offer.

We had the time. We were still looking for direction. I had established a firm grasp on what life was like for the coastbound inhabitants of Terra Australis, but there was still much to see.

Apprehensive, but willing, I caved, "Lead the way, then."

We ended up purchasing a used, yet sturdy, Mitsubishi Pajero. Once again, Karen kitted her out, we christened her *Mitzi*, and began educating ourselves about just how to make use of her.

We signed up for a four-wheel driving course that proved to be frighteningly educational. Growing up on a farm, I'd had my share of driving on dirt roads and fording small, innocuous creeks, and was capable of dealing with flat tires without calling them emergencies, but at no time had I ever faced anything that I would have described as dangerous.

"Where do you girls plan on going?" the teacher inquired to assess what kind of instruction we required.

We had gotten it in our minds to explore the Snowy Mountains. The High Country. Karen was keen to explore the fire trails that wound their way through the peaks and valleys of Australia's highest mountains. I still reckoned she was wanted the impossible, and our instructor didn't exactly calm my nerves. He explained what a serious undertaking we were proposing, and that if he didn't think we were fit for it by the end of our lessons, he wouldn't hesitate to say so. We needed to graduate his outback driving course before we were cleared to go.

"In the outback, your vehicle is your lifeline," warned the instructor. He made it sound so serious. "You have to know every inch of your four-wheel drive. You have to know how to be able to put every wheel within millimeters of where you aim it to go. One slip, and you could be dead. Tear up the transmission, and it could be days before you see another soul who can help you. You could slide off a cliff, and you're as done as a dinner."

Crikey. What was I getting into?

In the relatively controlled environment of this bloke's outback adventure track, he proceeded to conduct our trial by fire. We each took our turn, driving Mitzi through radiator-engulfing troughs of black water. We practiced crossing five-foot-deep trenches over bridges made of nothing more than two-wheel-wide planks. Up narrow, rocky trails, down steep, slick embankments. He even schooled us in how to recover our vehicle from getting stuck in various scenarios of sand and mud. He was our off-roading guru, proud and enthusiastic to help us get the most out of Mitzi, but also teaching us about our own personal limits as well.

"Never bite off more than you can chew," he urged us. "If you aren't prepared to deal with the consequences, then you shouldn't drive through it. The trip is over if you're dead. Now, go and have the time of your lives."

We had graduated!

twenty

There are few places I have visited in this world that have delivered the promised romance and beauty as that of the Australian landscape. By no means have I been everywhere, but I've often found that there have been times where I've been challenged to share in the same level of awe that the poets who came before meant to inspire. Perhaps there are times when I am too busy or distracted to lose myself to the spirit of transcendence, holding fast to reality that everything is the same. Too often, I have found myself numbed by a predictable world that holds nothing especially sacred or divine. Maybe Australia is, in the end, no different that any other place on the earth, made as it is of the usual stuff— rock, air, dirt and water—but nestled in her arms, I rediscovered spiritual contentment.

One of my favorite books as a young girl was Jean Craighead George's *My Side of the Mountain.* It is the story of a young boy who runs away from his New York City home and escapes to the solitude of the Catskill Mountains, where he learns how harsh, isolated, and nurturing life in solitude can be. The story resonated so much with my own young life, with my desire to run away from my own childhood troubles, my love of the outdoors, and my kinship with isolation, that I was drawn into his world as if it were my own lived escape.

Waking up in a serene, frost-dusted valley of the Snowy Mountains, I couldn't help but feel transported into a dream. In the High Country, the nights before winter are crisp and frigid. When the morning sun creeps over the towering ridge, the ice crystals that cover the golden grasses and red gum leaves glisten as they thaw, releasing the sweet, soft fragrance of eucalyptus into the air. Overnight, tucked into a much-relied-upon, state-of-the-art sleeping bag, my joints still would manage to stiffen from the freezing chill. The only remedy would be to force myself up and start a fire with my numb fingers, desperate for a piping hot cup of tea poured straight from the billy.

The whole world was plaintively calm, but not silent. Gone were screams of overhead airplanes and telltale sounds of human upward mobility (save us and our beastly four-wheel drive). Instead, we heard the sounds of distant cockatoos and kookaburras, yawning their songs to announce the day. Most mornings, I found myself compelled to step softly. Karen and I had become deft at rising in harmony with the nature that surrounded us, gradually making our way into the light, saying little between us, so as to lend our ears to the waking world around us. We were in no hurry to be anywhere but the present. The plan for the day might have been to make our way to the next camp, but that might be postponed because I had spent the best part of the dawn transfixed, watching a brumby mare grazing her way through the meadow. One day, I sat still enough for one to come within yards of our camp. Any sudden movement and she would snap her head up, nostrils fluming her white condensed breath into the icy air.

We were the alien visitors to her world. We learned quickly that the best reverence we could offer was leaving our campsite as we found it, seemingly untouched by human footfalls. There were times that we found ourselves in such a remote place that the only sign of the modern world was the narrow, rocky fire trails that led us there.

Every couple of weeks or so, we'd use a satellite phone to check in with our families. I could have been tempted to stay out there forever, were it not for the approaching winter. The trails that made our journey possible were dangerous enough in the dry days of summer; adding snow to the equation would have been far from wise. We had enough experience already in trying to travel tracks after rain to know that snow could trap us in the back country for weeks. Some passes were so treacherous that missing your wheel placement by a single inch could send your vehicle tumbling down the face of a mountain. Add a little water, and terra firma becomes terra calamitas. If you survive the carnage of twisted metal and timber, you might be stranded for days until help arrived.

After three blissful months, the rains chased us down from the hills and back to the hustle and bustle of Sydney. I had to admit, it was nice to get back to the luxuries of modernity. I got into the habit of thinking there was nothing unusual about having to dig my toilet every day and burn my toilet paper, but there's nothing as remarkable as feeling the cool porcelain beneath your backside to remind you that going it rough has its drawbacks.

Makeshift dunnies aside, I had been bitten by the outback bug and I wanted more of it. There was so much more of Australia to see! Getting back to city life, I was twiddling my thumbs, with little to occupy my time. Three years had passed since I had been counted among the gainfully employed, but my new job was all about soaking up the world. Back home, I was occasionally tempted to pull out my guitar and see what insights strumming might draw out of my travels, but doing so still came with twangs of sorrow. I never lasted more than a few minutes until I grew unsettled, reminded of the life that I missed back in the so-called real world.

My friends were astonished that I could afford to take such a long vacation. It was embarrassing to admit, but I had nothing to show for my previous life except for money. In those days, all I ever did was work. I bought a car and house and that was about it. I sold those, banked the cash, and tried to ignore the pleasure and the pain of watching my royalty checks come in. Pleasure, because I didn't have to worry about having to work for a good long while. Pain, because it reminded me of the past I was running from.

Money aside, my friends reasoned, surely I would get bored with doing nothing. It was difficult to explain, but that the kind of traveling we were doing was far from doing nothing. Though tranquil at times, every day in the Australian bush came with the prospect of a challenging and rewarding adventure. I wasn't done yet. I wanted more of it.

On our next trip, Karen and I decided to pull out all the stops and circumnavigate the whole of Australia. As I like to say, I left Sydney and kept heading left until I circled back around. We made our way up the eastern coast, past the highly populated areas that stretch from Melbourne to Cooktown, and up into the northernmost reaches of the continent. Once we made our way through the rainforests that let us know we entered into the monsoon realm of the Tropic of Capricorn, it struck us that we were about to see more of Australia than many Australians ever would.

The High Country is a cakewalk next to the demands of the Top End. I'd say the Snowies are practically cuddly. Not that I'd want to get into a tussle with an Eastern Grey Kangaroo (newsflash: They can growl like angry dogs and claw out your eyes if you test them), but at least a marsupial doesn't see you as prey. Respecting nature once you pass Cape Tribulation isn't just a quaint idea; it's serious business. Fording a river becomes a test of your courage, knowing that a giant crocodile could see you as a tasty treat. Even a brisk stroll through the bush has the potential of being a deadly affair, if you forget for a moment that this is the land of some of the planet's most poisonous snakes. It's not as daunting as it sounds, but it's not an undertaking to be handled lightly, either. As with all our remote adventures, we did well to educate ourselves about what to expect and prepared our skill set accordingly. At all times we carried with us a working emergency beacon, medical supplies, and, of course, sought specific professional instruction for first-aid care, in case the need should ever arise. The sage advice we had received from our former four-wheel-drive instructor wasn't just wisdom, it was a lasting gift that served us well.

The contrast of the slow, deliberate mountains, compared to the hot, rugged roads of the less traveled north, at times, got us wondering what on earth we had gotten ourselves into. The unpaved roads of Cape York, exposed to the hellish wind and monsoon rains, are the most unfriendly, bone-jarring paths I have ever traveled. No matter how much mankind attempts to smooth them, the dirt and rock are eroded into uniformly dispersed channels, similar to those of an old-fashioned washboard. The choice becomes either traveling at a woeful snail's pace, letting each trench swallow your tires in a nauseating bucking effect, or race over the top at breakneck speed in an attempt to ease the worst of the pain. It didn't matter to me; each option nearly drove me mad. I opted for the latter, choosing to make the misery of it end as quickly as possible. Kilometer after dreadful kilometer, the journey to the tip of Australia's northern most point left us parched and bruised, and our dear Mitzi just as battered. We would later discover that the vibrations were so violent that they actually sheered the engine-mount bolts off. It was a miracle that, with all our bouncing, the engine block didn't bounce right out onto the ground. Cape York definitely taught me the meaning of the Aussie term *hard yakka*.

No worries. We just bolted the engine back on and kept heading across the Top. Most of the north was about the miles. Everyday, our work was navigating our way across the long flat plains that sidle up against the Gulf of Carpentaria. Into the Northern Territory, we spent time soothing our weary bones, literally, under the shade of the coolabah trees beside billabongs. In Western Australia, we trekked through the ochre-drenched Gibb River gorges and fished for barramundi in the crocodile-laden, brackish waters of the Ord River.

WE MADE OUR camp many a night with no other living soul around but each other. The height of extravagance would come on the days one of us would manage to catch a recognizable fish from the ocean. For every barren stretch that seemed to make Australia such a desolate and hostile place, we always managed to find an oasis that made the hardships all the more nobly won.

There were times when I questioned the wisdom of two petite lesbians going it alone, so far removed from civilization. Beyond coping with our physical limitations, I was nervous that a rural country bloke might not take kindly to our being together. Back in Sydney, being gay is hardly remarkable. But if country folk in Oz were anything like what I encountered growing up in Kansas, I feared that prejudice in such a remote place had the potential to manifest into unwanted and hostile confrontation. For the few times that we were around other people, I tried to keep a low lezzy profile but, every once in a while, questions were asked.

I had initially avoided the outback pubs, thinking they were dens of respite reserved only for the most hardy of Aussie blokes, but after weeks of lukewarm Victoria Bitters from a can, my lips ached for a thirst-quenching, ice-cold draught beer. Yankee lesbian or not, I wasn't about to let my nerves get between me and a pint.

I'll never forget the first time we walked into a dark shed of a remote pub. Before I had a chance to order my drink, the old dusty cobber leaning against the ancient wood bar looked us each up and down from head to toe.

"Yooz two togetha?" he croaked from over the top of his brew. You could tell by his tone he wasn't asking if we were acquainted, he was asking if we were *together*.

"Yup," I said. His eyes narrowed, pinching back what seemed a retort of some kind. I needed a preemptive strike. I saw there was a small tube television airing the latest rugby league match between New South Wales and Queensland. We were in New South Wales at the time, so I let my patriotism fly. "Go the Blues! What's the score?" That's right, old man; I know what's going on.

With that his head tilted to the side, as if to readjust the screws that kept his heterosexual brain safely in his skull. Just before my internal tensions reached their peak and forced me to withdraw, he busted out in a huge grin and asked, "Whaddle you two sheilas have?"

Without a beat, "I'll have a schooner of Old, thanks!" Home, sweet, Aussie home.

Life is hard enough without knowing that you belong to someone, somewhere. Just a little bit of knowing that you're invited and welcome goes a long way to lifting the fog of loneliness.

The rugged, sweltering isolated interior of Australia managed to give me a glimpse of the difference between loneliness and solitude. There were some stretches of country where the only voice for days, besides Karen's or my own, was the squawk of a cockatoo. To break the silence with our words, at times, felt irreverent.

Some days were so hot and the sun so searing that the only thing left to do was to sit quietly, eyes closed, in the shade of a paperbark tree and wait for the stars.

In the beginning of our travels, so many thousands of kilometers ago, that silence drove me to tears. My mind would race with questions, with resentments and jealousy. Though Karen sat beside me through it all, I wept from a place of gut-wrenching loneliness.

Loneliness isn't as quiet as it sounds. For me, it was angry. I shook my fists. I cried. I shouted into every void for a return call of recognition, for acknowledgment. I accused. I judged. I cursed every soul and every little thought in my brain that said I was insignificant. I would have told you I was abandoned, rather than alone. Ignored. Cast out, even.

I wouldn't read Henri Nouwen's book *Reaching Out* for a couple of years, but when I did, my memories went back to my days recovering in the Outback. I understood him, when he talked about the differences between loneliness and solitude.

The agony of loneliness has always been the emptiness I experience when I reach out and feel nothing there. It is the desolate place where I am forced to acknowledge my own weaknesses. Whenever I have been frightfully suspended in that ever-widening darkness, I twist and flail, screaming, "*I don't want to be alone!*"

Solitude is different. It is much more quiet and restful. It's the place where, as Nouwen suggested, I could "claim [my] aloneness" and still find peace.

One day, under the cool, mottled shadows of the eucalyptus, I noticed those old tensions had fallen silent. I sat there, drunk in the ethereal space between wakefulness and dreaming. I kept my eyes shut and enjoyed the ceasefire.

I felt warmth cover the top of my hand. Like someone had gently placed their hand atop mine in a gesture of comfort. I smiled and let out a gentle, welcoming hum. I opened my eyes, expecting to see Karen, but there was no one there, only the silhouette of gum leaves dancing across my skin.

Maybe it was God? The wind? A patch of sunlight? Or maybe just my imagination? I didn't know and I didn't care. I was free from my usual compulsion to explain it. Beautiful and serene, it just *was*.

With another satisfied hum, I rolled my head back in submission, closed my eyes, and accepted the stillness there.

twenty-one

Our Australian expedition would take us six months to complete, leaving only the center and desert country for another time. All told, we had spent nearly three years traveling, and I was finally ready to set up a more permanent camp back in Sydney. I was so very fortunate to be able to afford what Karen called our "midlife retirement," but I was getting a bit restless. It was hard to admit, but I needed to get back to some kind of meaningful work that offered a sense of purpose.

I took a job at an antique shop that was within walking distance of my house. It had been over a decade since I'd worked nine to five. The rhythm of it felt good . . . for a while. Each day I'd come home, tired from moving furniture for hours on end, happy to take the aches and pains as a sign of usefulness. As an added benefit, getting amongst the workforce helped complete my assimilation into the Aussie culture.

I loved the Aussie bush. I was a pro at cooking snags (sausages) on the barbie (BBQ grill). I fell so in love with Aussie cricket (the sport, not the insect) that my friends affectionately called me a "cricket tragic," a term reserved for only the most diehard of fans.

And my Yankee twang had softened. After much teasing from friends, I realized that I'd started calling bananas, bah-

NAH-nas, and that was it. The only thing left was to seal the deal and finalize my Australian citizenship.

Clocking in, clocking out. Life wasn't exciting, but it was good.

One day, I got an email from my mom. She was excited about the fact that I was releasing a new record. I had no earthly clue what she was talking about. I went to the Internet to see what she could have possibly meant.

It turns out that Gotee released what I call a *posthumous* album of my live performances from the Back 40 Tour of years gone by. I had been off the grid for so long that no one had even bothered to get hold of me to let me know about it. I wasn't ready to call anyone back in Nashville, so I downloaded it from iTunes to have a listen.

I had all but forgotten that I had ever sung a note. Normally, I hated listening to my own records after they were finished, but I'd never heard anything but rough board tapes of my live shows, so I was curious as to how it had all come out.

Karen found me at my desk, headphones on, crying as though someone had died. I could barely speak. Tears streaming down my face, I pulled the headphones out of the jack and let the music spill out into the air.

"It's good." I trembled. I didn't want it to be. I needed it not to be.

She listened quietly for a while, reminiscing. "It is," she agreed. "Why aren't you doing that anymore?"

"I don't know." I was too dizzy to remember, but something in me sparked.

Not long after that, I had walked into a scene at work that would add fuel to fire. One morning I found my co-workers gathered around the front-desk computer, grinning and nodding their heads in an odd synchronized fashion. I could hear the faint sound of music that sounded strangely familiar. When they saw me, they all started to giggle.

"What are you guys on about?" I asked and walked around to face the computer screen.

To my horror, they were watching YouTube clips . . . of me! My face was red with embarrassment. "Stop it! Stop!" I scrambled, trying to take control of the mouse, but I was blocked.

"Why are you embarrassed? You're good," one of them said with sincerity and surprise. It wasn't exactly a secret that I had a career once upon a time back in America. Humiliatingly enough, I had little more to put on my résumé when I had applied for my job. Now, it was coming back to haunt me.

"What on earth are you doing here? Why aren't you playing?" The lot of them stood there looking at me like I was a complete idiot.

By now, I had my story down pat. As if by rote, I gave them my usual spiel about how I had drunk the American Christian kid Kool-Aid for a while, that I sang about it, and, now, had outgrown it and gotten on with my life.

"Yeah, but you're good."

"Play normal music, then," they all piped and interjected.

"Even if I did go back," I explained, "it'd probably be too hard to get fans when people figure out I'm gay,"

"Yeah, I dunno mate, seems like an excuse to me."

I was fooling myself trying to make it seem like the years I had spent putting my heart and soul into music was frivolous. Few were buying it, least of all me. No matter how far I ran away, no matter how I tried to paint a picture to myself or my new

Aussie friends that my former career was a just a fun, idle little adventure of the past, I could never shake the feeling that I was avoiding what I knew I was made to do. Maybe being a Christian rock star wasn't ultimately the best fit for me, but the voice inside me that longed to create and connect through music had never eased up. There was no measure of distance I could put between myself and the calling to sing that seemed sufficient enough to render it silent. It started to become clear to me that it was a lie for me to say that I didn't want to do it anymore. The drive was in me. I had made work of denying it for nearly five years by insisting that I wasn't interested, when the truth was that I had lost my courage.

I had lost the courage to be myself.

Whether it was music or even my faith, these things were a part of me, even if I didn't have clarity as to what to do with them. Whether I liked it or not, I lacked the fortitude to admit aloud that both had added to my own life's journey and made me the person I am.

I could talk all I wanted about how I was traveling the world in search of peace and personal understanding, but my Aussie friends consistently called my bluff when I made excuses as to why I wasn't practicing my god-given talent of being a musician. I didn't have to be great, but I owed it to the gift to at least try.

The joy of the collective Australian personality is the strong adherence to the social contract of giving everyone a reasonable right to have a *fair go*. You can be all manner of crazy, spiritual, intellectual, or godless. Gay, straight, Christian, Greek, Muslim, Yankee, a circus performer or a janitor. It shouldn't matter; no one person is better than another. Each individual is released to dream, achieve, and inspire. The personal challenge to each citizen who calls themselves Australian is to honor the privilege of making another's path as wide and peaceful as you imagine for yourself. So long as you are *fair dinkum,* honest and true in your personal integrity, no matter how nuts someone else thinks you may be (and if you are, you'll usually hear about it!), it is this social contract that helps define the intrepid Australian spirit. In many ways, to make excuses, to fail to try, is practically an insult to the very idea that all things are possible.

It took me a while to break the habit of letting my confused experience in the Christian music industry turn into a condemning judgment of my entire life. I wanted to erase my faith. Erase my talents. But I couldn't. These things were, are, a part of me. I was still doing my best to excise them through avoidance and minimization tactics, but they kept coming back, demanding to be recognized in moments that seemed like orchestrated interventions.

One such intervention took place in the office of Dr. Petros.

Dr. P. is a plastic surgeon I met in Sydney, who was supposed to remove a couple of potentially troublesome moles that had developed on my face. (Due to the weakened ozone layer over Australia and resulting potent nature of UV rays that sun-drench the country, skin cancer prevention is among the routine health concerns that every Aussie takes seriously.)

The architecture and design of Dr. P.'s clinic spoke volumes about how he viewed the world. The decor of his clinic had a clean, European feel. Every inch of the modern, fashionable interior design smacked of erudite perfectionism. His walls were decorated with photographs of beautiful, pristine faces of serious, steely-eyed models. Next to them, with surprisingly seamless continuity, images along the lines of Frank Lloyd Wright, Rolex, and

Bentley. Stepping into his faultless, sterile clinic made me feel like a thick and uninspiring Kansas girl. A fat, bumbling accident of nature that needed thinner thighs, bigger tits, and a better nose. I couldn't help but feel shockingly imperfect in this place. What did it say about my weak attempts to be vain by removing a couple of pin-point moles, when it was obvious only a complete overhaul would help such a sorry physical specimen?

Like so much of my Australian experience, I took comfort in my anonymity. He was to have no idea that I was a fat, aging version of a Christian superstar from America. I was just a chubby Yankee who wanted to excise a few moles before the inevitable black witch hairs started poking out. Judging by the office decor, this would be the least he could do to help me avoid the pitfalls of aging. And, who knew, maybe it was my gateway to a breast enhancement?

When I first sat down in front of his scrupulously arranged architect's desk, he grabbed my file, leaned back in his chair, and began scratching thoughtfully behind his ear.

"Jennifer Knapp?" He questioned as if I wasn't in the room. "Jennifer Knapp." Like a mystery he needed to unravel, he looked up at me and repeated my name again. "Why do I know that name? This is an unusual name for Australia. Why do I know this name?"

It had been years since anyone had treated me with any sort of recognition, so I was just as mystified as he was. Why on earth would he be so interested in what my parents named me?

"I don't know," I shrugged, clueless, "I'm just me." All I could think about was how fat and unkempt I must be compared to his typical clientele. I wanted him to pluck off my ugly moles and get out of there before he started critiquing my lumpy thighs.

"No. No . . ." he mused. "I know your name. You've done something. What are you? I've heard of you somewhere."

It finally dawned on me, but I hoped I was just being presumptuous.. *Oh God,* I thought. My face felt like it was filling with the blood of embarrassment. *Please . . . don't figure it out.* I wanted to be anonymous, especially here, in his perfectly manicured world.

"You're a musician aren't you? I've heard of you." He was politely triumphant, but was still trying to place me.

Finally, I confessed to my Christian music career.

"That's it! Yes! You had a record . . ."

"*Kansas?* The red one?" I felt defeated, reminded of the fact that this part of my history would never die.

"No, it was pale green?" he launched himself into reminiscence again. "You had long, Indian-straight hair . . . *A Little More* or something?" He named one of the songs off of the *Lay It Down* record and knew that he had pinned me down.

I had only done a few shows in Australia, and years ago at that. I asked how on earth he would even know of it.

He went on to tell me about his life growing up in a devoutly Greek orthodox family. The private schooling, the assumptions that he would carry on his family's religion, his own atheism, but strong appreciation for the beauty of faith.

I tried to keep him at bay. I didn't want to let him latch on to some perspective of me that represented what I wanted to leave behind. I kept minimizing my art, my contribution to the world, with every sincere recollection he offered of my work. I had more than grown embarrassed about what people assumed my spiritual identity was, even more so in Australia, where proclaiming that one is a Christian is tantamount to many as saying, "I'm a religious nut job." I wanted the conversation to go to my moles, to my thighs, to my less than average-sized tits, anything, except for this conversation about the past. But he kept moving forward.

As I listened to him continue on, I began to realize his interest in the conversation wasn't about me. He was actually telling me the story of his life. While I was busy internally processing my own ego, I was missing out on his account of his own history. In recalling the music, he placed himself back in his own journey, his own experience with faith, and was sitting here treating me to an account that was appreciative, contemplative, and far from the bitterness that I had come to frame my own experience.

He didn't know it, but he was schooling me. I was feeling a sense of conviction, being caught out as arrogant. For so long, I had seen the music as something for which I was wholly responsible. I hadn't accounted for the role that music takes on outside the creator. He went on remembering how the music reminded him of his Orthodox school days, the soundtrack of his life, how he would be in a band or two and play music in and around his church. The music that he heard, adopted, and created, was a part of his life's fabric. It had nothing to do with my person. He wasn't thinking about how I, as another person, had impacted his life, but rather, was telling me about where what I had created had fit into his own.

I sat there, stunned. For the first time in a very long time, I wasn't entirely ashamed. He took ownership of his faith experience. He was appreciative of my perspective and my art, but in no way made me the creator or instigator of his own journey with Christianity.

My mind went from chanting the hopeful mantra of *mole, mole, mole, please* to gradually joining in the first of many restorative conversations I would be afforded to process what I had experienced.

At some point, I blurted out my embarrassment of my history. I downplayed my faith to him, as I had done to so many other of my Australian friends, as if it were a phase. He would have none of it.

"Why would you be embarrassed? What you did was good. The music was good. You weren't cheesy. It seemed honest. Were you honest?"

It was a genuinely probing question, the kind that is meant to discover something unknown about another. It wasn't a setup, I was free to answer truthfully and felt I had no other option but to be honest.

"Yes. It was a season . . . and I gave my all. I wrote about my faith and my experience as a Christian. But I had to walk away from it," I found myself lamenting, "I was getting to the point where I didn't feel that I could be myself." Apparently my plastic surgeon was becoming my therapist as well.

Again, scratching behind his ear with meditation. "If you've done your work to the best of your ability, then you have no reason to be ashamed."

In that moment, he uncorked the years of torment I had attempted to bottle up inside. In my mind raced a thousand thoughts and sermons that I had failed to live up to. He made it all sound so reasonable and easy, essentially, "All you can do is be your honest best."

But I had. I had done my best, and it wasn't good enough. I doubted, I pined, I prayed, and I was still me. I was a gay woman, inspired by Jesus in ways beyond my ability to communicate, who failed to live up to the expectations of all that a Christian was supposed to agree with, believe in, and reenact. I was certain I could no longer be the standard-bearer of an institutionalized religion, but I couldn't escape the fact that my faith seeped into my art.

Somehow, we were talking about the career I was trying to leave behind. I grew frustrated and tried to turn the tables to him. Internally agitated, I asked, "What about you? You're a plastic surgeon. Your whole career is about making things perfect." I gestured to the trappings of subjective perfection that surrounded us.

I suppose he could have rightfully taken my question as an affront. I was flat-out judging him. All I thought a plastic surgeon wanted was to make people into his idea of perfection. I imagined that he was probably judging my B cup as inadequate in some way, even then. How could this man talk to me about appreciating one's best efforts and gifts when his entire world seemed built around changing anything deemed less than perfectly beautiful? His world made me feel stupid and poorly made. Another way to fail. I understood his idea of trying to be significant in the world, but I certainly wasn't seeing it through the lens of plastic surgery.

"Let me show you something," he motioned for me to come around to his side of the desk and look at his computer. In an unexpected move of intimate hospitality, I sat next to this stranger, elbow to elbow, as he proceeded to show me his heart.

On the screen, he pulled up a particularly gory slideshow of disfigured faces. I don't know if he thought I was capable of handling such gruesome pictures, or if he was in some way disregarding their shock to my system as a form of punishment for my not-so-veiled judgmental inquisition.

"Here." He pulled up a photo of an outback sheep farmer whose entire nose had been forcefully smashed and rearranged to the lower side of his jaw. Dr. Petros explained that the man had nearly died when an iron gate had slammed into his face. Truthfully, this before photo was an image of a man who was hardly recognizable as a human being. Of course, this man needed to get back into the form of humanity that made him somewhat socially approachable, but it was more than that; his nose was no longer a working nose. He couldn't even use it to breathe unless Dr. P. helped him surgically. It was hard to imagine anyone being able to recover from the state that I saw, but then Dr. P. showed me the after photo.

I could feel his humble sense of satisfaction. It wasn't arrogance; it was a profound sense of gratitude that he had used his hands and his skill to change that man's life. I couldn't help but share in his sense of amazement. The sheep farmer was a new man; he had his life back.

And so it was, picture after picture, of before-and-after photos whereby empathy forced me to recognize the challenge that many of these faced without the vision, skill, and passion of Dr. Petros. Not once did he brag about himself, nor did he present this display in a prideful manner. After nearly a mesmerizing half an hour, he closed down the screen, and simply and quietly said, "That's what I get to do. And I love it."

He was full. Not as a puffed-up man whose coffers were amply filled, thanks to the misery of others, but rather as a man comforted by the irony of living in a confusing world, that maybe, just maybe, he had something to give others that would help them in this life.

I exhaled a peaceful, "Wow."

"Now," he said, renewed and on task, "Let's have a look at those moles . . ."

I had never felt such misplaced arrogance and vanity in all my life. It was starting to feel like there was a not-so-silent conspiracy happening around me that was forcing me to contend with the reality that I was missing my true calling. The hits kept coming.

All of a sudden, it seemed like half of America's touring artists had inundated Sydney. Bonnie Raitt came through. Kelli Clarkson was on a tear. Ani DiFranco was making the rounds through some of the best songwriter festivals and winery venues. It was like I was waking up and I was surrounded by musicians. Lady Gaga was bouncing around the streets in her underwear and making all the papers, while some poppy chick named Katy Perry was making the airwaves singing some upbeat song about kissing girls and liking it. I tried to block them all out, as my thoughts began to join in the litany of others' questions.

Why, exactly, am I not singing anymore?

One day I turned on the telly and I got the shock of my life. There, in living color, was the adult version of the young girl I had hoped to mentor back in the days of Alabaster Arts.

"Oh, my God, Karen, come over here, look. That's little Katy Hudson!"

"Get out!" she said, as she came closer. The shoe had finally dropped. Katy Hudson had changed her name to Katy Perry, died her blonde hair black, harnessed her boobs into a perky short dress, and taken the world by storm.

Once upon a time, the feelings that would have washed over me would have been laden with guilt and shame, but what was happening now was unfamiliar and new. I wasn't sad, or embarrassed. What I felt wasn't grief. It took me a minute to put my finger on what I was feeling.

As the music played on and Katy strapped on her dainty Taylor guitar, it hit me. I was jealous! Mad, angry, climb-the-walls, stir-crazy jealous!

It came to me in a rush of adrenaline-fueled rage.

Your whole life you've always had music! My thoughts barked and howled.

You are the only one keeping it from happening!

It's your gift!

Use it! Use it!

My eyes grew wet with tears. "I used to do that," I said plaintively to Karen.

A pregnant pause, then she offered, "You still can."

Through all my anger, all my tears, all of my self-loathing attempts to sabotage my own gifts, Karen never gave up on me. She had waded through years of silence, arguments, torment, excuses, and frustration propelled by the fleeting hope that, one day, I would return to the music that had fueled my soul. I had obsessed for so long about my own fate that it had never even occurred to me how sustaining her hope had been.

I began to soften.

I finally dusted off my old Taylor 810, twisted her knobs back into tune, and tempted myself to sing for the first time in what seemed a thousand years. I began to write. It was slow and awkward at first, but it was familiar. Like the old days, I'd wander around the house, guitar strapped on, singing this song and that. I let my voice open up and lead me, stringing nonsense words together until they formed a thought complete enough that I could chase it.

It was uncoordinated and cumbersome at first. My calluses held only a sliver of their former protective strength. My throat was weak and scratchy. I would fight my mind more than my body.

At times, the voices of the past would creep into fits of borderline schizophrenia.

You'll never do this again.

God will smite you.

You suck.

I fought them.

I will.

Let him.

I don't.

There were days where the exercises where less musical and more therapeutic sessions of reparative psychology. For every negative thought that entered my mind, for every good reason that I had to not proceed, I used my strength to counter with a positive reply. I took the idea of performing again off the table, trying to convince myself that all I was doing was just getting back to playing again for my own personal good.

I had joy in my life. Love. Energy. Hope. I couldn't pretend anymore that I had nothing to sing about.

Music was the gift of my life, the one thing that had given me courage, peace, and purpose. I didn't have to make a job of it; I just needed to sing again. Who cared what came of breaking out the guitar and writing a song or two? For the moment, all I had to do was let it fly.

Before I knew it, I had a decent handful of new songs. A door began to creak open, rusty though the hinges were. Maybe, just maybe, I could perform again?

With my partner's encouragement, I quit my job and dedicated three months to setting up a small home studio, writing, and recording a demo. I couldn't imagine where this was going to lead. If my mind wandered too far ahead, I got nervous and was taunted by the fear of failure. I had to block it all out and for now, simply play.

There were so many unknowable questions that challenged any hope for a comeback.

Would there be any interest? An audience?

What about being gay? Will it kill my chances?

Can a former Christian artist even have a mainstream career?

All those questions had to be put to the side. I put up a self-preserving curtain between me and any hoped-for future, dedicating my endeavor as a Christmas gift meant for my family. My Grandpa Gray had always said that he wanted me to make him a recording of just voice and guitar, and now was my chance to honor him. I had written a song for him many years ago that had never made a record. I had never dared play it for him, but now, I was finding that I finally had the courage to share it. The modest goal kept me focused and I completed the task in time to send it out for the holidays.

My family wasn't the only ones to receive it. I mailed a copy to a Nashville manager friend of mine, Mitchell Solarek. I put the CD in a plain envelope and stuck a Post-it Note to it, with the simple question: "Do these suck?"

His response was: "No. Get back to Nashville."

twenty-two

$\mathcal{J}$ had no idea what to expect when I returned to Nashville, either professionally or socially. For the first time, in a very, very long time, I was excited about the idea of returning to the music profession, but there was a lot that scared me.

Professionally, there was no guarantee that I'd have a career after a seven-year layoff. I didn't have any interest in returning to CCM, and the reality was that outside the Christian music industry, I was relatively unknown. Despite the years of experience and over a million records floating around the world with my name on them, I was essentially coming back as a new artist.

I was energized and ready to take on the career challenge, but as a real-life human being, I was freaked about how people were going to react once they found out I was gay. All those years ago, I had left Nashville under a shroud of darkness, unable to cope with what to do with my faith and terrified by the potential public shaming I'd receive if people knew I had fallen in love with a woman. I left many friends without saying so much as a goodbye. To many, I had simply vanished.

I was hoping that my seven-year absence would help me slide into town under the radar for a couple of reasons. The most obvious, of course, were the concerns I had about how gayness might affect my future, but it was more than that. All the questions I seemed sure to face were deeply personal, and I wasn't certain how I was going to handle it.

Coming back was scary because it meant that I had to face my fear of failure. When I had left CCM all those years ago, I left defeated. I had never felt fully embraced or comfortable amongst the paragons of Christian culture. I never felt like I adequately lived up to the expectations of what it meant to be the so-called right kind of Christian. I truly believed that I didn't deserve to have the career that I had. Spiritually, I left feeling like a charlatan. I was supposed to be a role model of the faithful Christian woman, but I couldn't do it. What was worse was that I didn't *want* to do it. Then, to complicate matters, I fell in love with a woman. Even according to my mentors, I'd failed to honor the best of God's plans for me.

I suppose I had underestimated the length of the shadow cast by my CCM career, because part of me hoped I could erase it as though it never happened. I didn't realize it until I started plugging back in, but to the wider public, my absence actually took on a CCM cultural buzz. For the last several years, social media had been trying to solve the mystery of my supposed disappearance.

It's both hilarious and heartbreaking to see how the Internet has evolved into the thing that lets you eavesdrop on the people talking behind your back. What's even crazier is how some people think everything on the Internet is true.

Facebook, Twitter, MySpace, and Wikipedia . . . When I finally dared to log on, I was blown away how so many strangers were writing the so-called facts about my life that they couldn't possibly have known. I was so off the grid that only my family knew where I was.

Over the years, my mother periodically would receive calls from complete strangers who sought to get the lowdown. Despite the fact that I had spent the entire last year of my Christian career telling everyone who would listen, print, and record it, that I was retiring to a private life, there were those who ignored that request. Unable to find me, a few sorry souls invaded my family's privacy by pushing them to reveal my fate. My mom told me how one time she'd had to hang up on a persistent woman who called her place of business, telling her that God had a message for me and demanded to pray with her on the phone. "Let her be," Mom said, and hung up. Without my having to ask, Mom guarded my privacy as if it was her own but, eventually, I was going to have to face what I had long tried to avoid.

There were so many interesting, highly detailed versions of my cyberlife that I wondered if I were the doppelganger of the so-called real Jennifer Knapp. Some reported that I had gotten married and had babies. There was one account that I had throat cancer and had to retire. There were threads that reported sighting me living a quiet life in Seattle, and a few swore that I was dead. The most gut-wrenching was the widely held conspiracy theory that I was forcibly ousted from CCM because I had been discovered to be gay.

What bothered me about all the ugly whispers and gossip wasn't the inescapable truth of my sexual orientation, but rather, how so many Christians chose to speak so cavalierly about a real person they knew nothing about.

"I know Jennifer and she would never be gay. She's a true woman of God."

"Everybody knows you can't be gay and Christian. If she is, then

I'm burning every record of hers I own. The Holy Spirit cannot dwell in a person who chooses sin."

I wondered sometimes if the people who wrote those things realized that I would end up reading them.

It hurt. As if it were only fitting that a gay person recuse themselves from the faith community due to the obvious disgrace of being gay. I couldn't deny being gay, but I wasn't a disgrace. I wouldn't have come back to Nashville if I had anything I wasn't ready to be held accountable for. Yet, at the same time, I wondered what the right thing to do was. Should I or should I not talk about being gay?

The hurt part of me wanted to shame those who spread rumors without true knowledge. Part of me wished that I weren't gay just to embarrass the know-it-alls who filled themselves with pride over information that wasn't theirs to relate. Daydreaming of it helped for a moment, but it wasn't lasting or reflective of the honor I had for my partner. No matter how things played out, I knew I couldn't lie about being gay. I didn't have a closet to run to. I had family (on two continents) that knew who I was, and a partner, and every single friend that I kept in touch with knew it. I wasn't prepared to change my life just so I could keep a secret.

The irony was that I was living with more integrity outside of CCM and Christian culture than I had been when I was immersed in it. Apart from my woeful conversation with mentors Rolly and Sandy, I had never lied about what I believed, who I hoped to be, or who I was. It's true, I definitely learned to kept my differences to myself, but I did my very best to live faithfully as a Christian. I aspired to lead well and with honor, but there's only so much that is appropriate to share in public spaces. When

I couldn't talk about the things that were private, I struggled under the weight of feeling ungenuine.

It was like being on stage, or how you don't walk the same when you're aware that you're being watched. All of a sudden, you start thinking about it and getting confused as to how your arms swing naturally at your side. You're overly aware that everyone is watching and it's hard to be your honest, free-flowing self. Away from the spotlight, I was more relaxed and less self-conscious. I wasn't constantly assessing my every movement and motivation. I decided to just live.

I lived openly, and it was good for my soul. I didn't spend time hiding my sexual orientation. I didn't advertise it either. It wasn't like I walked into every new room and introduced myself saying "Hi! I'm Jennifer and I'm a lesbian." If it came up, great. If not, then, I let it ride. I was just me.

It was the same with my faith. I didn't hide my faith, but I didn't dodge it, and I stopped trying to manufacture an outward appearance for the sake of others. I didn't make a conscious decision to *be* Christian. I tried to live out my faith as though I were walking alone and no one was watching. What ever my faith was, it was.

The thing was, I was getting back to the stage, and the spotlight was starting to heat up. Word spread fast that I was back in the studio. We were getting calls from Christian retailers and radio stations asking when to expect a release, on the assumption that I was, of course, going to sing for Jesus. Churches began to queue up, requesting that I return to perform all their favorite, faith-inspiring songs. The mounting fervor left me with that unwanted, yet familiar, tension of failing Christian expectations. People were excited about my return, but at the same time, spoke with a familiar nervousness, alluding to, but never fully daring enough to ask me the million-dollar question: *Are you gay?* In front of my face, everyone smiled, but when I turned, speculative whispers tickled the back of my neck like a zephyr.

What was I to do with the swirling vortex of gossip? It was a quandary yet to sort itself out. Did I proceed with my life as usual, as if there was nothing at all unusual about me? Or did I need to announce "Lesbian rock star! At your service!" every time I took the stage? Sarcasm aside, it was important to me to take time to consider what might be the reasonable course of action in being forthright.

Rather than speculate or force the issue, I decided to take things one step at a time. I had a lot on my plate in preparing for public life again. I hadn't performed in public in nearly a decade. My musical muscle memory was still there, but my calluses were microscopic. My vocal chords were weak and needed practice to strengthen. I had to finish writing and recording a new record. I had to figure out a business plan. I was also going to have to figure out how I was going to handle the Christians. I wasn't going to back to CCM, but my faith was a part of who I was, and I wanted to reconnect with the fans that were willing to come with me.

To get back in touch, I was going to have to knock on a few church doors.

To say that I was scared of the church is an understatement. I was terrified.

First, did I mention that I'm gay?

I knew what Christians thought of and did to gay people. Gays get pulled aside, special prayers "of concern" are said, and if you're not careful, you get carted up to the front of the sanctuary and sweaty hands are laid upon you to cast out the demons.

All I had ever seen, known, been preached to, warned, and instructed echoed that gay is *wrong.* I'm not talking a little off the beaten path or unconventional—we're talking corruption of the soul. Good, God-fearing Christians are supposed to struggle against homosexuality and feel the turmoil of the Holy Spirit. As a woman, I was supposed to want to pray it away, change, be straight, submit to a man, and have babies.

I was afraid because, the truth of it was, I didn't want any of that. I didn't struggle to accept my sexual orientation, I struggled against the embarrassment that my nature was not what others insisted it should have been. In fact, it wasn't until I met my proper soul mate that sacred love even began to make sense. All of a sudden the fear of my own body, sex, and love came into alignment. I wasn't ashamed or suspicious of love; I welcomed it. The idea of being a faithful, healthy, and loving partner didn't seem as ridiculous or impossible now that I wasn't trying to squeeze it into gender expectations. Love is sacred. Love is love. Isn't it?

I was afraid because admitting my truth meant questioning everything that I had ever been taught by my church.

I was afraid because I feared what accepting my sexual orientation said about my faith as a Christian. All I had ever heard was how bad Christians lost their so-called struggle with sin. What did it mean that I wasn't interested in fighting? What did it mean if I didn't agree?

The Christian world sat poised to judge the validity of my entire spiritual life, experience, and personal character solely based on the gender of the person that I was most attracted to, and there wasn't a thing that I could do about it but face the music.

I was scared because I was afraid that *they* might be right. I couldn't find a way to say out loud, "I am gay and I am a Christian." Because, though Christianity is the mother tongue of my spiritual life, I had only ever been told that I had to be one or the other.

I was afraid, because I knew I was gay and, by that measure alone, I believed that I was no longer allowed to claim my Christian faith.

I was scared because I thought *they* had the authority to say so. Who was I to say otherwise?

It was so hard, because coming back to Nashville was drumming up my old personal, religious turmoil again. I was desperate to find a way to create some space for what was really true about my journey, but I didn't yet have the words to describe it.

I just knew I wanted back on the horse. I wanted to play, but I simply wasn't ready to make a theological defense of my existence. I knew that I was finished with the Christian rock thing, but I also knew that I was offended at the idea that my sexual orientation was the reason that I wasn't there anymore. It just wasn't true. I wanted to believe that if I was inclined to sing Christian music again, I would have done so regardless of being gay. I still secretly wondered if something in me had broken, because I didn't want to.

I had to keep reminding myself to focus and not be distracted. I was back because I was a musician, same as I ever was. Independent of my faith and sexual orientation, I wanted to sing, and that was it.

I wanted it to be clear that it wasn't altering my course from

CCM because I was gay. I wanted my intentions as an artist to be understood, and I wanted to be transparent in that what I hoped to achieve as a career songwriter lay beyond that world. My aspirations were not to just write songs about my faith; I wanted to write about everything. All of life's simultaneous beauty and brokenness. I wanted to be able to end a story in defeat if the narrative called for it. To be free to lose hope for at least three minutes of unredeemed free-falling. If Jesus were to ever inspire a lyric again, He'd have to hold his own without the predictable clichés.

I didn't want to speak ill of my past musical life, but I really needed to move on. I didn't just need to change my environment; I needed to change my language, too. The person who was returning was not capable of living in that place or speaking with that voice any more.

It was difficult to watch as people's faces went from smiling to gloomy, once I confessed that my return was not the prodigal tale they imagined. It was my first round of experiencing the disappointment aimed at my spiritual character. I didn't want to sing about Jesus anymore, and that made me suspect to some.

I did several interviews with Christian journalists who sought to make sense of my departure and return. Reporter after reporter stuttered and stammered on the other end of the line, asking every question under the sun, probing to ascertain if anything legitimate remained of my faith, but when they would reach the moment where they had the opportunity to ask about my sexual orientation, no one was able to pull the trigger and ask me plainly. On more than one occasion, I was reminded that there were many rumors surrounding why I had left CCM. I always acknowledged that I was aware of speculations, but I offered no confessions. It was important to me that people understood the one thing I had left to say to a Christian audience—that I couldn't work in a world where I felt pressure to be anything other than myself. I couldn't believe that no one asked me what self I needed to be! I thought I was throwing the door *wide* open, but not once did anyone actually ask me to clarify whether I was gay.

One of the CCM journalists printed that I had purposefully lied to him when I failed to offer a confession without a direct question to the effect. I was livid when Jesus R. Murrow reckoned it any business of his, or anyone else's for that matter, to expect me to reveal personal information, if he wasn't brave enough to ask the question in the first place. I'm not saying that I'm proud of that attitude, but therein lies the rub.

Is it anybody's business to ask something so deeply personal about someone else? When is it appropriate or necessary for me to disclose intimate details about my private life to a complete stranger? What difference does it make to my calling as a musician to reveal what genders I do and don't find sexually attractive? By not publicizing the truth about my sexual orientation, was I complicit to a conspiracy that implies being gay is in any way something to be ashamed about? What should it matter whether I was in or out? Was there truly a need to declare such things so publicly?

I wanted to know if there were answers to those questions, but I had to live it out to start learning.

It bothered me when that reporter called me a liar. I didn't lie. I didn't feel too great about taking advantage of his lack of skill either, but if he imagined using me to advance his own career, I figured he should at least have to work for it and ask the direct question.

Here we all were, hemming and hawing, like we didn't know the score. I wasn't ashamed of who I was, so why didn't I just say it? We both knew that Christianity, as a religious and corporate body, struggles with homosexuality, but if he wanted to write about it, then I hoped he would ante up and face the topic head on.

My previous fears started to get pushed aside by the part of me that was itching for a good, honest fight. I was done moving sideways. If I expected people like Jesus R. Murrow to be direct with their intentions, then I needed to back it up by living up to my own expectations of honesty.

That was the thing. Honesty. The rocky road to discovering myself had nearly loosened all my screws, but the time away afforded me the space to tighten them up again. I was comfortable enough in my own skin to be frank about what I saw. I knew that choosing to be honest had the potential to cost me a livelihood, but I wasn't going backward and having it cost me a life. It was a hard path, but it was good to learn: I am me and I am not ashamed. Why should I keep that bottled up inside?

I couldn't.

When I am set free, when I am myself, the truth of it shows up in my music. There have been times when I wished that I could hide it, but I've never been able to. The passions of my heart have always spun themselves into the fabric of the music. The God I see, the God that captures my amazement and imagination, always shows up. The God I doubt, the God I fear, heckles me and dares me to reach for a light in the darkness. The people I love, the dreams I dream, the person I am, has always flowered most in the fertile soil of truth.

I had hidden away for too long, fought too hard to find

peace with my own person to give up by going back to a place that was less than honest. All I have ever wanted is to create a safe space for people to find a pathway to hope. Murrow had at least one point that I began to appreciate. Right or wrong, the Christians that had supported my music career, those who still called themselves fans, wanted to know if I was still the same kind of soul-searching person that they had once known. Now, they were about to find out.

By the spring of 2010, the loose plan started to take shape. In March, I'd start touring nationally. In April, I'd do some interviews during which I specifically discussed my sexuality. Then, in May, we'd release *Letting Go*. My first record in nearly a decade.

My first tour back was going to be a three-month stretch with a rabble-rousing, fringe Christian artist named Derek Webb. I wasn't all that keen on the idea in the beginning. I really wanted to get away from the CCM scene, but Derek insisted that we get together and chat about it over coffee. He emailed me a copy of his latest record, *Stockholm Syndrome*, and said I should give the idea a chance before I blew him off.

I didn't know it, but Derek was getting in some hot water for openly encouraging Christians to rethink their religious bias toward LGBT people. In particular, he wrote a song to none other than Fred Phelps of Westboro Baptist infamy to get his point across:

> *How could you do this to me*
> *How could you tell me you love me when you hate me*
> *Freddie, please*
>
> —Derek Webb, "Freddie, Please," *Stockholm Syndrome*

I found it interesting that Derek didn't seem to be angling for me to make any confessions. It was unusual for most of my conversations at the time. He didn't ask me if I were gay. He didn't ask me to explain how I could call myself a Christian. We just sat down and started talking. We talked about what our experiences had been like in CCM. We talked about music and our faith. But, mostly, he wanted to welcome me back to the life of an artist.

He encouraged me to remember that many of our fans were cut from the same cloth and that I didn't need to be afraid to be myself. He wanted me to know that he was a friend who wanted to help me reconnect.

Derek's gesture was a genuine invitation unlike any I had received in my career. He was offering his hard-earned platform for me to get back on my feet. We really didn't know each other that well. He didn't owe me anything, yet there he was, standing up as a Christian man in Nashville, a known CCM artist, willing to put his reputation on the line to do his part in helping a fellow artist and friend succeed.

I could hardly believe that a person could do such a thing without ulterior motives. I kept waiting for the other shoe to drop, for something bad to happen, or for Derek to pull out. Instead, in the lead-up to the tour, we found ourselves jostling over who was going to open the show. Normally, artists fight to be the closing act, but Derek and I argued that the other should take it.

I said that I hadn't done a tour in years and there was no reason for me to close the night. Not only did I fear I lacked the stamina to play a closing set, I worried that audiences would be disappointed if Derek wasn't treated as the main attraction. I didn't think I was a strong enough artist to warrant the arrangement. Derek disagreed all the way to sound check of our first show.

"Yeah," he said with an easy grin, "I think it's better that I open." With that, he finished his sound check and the order was settled. He played his set and I sat in the dressing room chewing at my fingernails, imagining the whole time that the audience was going to walk out after Derek had finished.

I don't remember the city of our first show. I just remember the picture of walking out onto the stage, my knees a little wobbly, the stage bright, the room dark. My name was announced and, as usual, the applause started as I walked to the center and put on my guitar.

When I looked up, I realized that this was no ordinary welcome. The crowd was on their feet, clapping and cheering with electric enthusiasm. I stepped up to the mic to say "Thank you," to quiet the crowd so that I could start, but the crowd wouldn't stop. They kept cheering and cheering. Before I could sing a single note, the room had risen to a standing ovation to welcome me back. I tried to quiet them, but they wouldn't be denied. It went on longer than any applause I can ever remember receiving. I tried several times to get on with things, but still they made me stand there and accept their appreciation.

Part of me didn't want such a big deal to be made because, when I finally allowed myself to take in the extraordinary scene, my eyes welled up with tears and my throat tightened to the point that I feared I wouldn't be able to sing at all. The raucous reception continued until the crowd knew I had fully received it. I had to put my hands over my face to try to keep all the emotions from spilling out.

After so many years of self-imposed silence, after years of

thinking I had no more music to offer nor any good thing to give back to the world, I found myself in a room full of people who seemed to acknowledge that I had returned from a very dark place and survived.

It was humbling. To receive their support was a privilege and an honor. I was so overwhelmed that they invited me back to do such a seemingly simple, yet life-giving, thing. They asked me to sing. It was the one thing that I feared I might never be given the chance to do again and it was theirs, for the moment, to make possible.

Though the news of my sexual orientation had yet to be confirmed, it was clear to many that I was not the same artist that had left those years ago. I had done several interviews in which I spoke about why I was moving on from Christian music, and even tried to talk a bit about how my faith was evolving. I could talk about my CCM burnout and my experience with Christian culture with relative ease, but when asked about what my spiritual evolution was *exactly*, I found myself tongue-tied as to how to respond. It was true, I had stopped going to church entirely (a news item I was careful to omit), but I had never stopped contemplating my spiritual life. The truth was, I had shifted away from the Evangelical Christian theology and practice, but I was terrified to talk about my specific personal views in public. Simply leaving the Evangelical tradition was grounds enough for the Christians who raised me to say I wasn't Christian anymore. But gay? Everything that I had ever been taught said that was a deal-breaker.

One might argue that I had lost my religion, but no one could take away my faith. I struggled (and still do) with the language of how to express the inner, holy, transformative experience

I had when I decided to follow Jesus. This kind of following is an act of *faith* that is different from *belief*. *Beliefs* are the certainties you're encouraged to hold *about* Jesus so that you can stay a voting member in your church (orthodoxy, according to Harvey Cox in *The Future of Faith*), but faith is the thing that changes the human heart.

When I saw *that* Jesus, I wanted to be like Him. Loving. Created. Good. Mindful. Open to the miraculous. Forgiving. Giving. Gracious. Loved. Compassionate. The day that I opened my heart to the invitation to accept, receive, give, and honor those sacred, holy things was the day that my life changed forever.

How could I ever have imagined how that one spiritual experience could have led me on such an odyssey? I had always tried to follow. I had always tried to listen. Now I was back in America, back on the road, and back on the firing line.

On stage, I didn't say much about Christianity. I was happy to play a few of the old songs, but mostly, I needed to get onto the new stuff. By the end of my set, you could feel people leaning in, urging me on to tell my secrets, if I had any, or explain more, but I kept mostly to the music and expressions of gratitude.

After the show, the pressure of our weighty reunion continued to build. I barely played for an hour on stage, but the conversations with folks after would go on for even longer.

I listened to story after story of how others had made journeys similar to my own. Many people talked about how they fought to keep hold of their personal spiritual experiences while others in their church insisted on judging their validity. Some were kicked out because of supposed sin, others for differing theologies, and more than enough just left because they felt like they couldn't trust their faith community to love them when the going got tough. In all, they were the collective stories of the times when we need hope, faith, and our communities most.

Some shared stories about how they had moved on from the church after nightmare divorces, others disgruntled by the way those who shared the label *Christian* simply made them embarrassed to use the term. But the most personally heartbreaking of them all were the countless number of LGBT people who told how revealing their sexual orientation had cost them so dearly.

Even those who had never had sex, and had only admitted to being same-sex attracted, were getting pushed out of their churches. Singers were getting kicked out of choirs. Teenagers were being ostracized from their youth social groups and Bible studies. In extreme cases, adults and teens alike who sought a so-called God's correction were subjected to reparative therapies and exorcisms.

On more than one occasion, I had a young adult share with me how their religious parents told them that it would be better for them to douse themselves in gasoline and light a match than to be gay.

How can that possibly be okay? What can you say to soothe that kind of suffering except to hold a person in your arms and help them grieve? The only thing I could think to do was wrap my arms around those damaged souls and whisper my own confession, "I know; I get it. I'm gay too."

It was a good start, but I wasn't saying it loudly enough.

twenty-three

As crazy and premeditated as it sounds, I had to plan and schedule my coming out. When I returned to the States and to Nashville, there was no question to those around me that I was in a same-sex relationship. It wasn't a secret so much as it was a question of just how fast the details of my private life were going to spread. There was clearly an expectation that I would come clean, but the question was, how, when, where, and to whom I could tell that story in order to tell it well and accurately.

So many reporters had expressed their interest in breaking the story to the point that it became unmanageable; so, my manager, publicist, and I decided to pick one gay, one Christian, and one mainstream media outlet for the inevitable exposure.

In March 2010, I did three interviews, one each with *The Advocate, Christianity Today,* and Reuters. They all agreed to post at the same time, so that we could attempt to control the chaos that seemed likely to ensue, but my story kept getting pushed back. Meanwhile, the tour with Derek kept moving on, the standing ovations kept coming, and the after-show talks were still heavy with the weight of what I knew I wanted but was not allowed to say. I was on lock-down, unable to openly speak anything of my own truth until the media reported it.

A whole month went by, and we were now into April. I didn't know how much longer I could keep my nonsecret from seeming like avoidance. Fortunately, the news was planned to drop that first week, but then pop icon and lust-magnet Ricky Martin came out. Unable to compete with that kind of star power, I got bumped!

As my young nephew Jarrod once said, "You're not Lady Gaga famous," speaking carefully so as not to burst my bubble, "but you *are* 'mostly' known." (This was his summation after he Googled me and found I had a better-than-average presence in the Internet universe, but was still lacking in true star power.)

I suppose the good news was that the journalists really wanted to make sure people heard the story enough to wait Ricky out. The bad news was that their hopes of national coverage hinted of the storm that was to come. Apparently, nobody wanted to miss the opportunity to watch the Christians freak out over a so-called sex scandal.

For several weeks, my story was delayed, and life went on as usual. The tour was going well, but I wondered for how long. Our audiences were strong and enthusiastic about my return, but I knew the majority were Christians. But what *kind*? Despite the clandestine conversations and even those who seemed as though they might still accept me, there was no way to know until I spoke my truth plainly.

I had taken a break from the tour to go camping for my birthday. For two weeks, my publicist kept insisting that the story would land any day now, but I had to stop waiting for the phone to ring and get on with my life. To ease my growing anxiety, I took a weekend to retreat to the quiet outdoors.

April twelfth, my birthday, was particularly beautiful. Apart from a phone text I got from my mother, the day was quiet enough to imagine that Karen and I were the only two people in the world. Nestled in a narrow valley somewhere in middle Tennessee, I was no one of any importance or consequence. I was just another flower on the hill poised to soak up the sun. The spring nights were still crisp and cool enough to forget that I had this strange alternate life somewhere back in the hustle and bustle. My phone had gone silent and I did nothing but quietly count the minutes as they slipped by.

The next day was more of the same. I was standing waist deep in the lazy waters of the Caney Fork River, trout fishing when suddenly, my phone began techno-chirping from deep in my pocket.

I hauled my fly line back to a submissive length and tucked my rod underneath my arm. Bothered by the interruption, I grumbled while I fossicked through the copious supply of vest pockets, certain that when I pulled it out I'd probably learn nothing and drop my iPhone in the river just for the trouble.

It wasn't nothing. It was a text from my management: *It's official. You're out.*

Weird. I swallowed the lump in my throat. Nothing about me had changed, and yet everything felt as though it was about to. I was officially a woman of controversy.

The river coursed around me. Downstream, a fish mocked me by flopping out of the water. It was Saturday, and all that business was a world away. Whatever lay ahead, it would be Monday before I could see it.

I put my phone back into my waterproof waders and cast another line. That was that, I thought. Career 2.0 might be over before it even started.

SO, THERE IT was. The door was now open for complete strangers to talk about my sexual preferences. Conservative Christians sounded the alarm. Internet social networks were buzzing, article comments were crashing Web pages, and sermons were being posted on YouTube directed toward me personally about the evils of homosexuality. I ignored most of the Internet junk and asked my friends and family to do the same. It was harder, however, to ignore the lines of communication that were necessary for my work. My Facebook pages, phone lines, email, and even snail mail received hundreds, if not thousands, of responses.

I got everything from "Burn in hell lesbo!" comments to gay wedding announcements.

All in all, it wasn't too bad. Most of the correspondence I received was split neatly down the national average of fifty-fifty in terms of support and disappointment. Unfortunately, almost every negative, ugly letter came from a person who made a point of identifying themselves as Christian. There were a few letters of support from people of faith, but the challenge of affirmation is that it rarely has the volume to compete with the outrage of anger and disappointment.

The inevitable crush of those concerned with supposed Christian rightness had to be made known. Christian radio stations made it a point to remove my songs from their playlists. Christian bookstore chains deleted me from their search engines. Religious leaders wrote editorial blogs, gave sermons, and encouraged faithful Christians to keep tight to the teaching that homosexuality is a sin.

The unfortunate thing is that none of it was surprising. I expected it. I had seen others judged, labeled, and discarded by those who claimed to speak for God. I did my best to brace for the impact, but nothing prepares you for the way it actually feels when it happens to you.

April fifteenth, two days after G Day, Derek and I were back on the road and performing in Tulsa, Oklahoma. I was excited to be back in the Midwest. These were my people, the same kind of folk that I grew up with, not two hours to the north. I had been looking forward to a homecoming of sorts, but I had heard that ticket sales were poor. Even worse, people were calling to cancel their tickets after they confirmed that I was gay. Our show got demoted from a ballroom venue to the smaller spillover bar area, and there was some talk of canceling the show altogether.

When it came time to do the gig, fewer than fifty people showed up. Derek on his own could draw more people than that, so I was embarrassed that he had to suffer the blow with me. It was clear that it was my fault that nobody dared to come. There were so few people there that it almost seemed silly to turn on the PA. Still, we went ahead as planned and tried to give the best show possible to those who braved the controversy.

I was grateful to those who came, but it was hard not to feel humiliated. I had traveled a long way, fueled by the encouragement that the gifts I had to offer were of value, and now it looked like being gay was a complete disqualification. I tried to keep my head up, but it was so hard to push back all the negativity that flooded in.

You'll be punished for living a life of sin. The inner voices started in.

God cannot live in a person like you.

You will lose your voice if you give into homosexuality.

I tried to fight them but, in that moment, I wept over the fear that maybe it was all true.

After a few nervous and less than spirited performances, someone from the room asked if I would sing "Martyrs & Thieves." It was one of the few songs off *Kansas* that I still felt I had enough Christian integrity to play, but that day I was afraid it was slipping away from me. I didn't feel worthy enough to sing it. I didn't want to, but there were only a few people there and it felt rude not to try.

> *There are ghosts from my past who've owned more of my soul*
> *Than I thought I had given away*
> *They linger in closets and under my bed and in pictures less*
>   *proudly displayed*
> *A great fool in my life I have been, have squandered 'til pallid*
>   *and thin*
> *Hung my head in shame and refused to take blame for the dark-*
>   *ness I know I've let win*

My voice cracked as the tears rolled down my face. Really, I was only able to sing intermittently. A few kind souls in the audience sang along to fill in what I was unable to sing. I don't remember if I managed to actually finish it. I just played and let myself remember the days when I wrote it. Alone, in my bedroom, back in Pittsburg, praying for a new lease on life. It was my prayer then and it was again. I couldn't hide it. Everyone in the room knew why I was crying. I had been shunned.

After the show, a few of the people that came wrapped their arms around me and gave me the warmest, most genuine hugs.

For the first time, we talked openly about the cost of being gay in a Christian setting. No one whispered. That night they shared the sorrow of the loss with me. Derek stood up straight next to me that night, the same as every night before. Together, their compassion got me through the pain of getting punched on an old wound. I let my heart dare me to lead me with the music. I volunteered to be exposed. Why? Was it worth it? I wondered if the pain of it was a sign that I'd truly shared something meaningful, or if coming back had just been a mistake.

It was hard to push back thoughts of giving in and giving up. It wasn't that people stopped liking my music; it was personal now. *They* didn't like *me* anymore. I was being rejected for things about myself I could not change.

The most devastating rejection that I would experience would come in the form of a package sent to my fan-mail box. I was getting a steady stream of encouraging letters to accompany the ones that expressed disappointment in my character. Most of the sad stuff came in the form of letters, while the larger packages I received usually turned out to be interesting welcome-back gifts like books, art, or music. One day, a puffy package had arrived, labeled with what seemed the girly-scrawl of a young teenager, whom for the sake of anonymity, I'll call "Julie."

I tore it open in anticipation of something wonderful.

Inside were several of my CDs. The jewel cases were well-worn, the shiny-silver playing surface of the discs scratched from a decade of listening. I had assumed that Julie sent them so that I would sign and return them but, as I read through the accompanying letter, it became clear that she wanted nothing of the kind.

Julie went on to explain how I had completely destroyed her

enjoyment of the music that she once held so dear, and that she wanted nothing to do with my music any more. She only listened to *Christian* music made by *Christian* people. Since I was gay, she explained, it was obvious that I was not a Christian. According to Julie, and the many others who were now letting me have it, no one can be gay and Christian.

She sent the records back because she no longer wanted them and she didn't want anyone else to hear them either. She could have just thrown the music away or quietly moved on. Instead she needed to make a point. She wanted me to know how disappointed she was that I failed to be the Christian she imagined I had promised to be.

It worked.

I was crushed, heartbroken, and angry all at the same time. I wanted to give into the physics of anger and scream over the hurt of rejection. I wanted to hide my face and quit. I wanted to drive to Julie's house (after all, I had her return address) and ask her where the hell she thought she got off judging me? When anger would give way to tears, I found peace in absorbing her blows. I wanted to wrap my arms around her, hoping to be a friend when she needed one most. I shuddered when it hit me that she might be having an experience in her own life when she didn't feel accepted and loved for who she truly was. I didn't have any answers, but I knew what it was like to be unwanted.

Through both the anger and the pain, all I could think of was divorcing myself from Christian culture. I didn't want to live with people who insisted that I was a failure. Rather than being the community that reflected the compassion that I had experienced in Christ's Christianity, it had transformed into the one place where I felt most unsafe and unwanted. Christianity had turned into the place where my faith, my loves, and my personal experiences were constantly being assessed and judged instead of being nurtured.

Julie's act touched on the one secret that I still carried in my heart. In public, I could still claim to be a person of faith, because it was true. I was. Yet I still feared that Julie was right in that I no longer had the right to describe my spiritual experience as Christian.

Like so many other Christians of my time, I couldn't see how to describe my faith as *Christian* without attaching so many of the beliefs that were demanded by the church and my peers in Evangelical culture. A Christian had always been described to me as a person of belief, and that the measure of one's faith was evidenced by the ability to believe in the unbelievable.

For every fact I failed to swallow whole, for every doubt and question I had about the story and theologies that had been handed down to me, I could not, for the life of me, go without exploring for myself. I *followed* because, at times, my struggle was with unbelief.

I don't know that *what* I believed about Jesus had actually changed as much as my willingness to confess that I had no idea *how* to believe any more. I could no longer tick the box that said *Christian* without feeling as though I had failed the test of my religious experience. I wasn't willing to relinquish my spiritual experience with Christ. My life had been transformed by faith, and Christianity was my native tongue. The Julies could try, but there was no sending it back or erasing it, even if I found myself in a new struggle of explaining my experience to others in a way that they might understand.

INSIDE OF TEN days of my national coming out, a very public, fever-pitch debate about the legitimacy of gay Christians had brewed into a big enough storm that CNN's *Larry King Live* decided to use my life as the lightning rod.

When I agreed to the taping, I did so naively thinking that I was simply to be extending the narrative of my own journey. I anticipated that my faith would be a portion of the conversation, but hardly the headline. I was still underestimating how offensive homosexuality can be to the core beliefs held by many conservative Christians.

As counterpoint to my story, CNN invited a Southern Californian Evangelical pastor, Bob Botsford, to represent the conservative Christian voice. Pastor Bob held the predictable line that deemed homosexuality a poor "lifestyle choice." He cited scripture after scripture as evidence, finite and complete for his side of the argument, but I had nothing more than my own lived experience. I had no smart retort or Biblical reference to justify my being gay; I just was. When called to answer Pastor Bob's assertion that I couldn't be gay and Christian, all I had to offer was the simple request to be respected as a human being.

"I am comfortable with the parts of me that you don't understand," was all I could manage. The simplicity of it seemed too mundane to be sufficient a defense against Pastor Bob's arguments to the Godly order of things. What more could I do but ask to be acknowledged for being present and accepted for who I was and not judged to be less than a credible human being, regardless of my sexual preference?

The question of so-called homosexual choice made its expected appearance, and I found myself floundering to answer the age-old quandary. I'm attracted to a woman—what else is there to say? I just *knew* I was gay.

Pastor Bob insisted that being gay was a choice, but Larry posed the obvious question I had never thought to ask.

"How did you know you liked women?" Larry asked, catching him off guard. "How did you know you didn't like boys . . . *romantically?*" Of course the query was meant to unsettle him but, at the same time, Pastor Bob might have done well to understand this was just the same kind of implied insult that I and gay people everywhere experience almost daily.

Bob stammered and fidgeted, unable to find the words that helped him describe his own sexual awareness without a Biblical quote, the same as I had. It's not easy, but sometimes the answer is as simple as considering your own experience.

The conversation deteriorated for Bob from there. All he could say was that was the way God made everyone and then he said it . . . the worst and most tired cliché of them all: "God made Adam and Eve, not Adam and Steve." His hands started to shake and his face went pale. He had been rigid and proud before, but now he seemed to have lost his zeal.

It wasn't surprising that Bob couldn't describe his assurance of his sexual orientation. He'd never truly been asked to explain his attractions before that moment. One could argue that he was safe, because he never had to defend his straight sexual orientation to a greater majority.

Under the hot lights and on national television was hardly the place to expect him to reach any epiphany. I had had seven years to formulate my own convincing defense of sexual orientation, and still needed Ted Haggard and Larry King to come rescue me.

We ended in an impasse, as these so-called public debates often do. Pastor Bob had done little more than make it clear that his church was for straight people, and that I was only welcome if I repented. Behind the scenes, Bob kept insisting that he and the two beefy strong men he brought with him were only there because they loved me. He let me know that he was praying for my life to have peace.

To my surprise, I was finding that I was actually feeling more peaceful, but probably not in the way that he had imagined. I actually found that the anger I had toward his theology was easing and, instead, was just feeling sorry for him. He really was a nice guy and I truly think he meant well, but his choice to be religious had usurped his heart. It was like he'd never actually met a gay person who wasn't broken to pieces by being gay. It didn't make sense in his world because all he had ever experienced were gay people who disappeared from his church. After what I had seen, it was no surprise that he had probably never seen any come back. I was the same—unable to walk back into his world because I wasn't able to be who he wanted me to be. Yet, here I was, somewhere out in the margins, still holding on.

"Bob, I didn't lose my faith when I realized I was gay, but it took a lot of faith to tell the truth. All I ask is that you be the kind of guy who gives me the space to sort it all out safely," I said. Maybe no one had ever asked him that before, to step back and agree to disagree. Maybe he'd never been in a place in which he was outnumbered and left feeling alienated.

Only he has the right to tell his story, as I have the right to tell mine. Who knows what his takeaway was, but mine was one of feeling uninvited to his party. I didn't want him to feel the same. I invited him to come to my show later that night. I told him I would put him on the guest list so that he could come see and hear for himself the kids who were showing up at my concerts battered by the so-called love he was offering.

"Please know that you are welcome to come. Stand beside me and listen. There are a lot of gay people who still share the same faith that you have. Maybe you would like to meet and hear from some of them?"

He never came.

twenty-four

*I*t was disappointing that Pastor Bob couldn't show his intended love for me in a way that would have really made a personal impact. He could have met me in a place where I lived and prospered. He could have listened and opened himself up to an invitation to see the world where music was cultivating hope in my life and in the lives of others. I could have talked until I was blue in the face about how I was the same person as I ever was, even though he now knew I was gay, but nothing replaces showing up and seeing for oneself what is actually happening. Instead, we parted ways, and haven't spoken since.

I can't sit here and judge only him, though. I had been just as complicit in the segregation between my old life and the new. Despite the fact that there were many churches asking me to play, I couldn't see a way to feel safe there anymore. Christian fundamentalism had left me so fragile and defensive that the last place I wanted to be was in a position to have to explain, justify, or exonerate my faith to a crowd of witnesses.

I couldn't play every Christian song I had ever written, but I had reclaimed a few. If people wanted to hear them, I insisted, it would have to be in bars, theaters, and coffeehouses, but there was no way I could walk into a church. It didn't matter that there were many faith communities that called me, wanting to show their support by gladly offering me a place to play. I continued to deny their invitations, embarrassed that I couldn't share my faith the way I once had.

I answered every Christian's request for a concert with as gracious and honest a reply as I had: "I'm sorry, but I'm not playing churches anymore." I needed a break from the public pressure to explain my faith and orientation. Really, I just wanted to focus on my music career. "Thank you for the appreciation and support. Truly. I hope you'll come out and join me on the road!"

The thing that I didn't yet comprehend was the fact that there were some churches that simply wanted to be a part of helping me get back on my feet. They were aware of how hard it was for an LGBT person to come out in this world, never mind the devastating experience that so many have had when religion was in play.

Despite many requests from faith communities that hoped for a full evolution of my return, I continued to resist. Beyond the solidarity of coming out, I felt I had nothing left to offer the church.

It was easy to take part in the kinds of conversations that I had at my shows outside the church walls. Outside the earshot of those who saw fit to correct every misstep and doubt, I found many people who were just as bewildered, yet eager, to process their own spiritual journeys. So, why was I so adamant that it wasn't possible for me to do the same in churches that were inviting me to bring that conversation to their neighborhoods? I began to wonder if I was rejecting genuine gifts of hospitality when churches asked me to come and play. Perhaps I was limiting the potential of LGBT faith by failing to offer some portion of my own experience to those who asked me to share it?

Part of what changed my willingness to engage was an encounter I had with Pastor Mark Tidd of Highlands Church in Denver.

Highlands was preparing to host a small local conference bluntly called "The Church and Homosexuality," and they were calling in speakers capable of adding to the conversation. Initially, I turned up my nose at the idea that I had anything to contribute. I was well on my way to severing what few remaining ties I had with organized religion, and was looking forward to the peace and quiet of less religious rhetoric in my life.

As, usual, I fobbed off their requests on my management team, reiterating my lack of interest in playing any music inside the church. The last thing I wanted to be was the subject of another unresolvable public debate over Scripture, outdated church traditions, and theology. Enough eloquent, biblically examined cases have been made by scholars and clergy alike that suggest homosexuality is neither sickness nor sin. I'd read so many books on both sides of the aisle only to be left feeling as though my lesbian arms had spread between the two and my life was being used as a tug-of-war rope.

I couldn't see how yet another debate was going to break the impasse enough to heal the wounds that I or any of my LGBT friends carried. The assumption that Tidd and his church wanted to wade through the quagmire was less than appealing.

Pastor Tidd was insistent though, and kept calling. After several emails and phone calls to my camp, it was clear that Highlands wasn't going to go away. I decided to speak with Mark directly, hoping to appeal to his pastoral side. Perhaps after a personal conversation, he could hear my voice and understand I wasn't the person that he was looking for any more than he or his church was what I was interested in.

We ended up chatting for over an hour. I listened as Mark shared with me the background of how Highlands came to be. How along the way he had personally experienced revocation of his ordination by openly supporting his LGBT members. How he and his church were rebuilding after they theologically came out, having lost the support of their parent denomination and funding. He spoke of how his own journey and the lives of the people in his community had been hurt through adverse judgments and theologies that sought to separate LGBT people and their allies from spiritual community. It wasn't that Highlands was a gay church, though there are many members who happen to be.

"These guys are serious about their faith," Mark explained. "We just want to be a place where everyone knows they are welcome to be who they are." The fact that sexual orientation was a recurring theme among the damaged Christians walking into Highlands encouraged Mark to want to listen more and speak less.

Pastor Tidd seemed to express a desire to be a part of a community that helped people discover the joys of a spiritual life and all that comes with it, rather than be the enforcer of by-the-Book Christianity, if there is such a thing.

Mark asked me if I was willing to share a picture of the journey I had experienced in my life. He released me from any obligation to have a neat and tidy explanation of where I stood. He didn't ask me to define my faith, instead he asked me to tell the real story of the adventure. In fact, what he hoped I would be brave enough to share was the doubt and the insecurities—the unpolished truth of my Christian experience.

"What has that been like for you? Tell me in your words. If

you come, I'll take responsibility for making a safe place for you to tell it. You don't have to be a Christian if you're not there anymore. You can be angry, cuss, cry—it doesn't matter. Just tell it like it is," Mark offered, "I hope it can be a gift for you to share what you've been through." He hoped that maybe, in doing so, we'd all find the ways in which we relate and could share our faith rather than argue about how we are different or who was right.

Mark's invitation finally sunk in. He wasn't asking me to do a gig or incite a particular school of thought; he and Highlands were simply interested in hearing my story. They were offering hospitality, not debate.

"I do hope you will come. We would love to be a friend," Mark humbly appealed.

Truth was, I hadn't been to a church in years and was intimidated by the thought of standing in a sanctuary. All the communal praise and worship music, Jesus talk, and prayer, was a welcome distant memory. For years, I'd adopted the "where two or more are gathered" idea of church, where a strong beer and long buzzy night of hashing out my faith experience with friends in a bar was much more rewarding than feeling like a Sunday morning disappointment. I imagined myself to have moved beyond such trivial expressions of spirituality and traditional practices, but I was also curious. I wondered if it was still possible for a church to be a community that served its people's spiritual needs before serving denominational politics. Mark said he thought that might actually be happening in Denver, but I'd have to come for a visit to find out.

And so, I went.

Most conferences of this sort have a habit of only inviting well-practiced and skilled speakers who are there to help solidify some sort of finite conclusion or ideal for the cause. This is especially true when it comes to Christian meetings, where there is typically a great deal of effort in securing the talents of those who uphold a particular religious teaching and who also have the charisma to inspire those listening to walk out clutching certainty rather than doubt. Highlands took a different approach.

Instead of building a curriculum that prescribed what all who attended *should* believe after the event, it was presented more as an opportunity for everyone involved to contemplate and consider how the ramifications of our beliefs, traditions, and theologies actually played out in the world around us. The topic this weekend happened to be centered around the church and homosexuality. Rather than defining what the outcome should be, they wanted to compile the realities—the lived stories—of those who had been experiencing this complicated dynamic. Rather than a school of instruction, the symposium was more like a storytelling convention where those who shared did so by telling the story of their personal journey through the maze. The rules were relatively simple and elegant. Speak to share, not to preach. Listen to hear and not to judge.

Though I arrived ready to participate and prepared to be a focal point, I soon found myself in need of listening far more than speaking. I listened as one woman told the story of how her religion-inspired rejection of her lesbian daughter ended in the tragedy of suicide. An African-American pastor spoke of how his coming out shaped not only others' perceptions of his faith and cultural identity, but how that experience affected how he saw his own life. There was a passionate lesbian, who was finishing divinity school, and wondered aloud where her passion for serving God and the church would lead when her truth was fully revealed. Rounding them out was an ex-gay reparative therapy sur-vivor and one former Christian music rock star . . . all of us with tales of paradoxical joy and suffering at having found ourselves to be people of faith in an environment that had worked hard to si-lence the telling.

I listened to others tell of their experiences, and I was struck by one statement that would resonate with me for months and years to come. It came from the gay pastor's coming-out story of how he was confronted by one of his church board members. Upon his revelation, the board had convened and reached the conclusion that a gay pastor was no kind of pastor for their church, and he was asked to resign. All involved began to mourn the supposed fall of their beloved leader. After the decision had been reached and each went their own way, a man approached the now-discarded pastor and said, "Pastor, we all knew that you were gay, but why did you have to come out?"

I teared up when I heard those words. I recognized them from the many angry letters, returned CDs and, uncomfortably public blogs aimed in my direction. So many words of admonish-ment, disappointment, and disgust, but I had never heard it put so plainly to the point. In essence, we can only accept gifts from people who are straight or have yet to declare.

Yes, it's incredibly sad that a gay man lost his job and his spir-itual community. Tragic, even. But what stands out to me is not the argument as to whether it is religiously acceptable to be gay, but rather that when the time came for a community to share in the journey of one of its members, the answer was, "No. We would prefer your silence rather than consider how we can rise to the challenge of loving you as you are."

So much of the story of LGBT people living in the shadows

of religious bias is that the story has been so one-sided. The religious conservatives have had plenty of face time to describe their views. We've heard so much rhetoric as to the Biblical grounds that justify marginalizing nonheterosexual people, but we've heard so little about the deeply spiritual, soul-searching experience of those who have been victimized because of it. As a gay person, I've experienced others' attempts to pressure, shame, and preach me into silence. The end result was that, in my absence, I let others tell my story for me. That story was that gay people lose their faith and disappear in the shadows.

I had spent enough years in silence to come to a place where I could no longer ignore the voice inside me that longed to be heard. I had tried to convince myself of what others had alluded to, that it would be better for me to be quiet and fade into obscurity than to rock the boat. Yet, in doing so, I had only stifled my own passions. I lost sight of what I was made to do, what I longed to do, in singing, writing, and sharing my experience with others. I lost community. I lost connection. The gifts that I had to offer others lay rotting on the ground, unwanted and wasted. I had wasted enough. I was ready to live and tell the tales of my adventures.

What earthly good was my life if I was not out, living in the world, connecting, and sharing my story with others? By hiding any portion of my experience, I was sacrificing the opportunity to connect joyfully with others. When I finally opened the door, got dressed, and walked out, I may have found difficulty, but I also found support, love, and connection. When I dared to share a little of my journey with others, the story grew. I began to realize that my story didn't happen in a vacuum. It was alive and growing. That when I shared it, others joined in by sharing their own experiences. By hiding my story away, I was not only shortchanging my own experience, but I was also keeping others from finding a place out of their own silence.

We each long for some kind of community. We long for connection. For though we each have our own individual lives and experiences, it is not until we share those experiences with others that we begin to develop the wholeness of our story. We need witness and friendship to our being. To lock a portion of ourselves away, to cut ourselves off from spiritual contemplation, or to be ostracized and rejected is truly the most violent act against another human being that we can think of. It is why the idea of solitary confinement is so utterly devastating. To be shut into a black box, silenced and forgotten, is to be rendered into nothingness. To set the story free, to be heard, and allow it to be retold is the essence of our humanity—to know and be known.

No. I've had enough silence. I had somehow found the courage to sing again, and I wasn't about to be silenced about the joy of discovering love. I was grateful that I had a partner who loved me and supported me. Bemused that faith had kept me remarkably intact, I was humbled that I had a place in this world to sing. I had traveled thousands of miles in silence and had adventures aching to be spoken of. I consider it a blessing to have come so far and be healthy and fit enough to have the energy to share it.

Listening to the others at places like Highlands Church tell of how they had traveled helped me realize that if I was willing to share my story, doing so might help another person take hold of their own story. For me, it was a turning point. It took a good long while to work up the courage, to get over my own hurt and disappointment at being so poorly treated by Christians, but I was ready. I made the decision to take the risk. The next time a Christian, or anyone else for that matter, asked me what it was like to have the experience I was having, I would choose to engage rather than to walk away. The days of being silent were over.

twenty-five

*W*hen I walked off the stage in 2002, leaving CCM and public life for what I truly believed was forever, I thought that I really could leave everything behind me: every memory—the music, guitars, religion, good times and bad—all of it. If I could have erased my own mental hard drive, I would have. Instead, all I could hope for was to be forgotten in the public mind.

"Burn it all!" I thought. I didn't want to be reminded of any of it. I tried to ignore my own memories of my public life, but the one thing I couldn't avoid was my name. It got to the point at which I hated seeing my name in print, and even loathed having to write it down.

For a while, I grew obsessed with the idea of changing my name, convinced that I had corrupted the one my mother had given me. It had become the symbol of a life I needed to leave behind. I was angry and embarrassed every time I saw it or heard it. Even after I left public life, I feared its use. Too many times I sat trembling in places like doctors' offices, dreading the moment when my name would be called aloud among a room of strangers only to be found out as *that* Jennifer Knapp. I longed for the day when writing my name on a blood sample was just a sign of ownership and not a chance to be mistaken for an autograph.

How I hated my name.

The words *Jennifer Knapp* took on a life of their own. She had come to be a person, apart from the *me* I saw myself to be, and yet had attached herself so tightly that there was no telling where she ended and I began. Those two words, that name that had once been mine, came to stand for something or someone I didn't recognize. Their association to me left me feeling embarrassed, angry, and humiliated. Saying my name in public now had consequences.

I felt like a prize idiot. I regretted that I had ever used my own name to be a Christian rock star.

How could I have been so stupid? Why didn't I make up a stage name?

The remorse started in wishing that I had drawn a more definitive line between my private and public life, then slowly added momentum, death-spiraling into darker thoughts that I had used and brought shame to my entire family by having used my name.

This psychosis was all part of the mental haze back when I was making the exodus from CCM. I needed fame to stop immediately so I could have some quiet, alone time and figure out my life in private, yet I couldn't see myself as capable of escaping anywhere without having to use the actual name I was running from.

I spent time piecing together the prospective aliases for my new life. I picked out new first names and other family names from both my and my partner's families. I practiced writing them down. I even rehearsed introducing my newly named self in a mirror to see if the name fit as I imagined. I tried on dozens of new names, but they were all just cumbersome masks, layered on top of a person whom I couldn't rename or outrun.

When I really sat down and thought about it, I just couldn't do it. This was my name. This was the name my mother gave me.

When I imagined going to my mother and asking her to call me by some other first name, the whole idea seemed silly and even a little offensive. She loved me and was proud of me. How could I tell her I was ashamed of the person that she had always known? What kind of person was I anyway, to take what she had given me, ruin it, and then think that by simply renaming the package, I could change her impression of the contents within?

Then, all of a sudden, I realized, this wasn't just a name game. It took working through the ridiculous fantasy, but there it was, a truth that I could not escape. I had to live with the life I had. No change of name could change what ailed me.

The name was just the reminder of a life of which I had grown extremely self-conscious.

Obviously, I decided to keep my name, but when I moved to Australia and began meeting new friends, I kept my last name to myself. When asked about how I paid my bills I would grow sweaty and anxious.

It seemed weird to lie about such an innocuous thing, but I wanted to say anything but what became my usual terse reply: "Music."

It's the kind of response that people always want to know more about.

"Oh, yeah?" their eyes light up and you can see the questions queuing up to form a conversation.

"What do you do? Sing? Write? Play? What instruments do you play?"

"Are you famous? Have I heard of you?"

The last question is one I've always found funny. There's the old saying that if you have to ask someone if they're famous, then they're probably not. I never really knew how to answer it.

"Eh. Kind of. I guess." What was I supposed to say? Part of me wanted to be proud of what I had accomplished. I mean, really, how often does that happen? How fantastic was it that, for at least a short while, I had a professional music career. I had a radio hit in Japan for God's sake. I'd never even been to Japan!

"Are you on iTunes? Can I Google you?" and finally, the name question . . .

"What's your full name?"

Once anyone had my full name, that was it. My secret was discovered. The real source of my embarrassment

"What kind of music?"

When I wanted the misery to end I'd just blurt it out and cut to the inevitable chase: "I was a Christian music artist." It was a confession.

My most favorite response ever was a man who excitedly shouted "Jesus!" after my admission.

"Yes," I said sheepishly, "I used to sing songs about Jesus."

"No, it wasn't a question." He went on, "I mean, Jesus!" It was an expletive of surprise. "You've got to be kidding me!" Then, his tone dropped, head cocked, and—*Oh God no, please don't*—piecing it together he asked—*Why do they always ask?*—"So uh, you're a Christian, then?"

It never seemed to matter how I answered that question, because the deck was already stacked. Everyone, and I mean *everyone,* has an opinion about Christians. Even self-identified Christians tend to respond with qualifiers to soften the blow, and I was no exception.

What is amazing is that, to this day, the reactions I get when

I tell people I am a lesbian don't even compare to the reactions of telling people I am a Christian. Honestly, I still find the declaration uncomfortable. Not just for others, but for myself as well. There is just *so* much *baggage.*

In my years away from music, there were two major fears that I came to realize were pinning me down.

First were the sincere reservations I had about public life. I grew afraid to play music because, in one way or another, doing so always led me to a place of sharing. Music was dangerous because I told it my secrets and it never kept them. The logic train connected music with public, public with coming out, and coming out having to face the religious fervor of those who saw me as a failure. It was a lot to untangle for what used to be the simple joy of finding personal fulfillment in music, and it was potentially a very risky endeavor to undertake.

I was willing to take the risk, but the whole point was that following music had to, in some way, be fulfilling enough to balance the challenges. I've always loved a good challenge, and I've never minded feeling the burn so long as there's some muscle to gain, but the *what ifs* were killing me.

My second fear was that the risks of answering my calling wouldn't actually balance out. If they didn't, what would I do then? Like any work that is hard, you want to know that more came of it than just calluses and exhaustion. You want to see if you can build something that can make the world a better, safer place.

That I chose to come back wasn't so much that I found a resolution for any of those fears; it was just that I was no longer willing to let those fears rule my life.

For the first, I had the good fortune to know life with music and life without it. As it turned out, I preferred *with*, so I made the choice to accept the adventure, rather than live out the rest of my life wondering what might have been.

As to any questions of purpose, how was I to know unless I accepted the challenge of the adventure?

Every step back was a tiny, sublime victory. From sitting in my home studio in Australia to mailing off the demo CD. From walking through the Nashville airport for the first time in seven years to closing my eyes in front of a studio microphone. I told the world I was gay and (fortunately, as far as I know) no one died. I even managed to release a record after nearly a nine-year layoff and, thankfully, it didn't die either. (In May 2010, *Letting Go* debuted on the top one-hundred Billboard charts. It was a first for any of my records to appear so high on a mainstream chart.)

It has been a blessing to be able to get back to the music that I love, yet it has also come with the unexpected surprise of returning, in a way, to the religious community where I first came into the spotlight. By coming back to music and coming out, I've had the chance to be a part of a movement to end religion-endorsed discrimination, marginalization, and judgment against LGBT people and their allies. In 2011, thanks to many requests to do so, I began sharing what has been my personal odyssey of reconciling sexuality through the lens of Christianity. I took what was a series of chances to say *yes* to churches and faith leaders who asked me to tell what life was really like coming out as a Christian. Those talks evolved into what I now call *Inside Out Faith*.

I use *Inside Out Faith* events to tell my story, but I hope it doesn't end there. Because for every kid that comes out, for every pastor who stands up, for every friend, mother, and religious denomination that tells the true story of love, the more we realize how much we have in common.

Really, it's all about story. To be oneself requires a vulnerability that needs love, compassion, forgiveness, and empathy to protect. We know that every single person who dares to come out of the closet does so at great risk. We share the truth about ourselves because we want to be known. We want to be known because we long to love and be loved. How is this anything other than the universal cry of the human heart?

When I reopened my guitar cases back in Australia, I had no idea what road would rise up to me. There was nothing to know except that it was my journey to take. All I could do was my part. I could only be honest about my life, live it, and sing through it. If there would be anyone to walk with me as a fellow weary traveler, I'd be lucky and glad to sing them a song. All I could do was offer the gifts that I had, and let the chips fall where they may.

Like Rainer Maria Rilke suggested in his *Letters to a Young Poet*, I confessed the truth: I was not whole without music in my life. Hidden away, I was not altogether myself. I was compelled to play even if no one ever listened again.

"Ask yourself in the most silent hour of the night," prompts Rilke, "*must* I write?"

My answer, even after Pandora's Box had opened, was still, "I must."

I must write. I must sing. I must love. I must have faith. All these things insert themselves into being who I am.

They are such little words: "*I am.*" Yet their power is immeasurable and the words that follow are life defining.

The entire world could, would, can, and will forever offer its opinions about how to be the best version of yourself that they imagine you should be. Yet none of us will ever be able to live any life other than our own. There comes a point where the only real thing, the only choice we really have, is the choice to be responsible for the journey that is our own.

I gave up on my journey once, and I can't imagine doing it again.

acknowledgments

With gratitude and a great measure of love, I wish to thank my dear friends and family who have been so important and encouraging in helping me understand the value of what it means to have a story and to share it. Without your kindness, selflessness, and courage I would never have had the strength, clarity, or patience to take on the writing of this book. Each of you has given so much in time, wisdom, love, hot meals, and a little grog, all in perfect measure. You have helped me shape a story out of what seemed like chaos. So, thank you, for everything.

To My Love, how you center me! I am grateful for you in my life. To my family on all continents for blessing me with a lifetime of endless inspiration and support. For those who make "family" a much wider notion than I could have ever imagined: Laura, Andreas, Ellis, and Nikolas Berlind; Mike Kimbrell; Kimble and Chris Bosworth; Ted, Amy, Amber, and Alyssa Gavin; Spike and Lea Mason. Thank you for years of getting me across the line.

Special thanks to Jeff Chu for introducing me to Beth Adams, who would become my intrepid editor. Beth, your upbeat charm and disarming courage got me going, your tough questions helped me suss it all out, and your patience convinced me of the impossible. Thank you.

For every story that is told there are those who inspire it, and for that my deepest appreciation rests with Daneen Akers, Marcy Bain, Keb and Stephanie Barrett, Margaret Becker, Meghann Bowyer, Tristin Burke, Lianna Carrera, Amy Courts, Kevin Cuchia, Jason DeShazo, Carol Dunevant, Joey Elwood, Wyatt Espalin, Chris Ford, Megan Gandy, Jessy Grondin, Ginny Guedes, Carter Harkins, Gareth Higgins, Taylor Hill, John Huie, Justin Lee, Laura Rossbert, Mitchell Solarek, Bonnie Taylor, Dana True, Mark Tidd, Nancy VanReece, Derek Webb, Angela Wilson, and the growing list of churches, leaders, and supporters that have fueled what is now Inside Out Faith.

I cannot fail to mention the *Knappsters* (pardon the catchall for the many names I will spend a lifetime trying to remember). You are a loyal fan base who held vigil that someday I could write again. You have shared countless stories, inspired, and cried with and sung with me when I thought no one should or would.

Thank you.

Yours, Jennifer.